Virtual Filmmaking
with Unreal Engine 5

A step-by-step guide to creating a complete
animated short film

Hussin Khan

Virtual Filmmaking with Unreal Engine 5

Group Product Manager: Rohit Rajkumar

Publishing Product Manager: Vaideeshwari Muralikrishnan

Senior Editor: Hayden Edwards

Technical Editor: K Bimala Singha

Copy Editor: Safis Editing

Project Coordinator: Sonam Pandey

Proofreader: Safis Editing

Indexer: Hemangini Bari

Production Designer: Shankar Kalbhor

Marketing Coordinators: Namita Velgekar and Nivedita Pandey

First published: February 2024

Production reference: 3100524

Published by
Packt Publishing Ltd
Grosvenor House
11 St Paul's Square
Birmingham
B3 1RB

ISBN: 978-1-80181-380-8

www.packtpub.com

In honor of my parents, Major Yusof Khan and Halimah J, whose unwavering encouragement and sacrifices made this journey possible. This book is a tribute to your love and resilience.

To my beloved wife, Neeza, who has been my constant source of support and inspiration. Your love fuels my creativity, and this book is dedicated to you.

To Donnie, Dottie, Fifi, Junior, and Precious for your companionship and unconditional love.

Foreword

When my friend Hussin Khan asked me to write a foreword for his book, I took a while to think about the best way I could do this. As a creative, I wanted to write something that the intended audience of the book (filmmakers, storytellers, etc.) would resonate with, which is the same reason why Hussin wrote this book – to help others get ahead in real-time filmmaking.

By 2021, there was a new renaissance of animated short films being produced, and Unreal was now not seen as just a game engine, but as a powerful tool to tell stories in the animation format. Even live-action projects got involved too, with the use of virtual production LED Volumes – this is where traditional back projections are not limited to a locked-off camera, but instead a real-time environment in Unreal Engine, synchronized with the real-world camera and stage. This enabled series and films such as *The Mandalorian* and *The Batman* to be shot during the pandemic, eliminated the need to travel, and so on.

This renaissance of content creation is why Hussin Khan's book is not only insightful and full of knowledge, but is also important in inspiring the next generation of filmmakers, as well as upskilling the current or even previous generation of filmmakers.

This is the book I wish I had when I started out – a book I can always refer to on my desk when I am stuck with something, or when I am trying to figure out a creative and technical problem. It will not only just solve the problem but also inspire other ideas to tell a story. If I had this book back then, I wouldn't have spent hours or sometimes days on the internet/forums looking for answers to problems, only to be more frustrated with confusion!

Yes, today, there are lots of tutorials online you can get for free, but now the opposite problem applies – there is just too much! Therefore, it becomes even more frustrating. So, to have a book that has all the things you need to know to get started in real-time filmmaking in one place is very helpful today. The way Hussin has broken down each category, and the way he succinctly conveys each step of a process, makes it clear that he is a creative himself. He has also collaborated closely with other creatives and has decades of experience, from animation to VFX to real-time filmmaking.

If you want to tell stories, whether linear (film), interactively (games), or hybrid with live action (virtual production LED Volumes), then this is the book for you.

This book has been written for anyone who wants to use Unreal Engine to create content as a professional career.

HaZ Dulull

Director/Producer at HaZimation

Contributors

About the author

Hussin Khan is an authorized **Unreal Engine Instructor** (**UAI**) with a decade of experience as an educator. As a former head of education at an Academy Award-winning studio, Rhythm & Hues, he was involved in the production of movies such as *Life of Pi* (2012), *2036 Origin Unknown* (2018), and, more recently, *Rift*, an animated movie made entirely using Unreal Engine by HaZimation. Currently, Hussin runs EFXCO Academy, a creative-based training academy in Malaysia, which offers professional training and certification in graphics and motion design, game development, virtual reality, and visual effects. He is also a certified instructor for Nuke and Unity. Hussin holds a firm conviction that real-time production stands poised as the next major breakthrough in the media and entertainment industry.

I want to thank the people who have been close to me and supported me, especially my wife, Neeza, and my parents.

About the reviewer

Deepak Jadhav, a Germany-based XR developer, holds a master's in game programming. With expertise in **Augmented Reality (AR)**, **Virtual Reality (VR)**, and **Mixed Reality (MR)**, he excels in creating enterprise applications for healthcare, pharmaceuticals, and manufacturing. Notably, Deepak develops digital twin apps for the manufacturing and healthcare sectors. Formerly a game developer for mobile, PC, and console platforms, he is proficient in C#, C++, and JavaScript, leveraging Unity and Unreal Engine for XR and game development. As a seasoned technical reviewer, Deepak offers insightful evaluations of Unity and Unreal Engine-focused technical book titles, drawing from his extensive experience to provide practical guidance for developers.

Table of Contents

Part 2: Production: Creating the Environment

6

Creating and Applying Materials to 3D Meshes   131

Part 3: Production: Adding and Animating Characters

7

Creating Actors with Unreal Engine MetaHumans   171

Part 4: Production: Shooting the Scene

11

Enhancing Set Dressing, Retiming Shots, and Adding Niagara Particles   293

12

Setting the Mood with Lighting and Adding Post-Processing Effects   321

Part 5: Post-Production: Adding Post-Processing Effects and Music

13

14

Appendix

Preface

Virtual Filmmaking with Unreal Engine 5 is the first Unreal Engine book to guide you through the complete process of virtual film production. Encompassing the full spectrum of filmmaking, this book demonstrates the use of an industry-standard tool used by studios such as Disney, Industrial Light & Magic, DNEG (formerly known as Double Negative), and Framestore.

Walking through the process systematically, you'll first collect references and create a simple storyboard to plan your shots and then begin to create virtual environments, importing 3D models and adding materials and textures to create photorealistic, dynamic worlds. Then, you'll learn how to create actors using highly customizable MetaHumans, mastering their import, retargeting, and animation. Finally, you'll bring it all together with cinematic lighting and camera animation, before exporting your film.

By the end of this book, you'll have honed your skills, discovered new tools for your toolkit, and gained the confidence to work on your virtual film projects using only Unreal Engine 5, leveraging Quixel Megascans, Lumen, Nanite, and MetaHuman technology.

Who this book is for

If you are a beginner to intermediate filmmaker, 3D artist, animator, visual effects artist, or virtual production professional with some basic knowledge of Unreal Engine, and are looking to delve into making virtual films and animations, then this book is for you.

You would benefit from having some experience of Unreal Engine, but a deep working knowledge is not required, as activities will introduce the relevant tools and features when needed.

What this book covers

In *Chapter 1, Getting Started with Unreal Engine*, you'll delve into the fundamentals of Unreal Engine 5, laying the groundwork for your creative endeavors.

Chapter 2, Understanding the Principles of Photography, Film Cameras, and Lenses, demystifies the principles of photography, film cameras, and lenses, providing a solid foundation for visual storytelling.

In *Chapter 3, Understanding the Art of Storytelling and Creating Your Storyboard*, you will explore the art of storytelling and learn how to bring your ideas to life through the creation of a compelling storyboard.

In *Chapter 4, Importing 3D Objects and Creating Levels*, you will be guided through the process of importing 3D objects and crafting levels, enhancing your ability to shape virtual worlds.

In *Chapter 5, Creating Environments with Quixel Megascan*, you will be introduced to the powerful tool Quixel Megascan, with a demonstration on how to create photorealistic environments using photogrammetry 3D objects.

In *Chapter 6, Creating and Applying Materials to 3D Meshes*, you will learn to harness the art of crafting and applying materials to 3D objects.

In *Chapter 7, Creating Actors with Unreal Engine MetaHumans*, you will explore the creation of actors using Unreal Engine MetaHumans, unlocking the potential to craft lifelike characters.

In *Chapter 8, Retargeting the MetaHumans for Unreal Engine 5*, you will discover the intricacies of retargeting MetaHumans for animation, ensuring seamless integration into your virtual world.

In *Chapter 9, Adding Animations and Facial Expressions to Your MetaHuman Characters*, you will add mocap animations and expressive facial features to your MetaHuman characters, enhancing the depth and realism of your digital narratives.

In *Chapter 10, Adding and Animating Virtual Cameras Using the Level Sequencer*, you will learn the art of adding and animating virtual cameras using the Sequencer, enabling you to craft dynamic and visually compelling scenes.

In *Chapter 11, Enhancing Set Dressing, Retiming Shots, and Adding Niagara Particles*, you will elevate your storytelling by enhancing set dressing, retiming shots, and incorporating Niagara particles for added visual impact.

In *Chapter 12, Setting the Mood with Lighting and Post-Processing Effects*, you will uncover the art of setting the mood with lighting and post-processing effects, bringing a nuanced atmosphere to your virtual world.

In *Chapter 13, Exploring Color Management, Additional Camera Settings, and Rendering Your Shots*, you'll explore the intricacies of color management, fine-tuning additional camera settings, and executing the rendering process to bring your film to life.

In *Chapter 14, Adding Sound and Finalizing Your Virtual Film*, you'll acquire the art of editing, seamlessly incorporating sound effects and music to elevate your project. The chapter concludes with the essentials needed to export your film.

To get the most out of this book

Software/hardware covered in the book	Operating system requirements
Unreal Engine 5.2	Windows 10/11
Blackmagic DaVinci Resolve 18	Windows 10/11, macOS, or Linux
Blender 3.5 (if you want to follow the Appendix)	Windows 10/11, macOS, or Linux

Download the project files

You can download the project files for this book from the following link: `https://packt.link/gbz/9781801813808`. If there's an update to the project files, it will be updated at the link as well.

For any help or support, you can join the author on the book's Discord channel: `https://discord.com/invite/QbCS2ed2bs`

Conventions used

There are a number of text conventions used throughout this book.

Bold: Indicates a new term, an important word, or words that you see on screen. For instance, words in menus or dialog boxes appear in **bold**. Here is an example: "Now, drag **DirectionalLight** into the Sequencer. Then, click the + **Track** button on the **DirectionalLight** track and choose **LightComponent0**."

> **Tips or important notes**
> Appear like this.

Get in touch

Feedback from our readers is always welcome.

General feedback: If you have questions about any aspect of this book, email us at `customercare@packtpub.com` and mention the book title in the subject of your message.

Errata: Although we have taken every care to ensure the accuracy of our content, mistakes do happen. If you have found a mistake in this book, we would be grateful if you would report this to us. Please visit `www.packtpub.com/support/errata` and fill in the form.

Piracy: If you come across any illegal copies of our works in any form on the internet, we would be grateful if you would provide us with the location address or website name. Please contact us at `copyright@packt.com` with a link to the material.

If you are interested in becoming an author: If there is a topic that you have expertise in and you are interested in either writing or contributing to a book, please visit `authors.packtpub.com`.

Share Your Thoughts

Once you've read *Virtual Filmmaking with Unreal Engine 5*, we'd love to hear your thoughts! Scan the QR code below to go straight to the Amazon review page for this book and share your feedback.

https://packt.link/r/1-801-81380-9

Your review is important to us and the tech community and will help us make sure we're delivering excellent quality content.

Download a free PDF copy of this book

Thanks for purchasing this book!

Do you like to read on the go but are unable to carry your print books everywhere?

Is your eBook purchase not compatible with the device of your choice?

Don't worry, now with every Packt book you get a DRM-free PDF version of that book at no cost.

Read anywhere, any place, on any device. Search, copy, and paste code from your favorite technical books directly into your application.

The perks don't stop there, you can get exclusive access to discounts, newsletters, and great free content in your inbox daily

Follow these simple steps to get the benefits:

1. Scan the QR code or visit the link below

https://packt.link/free-ebook/9781801813808

2. Submit your proof of purchase

3. That's it! We'll send your free PDF and other benefits to your email directly

Part 1: Pre-Production: Project Development and Gathering Resources

In this part, you will embark on a journey into the world of creative storytelling and cinematic virtual film production. In *Chapter 1*, you'll delve into the fundamentals of Unreal Engine 5, laying the groundwork for your creative endeavors. We then move on to *Chapter 2*, where the principles of photography, film cameras, and lenses are demystified, providing a solid foundation for visual storytelling. Finally, in *Chapter 3*, you'll explore the art of storytelling and learn how to bring your ideas to life through the creation of a compelling storyboard.

This part includes the following chapters:

- *Chapter 1, Getting Started with Unreal Engine*
- *Chapter 2, Understanding the Principles of Photography, Film Cameras, and Lenses*
- *Chapter 3, Understanding the Art of Storytelling and Creating Your Storyboard*

1

Getting Started with Unreal Engine

Welcome to the exciting world of virtual filmmaking!

This book offers beginners and seasoned professionals the ability to create complete virtual films using photorealistic 3D props, environments, and realistic human characters, all done by harnessing the real-time technology of Unreal Engine 5.

In this first chapter, you will learn what Unreal Engine is, what it is used for, and how you can start working with it. You will then learn how to set up an account with Epic Games and download Unreal Engine, before learning how to navigate and understand the user interface.

Overall, you will become proficient in installing and setting up these applications on a Windows machine.

So, we will cover the following topics:

- What is Unreal Engine?
- Creating an Epic Games account
- Downloading and installing Unreal Engine 5
- Launching Unreal Engine 5
- Exploring the Unreal Engine interface
- Navigating the Viewport
- Transforming objects

Technical requirements

To complete this chapter, you will need an internet connection and the following hardware (recommended by Epic Games):

- An i7, i9, Xeon, or AMD Ryzen/Threadripper processor with 16+ cores
- 32 GB to 64 GB of RAM
- A 256 GB SSD (OS drive)
- A 2 TB SSD (data drive)
- 2080 Ti RTX, 30 Series or 40 Series GTX
- 64-bit Windows 10 or 11

Before we get started, I must remind you that this book is about extremely high-quality 3D imagery. It is important for you to understand this before setting up Unreal Engine and risk being disappointed because of technical issues. This is because Unreal Engine, like any 3D graphics tool, requires a powerful machine; much of this power comes from the graphics cards.

As a result, if you want to enjoy the real-time experience of working in Unreal, you will need a computer that can handle the best settings and display. Otherwise, you will experience a very sluggish machine with a tendency to crash a lot, and nobody wants that.

If you are a devoted Mac user, you are just not going to have as good an experience as you would have compared to a Windows user. Much of this has to do with Epic Games putting more time into developing the engine for use on Windows. This is not to say it is not available on Mac, but many of the features, particularly rendering features to achieve photorealism, are not available on Mac machines, most notably DirectX 12 and Ray Tracing Cores on the NVIDIA RTX series of GPU cards.

At this point, you may be getting needlessly worried. However, I personally tried using the tools mentioned in this book on a lower-spec machine, and for the most part, I was able to work through it using very low render settings, so if you plan to learn now and invest in a newer, faster machine later, this book is certainly still for you.

Finally, you can find all of the project files for this book through this link: `https://packt.link/gbz/9781801813808`. However, we won't need the project files until the next chapter.

What is Unreal Engine?

Unreal Engine is a game engine developed by Epic Games, initially released in 1998. It is used to create high-quality, interactive 3D graphics applications, including video games, virtual reality experiences, architectural visualizations, and simulations.

The engine offers a wide range of tools and features to help game developers create visually stunning and immersive environments, including a robust visual scripting language (Blueprints), advanced physics simulation, artificial intelligence systems, and a powerful visual editor.

The main advantage that Unreal Engine offers compared to other digital content creation tools (such as Blender, Maya, 3ds Max, and Cinema 4D) is that it uses a method called **real-time rendering** (or **near-real-time**). This method renders each frame so fast that it appears to be created on the fly.

Other digital content creation tools must render each frame using a method called **offline rendering**; however, this is an extremely slow method of rendering and can sometimes take hours and even days.

Real-time rendering is the most important reason why you would want to make your 3D movie in Unreal Engine. It can produce photorealistic renders that are close to the fidelity of renders that are made using offline rendering methods.

You can also edit things such as atmospheric effects, Materials, and lights in your 3D scene and get near-instant feedback. This is an incredible time-saver compared to the traditional offline rendering methods.

Now that we know a little bit about Unreal Engine, let's take the first steps in accessing it.

Creating an Epic Games account

To get started with Unreal Engine, you will need to create an Epic Games account (if you already have an account, you can skip this section). To do this, follow these instructions:

1. First, navigate to Unreal Engine's website: `https://www.unrealengine.com`.

2. In the top-right corner, click on **SIGN IN** (even if you do not have sign-in credentials, you will still need to click on this).

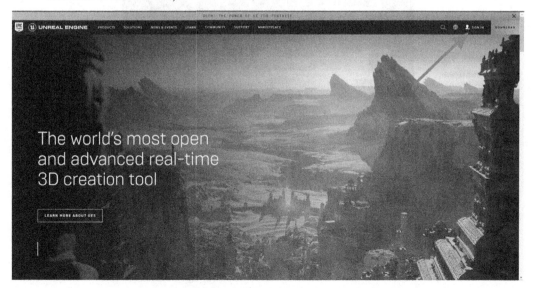

Figure 1.1: Signing in on an Unreal Engine web page

3. You will see a list of ways you can sign up. It is strongly suggested that you use an Epic Games account.

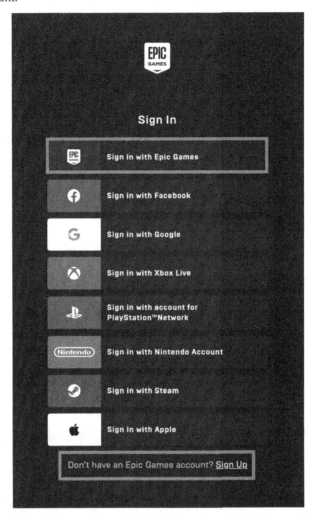

Figure 1.2: Sign-in methods

4. On the next page, you will be asked for your first name, surname, username, email address, and password for your account. You can opt to receive additional emails, but you will need to read the terms and conditions and tick that you have done so.

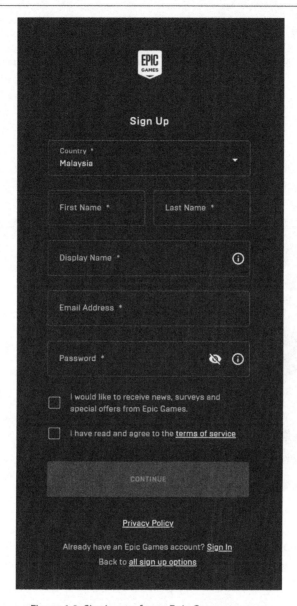

Figure 1.3: Signing up for an Epic Games account

5.   Once you have done this, a link will be sent to your designated email for verification. When you click on this link, you will have successfully created an account. You will need to be logged in whenever you plan to use the engine.

Next, we need to download and install Unreal Engine 5.2.1.

Downloading and installing Unreal Engine 5

Using your Unreal account, you need to download and install Unreal Engine 5.2.1. The application you are about to install is the Epic Games Launcher. This is where you install the engine and gain access to other features related to the engine, such as updates, plugins, scripts, models, and a host of many other assets.

To do this, follow these steps:

1. Once you have successfully signed in to Epic, you will see a page like this (the appearance of the page may vary, as the screenshot is from the latest marketing Material from Epic at the time of writing):

Figure 1.4: An Unreal Engine web page

2. Click on the **DOWNLOAD** button (at the top right of the screen), and you will be taken to the following page:

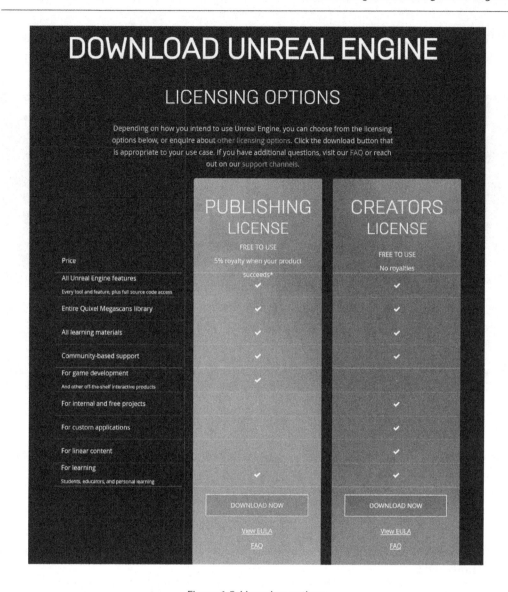

Figure 1.5: Licensing options

Since you've picked up a filmmaking book, there is a very slim chance that you will use Unreal Engine to create games, which is what the publishing license is for. Therefore, click the **DOWNLOAD NOW** button at the bottom of the **CREATORS LICENSE** column.

3. Choose where you want to download the installer.

4. Once the download is complete, double-click on the installer and then select **Install**.

When the installer has finished, you will see an icon titled **Epic Games Launcher** on your desktop. Clicking on this will open the launcher (note that it could take a few minutes to open the first time). Typically, it does not open fullscreen, but when it does, it looks something like this:

Figure 1.6: The Epic Games Launcher

From here, you will see a few tabs running along the top to the right of the Epic Games icon. Most notably, we have the following:

- **News**: The latest news about Epic Games and Unreal Engine
- **Samples**: Here, you can download free samples for learning and testing purposes
- **Marketplace**: Here, you can buy models, environments, and characters designed to work in Unreal Engine
- **Library**: This is used to find content that you have saved, purchased, or installed
- **Twinmotion**: This is an architectural pre-visualization application, with assets and presets designed specifically for architectural real-time pre-visualization

Select the **Library** tab, then click on the + sign marked in the following screenshot:

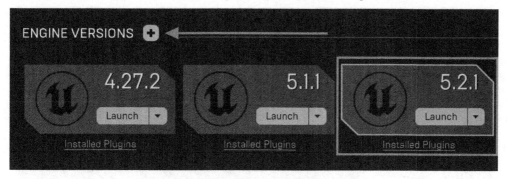

Figure 1.7: Installing Unreal Engine versions

> **Note**
>
> If this is your first time installing Unreal Engine, you may not have any engine versions available in the launcher. When you click on the yellow plus icon, you will be presented with options to install the engine you prefer. In this case, please install Unreal Engine 5.2.1.

The installation will take a while, depending on your internet connection speed.

Launching Unreal Engine 5

Once you have successfully installed the engine, click on the **Launch** button:

Figure 1.8: The Launch button

You will be presented with the **Unreal Project Browser** window:

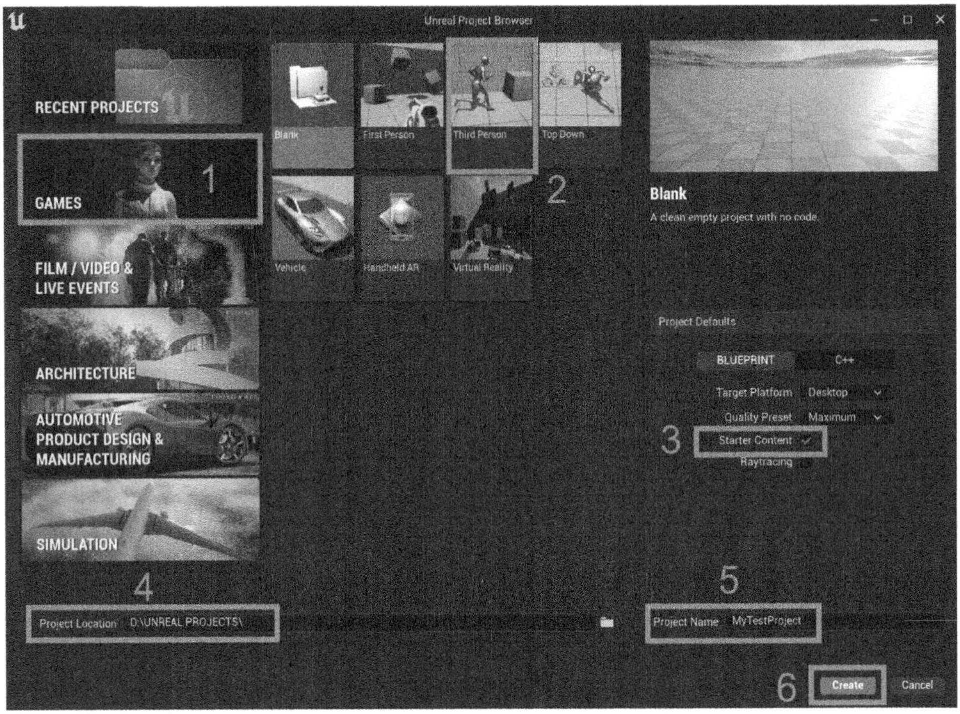

Figure 1.9: The Unreal Project Browser

The Unreal Project Browser allows you to open any recent projects and create new ones using a specific template. For this session, let us do the following:

1. Click on the **GAMES** category.

2. Choose the **Third Person** template.

3. Ensure you enable **Starter Content** (this will add additional content to your project so you can use it in your project).

4. Select a project location – I suggest you create the project in the largest and fastest drive on your system, as Unreal projects tend to get large as you work on them.

5. Provide a project name. Since this is a test project, let us call it MyTestProject. Unreal Engine project names cannot be more than 20 characters, nor can they start with numbers, and they certainly cannot have spaces in between the words. You can make use of underscores or hyphens to separate the words. For our example, I just capitalized the first letter of each word for legibility.

6. Finally, click **Create**.

After about a minute or two, you will be presented with the following screen:

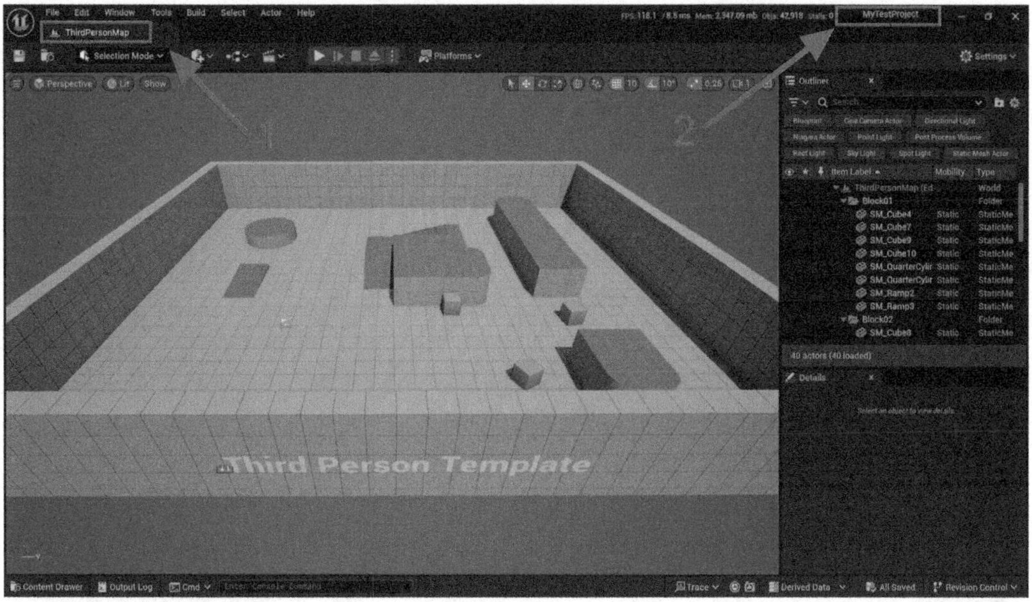

Figure 1.10: Third Person Template

This is the third-person project you just created, and you are currently in the **Level Editor**. Take note of the following:

1. **ThirdPersonMap**: The name of the current Level. You can create unlimited levels in Unreal Engine.
2. **MyTestProject**: The name of the project you just created.

> **Note**
>
> You may or may not get a notification at the bottom right of the screen. If you do, click on **DISMISS** and **UPDATE**. This is Unreal Engine's way of making sure your project is always up to date.

Congratulations! You just downloaded, installed, and created your first Unreal Engine project!

In the next section, you will start getting familiar with the Unreal Engine interface, and then we'll look at how to navigate the Viewport.

Exploring the Unreal Engine user interface

In this section, we will briefly take a look at the user interface and learn how to navigate in the Viewport. Unreal Engine's interface is divided into several key areas:

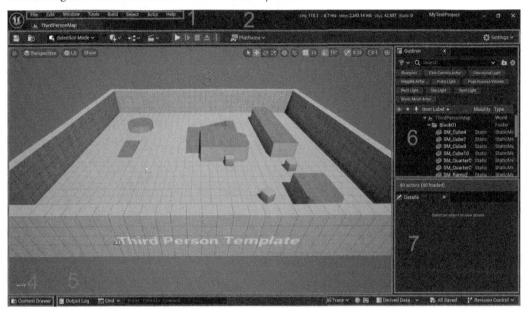

Figure 1.11: The Unreal Engine interface

Let's get to know these areas:

1. **Menu bar**: This is the standard drop-down menus, which consist of **File**, **Edit**, **Window**, **Tools**, **Build**, **Actor**, and **Help**.

2. **Main toolbar**: This area contains the most commonly used functions. This includes the **Save** function, the **Mode Changing** dropdown, the **Place Actors** icon, the **Blueprint Creation** icon, the **Add Level Sequence** icon, the **Simulation** icons, and the **Launching & Packaging** dropdown. Then, on the far right of the toolbar, there is the **Settings** dropdown.

3. **Level Viewport**: This is the most prominent area of all and where you'll be spending most of your time. It shows all the objects you have in the level.

4. **Content Drawer**: By clicking on this button, you will open the Content Drawer, which contains all the content you will use in your project. It will also contain all the imported objects, Textures, Materials, and so on.

5. **Bottom toolbar**: In this toolbar, you'll find the output log and the area where you can type in console commands.

6. **Outliner**: This panel mirrors the objects you have in the Viewport. It lists them in a hierarchical format. If you select any object in the Viewport, it will be selected in the Outliner, and vice versa.

7. **Details panel**: This panel gives you the properties of the item selected in the Outliner or the Viewport. This is where you will tweak and set the properties for each item.

Now that we have a basic understanding of the user interface, let us work with the Viewport and learn how to move around and use it.

Navigating the Viewport

To get started, let us first try to move around in the game world a bit by using just the mouse:

- Hover the mouse in the Viewport, and then click with the **left mouse button** (**LMB**) and start dragging the mouse forward and backward. This will allow you to navigate forward and backward in the Viewport. If you move the mouse left and right, the view will shift to the right and left.

- By holding down the **right mouse button** (**RMB**), you will be able to orbit (look around) the level.

- If you press and hold the **middle mouse button** (**MMB**), this will enable tracking (panning) around the level. You can achieve the same by holding down both mouse buttons (LMB + RMB).

Now, let's introduce some keyboard keys:

- While holding the RMB and pressing the Q and E keyboard keys, the view will shift upward and downward

- Using the RMB and pressing the W key will move you forward, the S key will move you backward, the A key to the left, and the D key to the right

- Hold down the Z and C keys with the RMB to temporarily change the field of view and zoom in and out of a scene

- To frame an object, select it and hit the F key

- Once you have framed an object (F), use the *Alt* key and LMB to orbit (tumble) around an object

- Hold *Alt* and the RMB to dolly the view closer or further away from an object

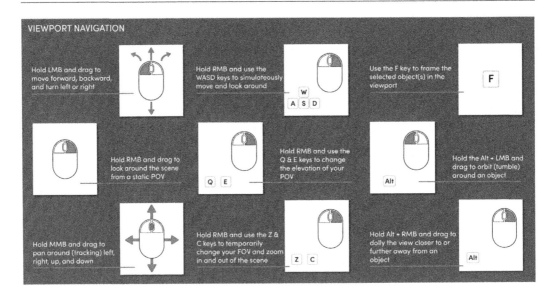

Figure 1.12: The Unreal Engine mouse-keyboard combinations

If you do not have any prior 3D application experience, it may feel a little awkward at first, but trust me – you will get used to it. In the upcoming chapters, we will dive deeper into understanding the user interface and the Viewport navigation.

Now that you can navigate the interface using the mouse-keyboard combination, let's learn how to manipulate objects in the Level Viewport.

Transforming objects

In this section, we will take a brief look at how to **transform** objects – and by transform, I mean moving, rotating, and scaling them.

The first thing to note is that in Unreal Engine, objects in the Level Viewport are called **Actors**. To select any Actors in the Level Viewport, you simply have to left-click once. The selected Actor will be indicated by an orange-colored outline, and the Actor will also be highlighted in the Outliner.

Here, select the middle blue cube in the Level Viewport, and press the *F* key to frame (i.e., zoom in on) the Actor.

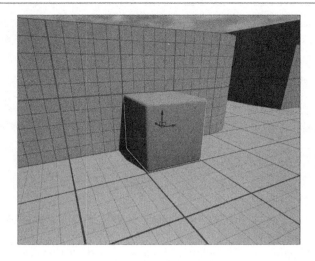

Figure 1.13: Selecting and pressing the F key on the blue cube

You will notice the three arrows in the middle of the cube. This is referred to as a **gizmo**, with the red arrow representing the *X* axis, the green arrow representing the *Y* axis, and the blue arrow representing the *Z* axis.

Now, use the LMB to select the gizmo and move the cube in the direction (or the opposite direction) of the arrows – this operation is called **translating**.

Other than **Translate**, there are other transform functions, as shown in *Figure 1.14*:

Figure 1.14: The Viewport controls

Let's review what these controls do:

- **Translate** (or **Move**) (**1**): Using this button, the selected Actor can be translated in the direction indicated by the arrows. The keyboard shortcut for this action is *W*.

- **Rotation** (**2**): Using this, the selected Actor can be rotated in all three directions using the Rotation gizmo. The keyboard shortcut for this action is *E*.

- **Scale** (**3**): The selected Actor can be scaled along all three axes using the Scale gizmo. The keyboard shortcut for this action is the *R* key.

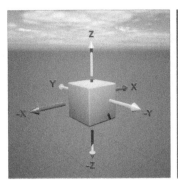 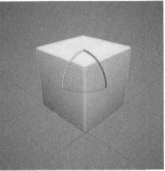 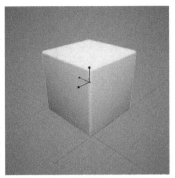

Figure 1.15: Translating, rotating, and scaling Actors using gizmos

- **Translation Snapping (4)**: This button will activate/deactivate (indicated by the blue highlight) the snapping feature of the translation. By default, translating an Actor will snap to every 10 units on the grid.

- **Rotation Snapping (5)**: This button will activate/deactivate (indicated by the blue highlight) the snapping feature of the rotation. By default, rotating an Actor will snap to every 10 degrees.

- **Scale Snapping (6)**: This button will activate/deactivate (indicated by the blue highlight) the snapping feature of the scale. By default, scaling an Actor will snap to every 0.25 units.

Go ahead and translate, rotate, and scale the objects in the Level Viewport to get yourself familiar with the tools.

> **Note**
>
> To get detailed information on Actor transformation, please use this link as a guide: `https://docs.unrealengine.com/5.2/en-US/transforming-actors-in-unreal-engine/`.

Summary

In this chapter, you successfully created an Epic Games account, downloaded and installed Unreal Engine, created your first project, and familiarized yourself with the user interface, Viewport navigation, and transforming objects (Actors).

In the next chapter, you will receive a brief history of filmmaking, before exploring the topic of cameras, both in the real world and Unreal Engine.

2

Understanding the Principles of Photography, Film Cameras, and Lenses

In this chapter, we will start thinking about the pre-production stage, first, by having a brief look at the history of filmmaking, and second, by exploring cameras. We will look at the key properties of physical cameras, including sensor size, aspect ratio, aperture, focal length, and depth of field, as well as the various camera angles and movements. Then we will move into Unreal Engine 5, helping you create your first virtual camera.

In this chapter, we will cover the following:

- Filmmaking history 101
- Understanding camera lenses and camera features
- Understanding key camera properties
- Understanding camera angles and camera moves
- Setting up cameras in Unreal Engine 5

Technical requirements

You will need Unreal Engine 5.2 installed and ready to go (please refer to *Chapter 1* for details).

The project file we will be using in this chapter is available at `https://packt.link/gbz/9781801813808`.

Filmmaking history 101

The history of movie-making can be traced back to the late 19th century, when the invention of motion picture cameras and projection technology made it possible to capture and display moving images.

In the early days of cinema, films were short and simple, often consisting of a single shot of a stationary subject. The first motion picture, the *Roundhay Garden Scene,* was shot by Louis Le Prince in 1888. The first public showing of a motion picture was on December 28th, 1895, by the Lumière brothers in Paris.

In the early 1900s, the motion picture industry began to expand rapidly, with the first feature-length films being produced. The first narrative film, *The Great Train Robbery*, was released in 1903 and was a commercial success. This led to the establishment of the first movie studios, such as the Hollywood studios, which would come to dominate the industry.

During the 1910s and 1920s, the motion picture industry continued to grow, with the introduction of synchronized sound and color film. The first feature-length film with synchronized sound, *The Jazz Singer*, was released in 1927.

During the 1930s and 1940s, Hollywood produced some of its most iconic films, such as *Gone with the Wind* and *Casablanca*. This period is often referred to as the "Golden Age of Hollywood."

In the 1950s and 1960s, Hollywood faced increased competition from television, and the film industry experienced a decline in popularity. However, the introduction of new technologies, such as widescreen and Panavision, helped to reinvigorate the industry.

In the 1970s and 1980s, Hollywood experienced a resurgence in popularity with the release of blockbuster films such as *Jaws, Star Wars*, and *E.T. the Extra-Terrestrial*.

The film industry has undergone significant changes due to the advent of digital technologies and the rise of streaming services. These changes have led to a shift in the way films are produced, distributed, and consumed, with streaming platforms becoming major players in the industry. With the advancement of computer hardware and software, game engines, such as Unreal Engine, are being used to create photorealistic, dynamic content for virtual production, full 3D animated series, virtual reality, and much more.

Let us have a closer look at the three main stages involved in filmmaking.

Understanding camera lenses and camera features

All films are told through a camera lens. This is because the camera is the primary tool that filmmakers use to capture the action and tell the story. The camera lens captures what is happening in a scene and the perspective from which it is being told. By choosing the right lenses and using them effectively, filmmakers can create a rich and immersive world that draws the audience in and tells a compelling story.

We are learning about the camera much earlier in this book because, like an actual film set, we will create our virtual world from the camera's point of view. As such, setting up cameras will be among the first things we will do in Unreal Engine.

There are several types of film and camera lenses, each with their own characteristics and uses. Here are a few of the most common types:

TYPES OF LENSES

STANDARD LENS   TELEPHOTO LENS   ZOOM LENS

Figure 2.1: Standard, telephoto, and zoom lenses

- **Standard lenses**: These lenses have a focal length of around 50mm and are designed to provide a field of view that is similar to the human eye. They are considered to be versatile and general-purpose lenses and are commonly used for portraits, street photography, and everyday shooting.

- **Telephoto lenses**: These lenses have a longer focal length, typically over 70mm. They are used to capture subjects that are farther away, such as wildlife, sports, or portraits where you want to compress the background. Telephoto lenses can be further divided into short, medium, and long telephoto lenses, with short telephoto lenses having a focal length of around 85mm, medium telephoto lenses around 135mm, and long telephoto lenses around 300mm.

- **Zoom lenses**: These lenses allow you to change the focal length, allowing you to zoom in and out on a subject. They are useful for a wide range of shooting situations, from landscapes and portraits to sports and wildlife.

TYPES OF LENSES

WIDE-ANGLE LENS   FISHEYE LENS   MACRO LENS

Figure 2.2: Wide-angle, fisheye, and macro lenses

- **Wide-angle lenses**: These lenses have a shorter focal length, typically less than 35mm. They are used to capture a wider field of view, making them great for landscape and architectural photography.

- **Fisheye lenses**: These lenses have a very wide angle of view and provide a highly distorted, curvilinear perspective. They are often used for creative and experimental photography, as well as some scientific and industrial applications.

- **Macro lenses**: These lenses are specifically designed for close-up photography and can focus on subjects at very short distances. They are commonly used for photographing small objects such as flowers, insects, and jewelry.

Now that you know the types of camera lenses, we will learn about the key characteristics of film cameras. The cameras in Unreal Engine mimic real-world cameras, so by understanding and adjusting these camera properties, you can keep greater control over the look and feel of your shots, and, ultimately, capture the best possible images.

Understanding key camera properties

Understanding key camera properties and how they interact with each other can help you take the best shots for your film. By understanding aperture, focal length, sensor size, and aspect ratio, to name a few, you will be able to create a cohesive and visually stunning film.

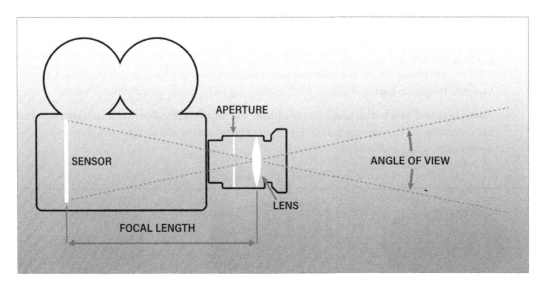

Figure 2.3: Key camera properties

Even if you already have prior knowledge of actual, physical cameras, stick around; you might learn a thing or two. If you're new to cameras and photography, fret not, all will be explained:

- **Sensor**: A camera sensor (also known as **filmback**) is the part of the camera that captures light and converts it into an image. The **sensor size** refers to the physical dimensions of the sensor, and it is typically measured in millimeters. The sensor size is important because it determines the angle of view and the depth of field of the image. The larger the sensor size, the shallower the depth of field. The smaller the sensor size, the deeper the depth of field.

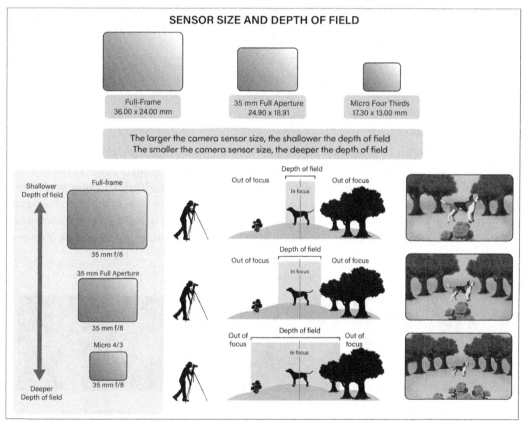

Figure 2.4: Sensor size and depth of field

- **Aspect ratio**: The aspect ratio is the proportion of the width of an image to its height. It is usually represented as two numbers separated by a colon, such as 4:3 or 16:9. The most common aspect ratios for film and digital cameras are 3:2, 4:3, and 16:9, but there are also cameras that can be adjusted to other ratios.

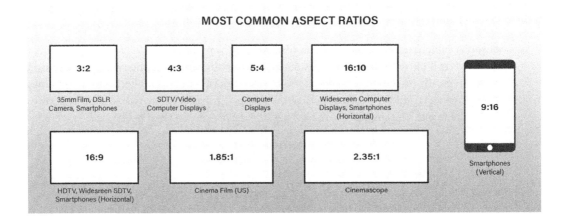

Figure 2.5: Most common aspect ratios

- **Focal length**: The focal length is the distance between the lens and the film or sensor when the lens is focused on infinity. This determines the field of view and the amount of background blur. A lens with a shorter focal length (wide-angle) will have a wider field of view, while a lens with a longer focal length (telephoto) will have a narrower field of view. In the following figure, the 24mm focal length has a wider field of view but the subject's face is slightly distorted, while the 85mm focal length has a narrower field of view and the subject looks much less distorted.

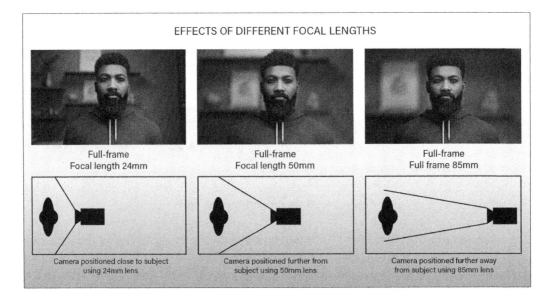

Figure 2.6: Effects of different focal lengths

- **Aperture** (also known as the **f-stop**): The aperture controls the depth of field, which is the range of distance in a photograph that appears to be in sharp focus. Aperture is inversely proportional to the depth of field: the wider the aperture, the shallower the depth of field; the narrower the aperture, the deeper the depth of field. A shallow depth of field means that only a small part of the image is in focus, while a deep depth of field means that most of the image is in focus. This can be used to control the visual style and to draw attention to certain elements in a scene.

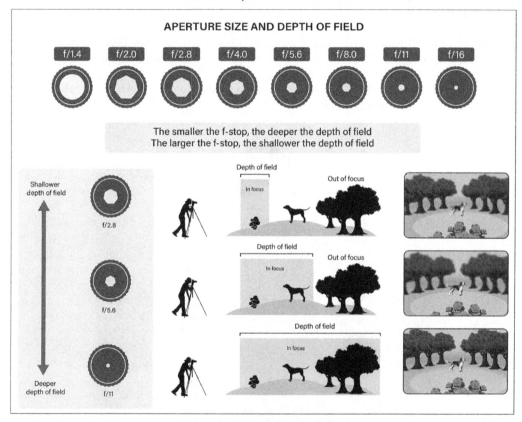

Figure 2.7: Aperture size and depth of field

It's worth noting that these are just basic concepts and there are more advanced techniques that can be used to control the sensor size, aspect ratio, focal length, and aperture in a scene. Understanding these concepts and how to use them to achieve your creative vision is a key part of photography and filmmaking. Now let's understand and learn about camera angles and moves.

Understanding camera angles and camera moves

Camera angles and camera moves are techniques used by filmmakers to create visual interest and convey meaning in a scene. By combining camera angles and moves, filmmakers can create a wide range of visual effects and communicate specific emotions or ideas to the audience.

Camera angles

Camera angles refer to the position of the camera in relation to the subject. Different camera angles can create different moods and perspectives. The following are some common camera angles:

- **High angle**: The camera is positioned above the subject, looking down. This angle can make the subject appear small or vulnerable.

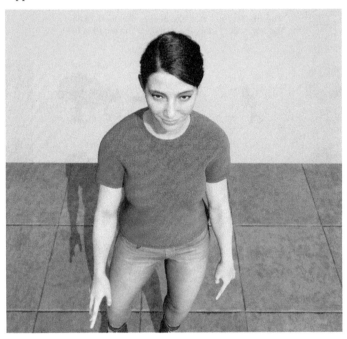

Figure 2.8: High camera angle

- **Low angle**: The camera is positioned below the subject, looking up. This angle can make the subject appear powerful or intimidating.

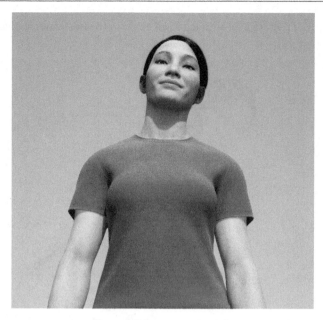

Figure 2.9: Low camera angle

- **Eye level**: The camera is positioned at the same height as the subject's eyes. This angle can create a sense of objectivity or neutrality.

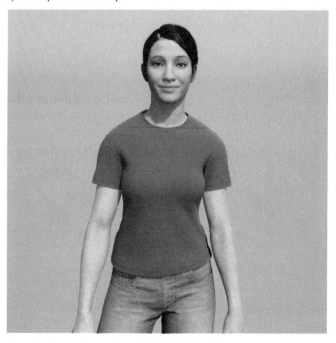

Figure 2.10: Eye-level camera angle

- **Dutch angle**: The camera is positioned at an angle to the horizon, creating a sense of unease or disorientation.

Figure 2.11: Dutch camera angle

Camera moves

Camera moves refer to the way the camera is positioned and moved during a shot. Different camera moves can create different visual effects and convey different emotions. Some common camera moves include the following:

Figure 2.12: Camera moves

- **Pan**: The camera moves horizontally from side to side, following a subject or revealing the environment

- **Crane**: The camera is mounted on a crane or a jib, allowing for smooth and dynamic movements

- **Dolly**: The camera moves toward or away from the subject on a track or a dolly

- **Roll**: By rotating the camera over its side on its long axis, you create a camera movement designed to deliberately disorientate the viewer and generate a sense of uneasiness

- **Tilt**: The camera moves vertically, up and down

These are just a few examples of camera angles and camera moves. There are many more techniques that can be used to create visual interest and convey meaning in a scene. Understanding these concepts and how to use them to achieve your creative vision is a key part of filmmaking.

So, now that you have a good understanding of camera lenses, camera properties, camera angles, and movement, let's jump into Unreal Engine and create your very first camera.

Setting up cameras in Unreal Engine 5

In this section, you will learn how to open an Unreal Engine project, create bookmarks, and create your first camera. To follow along, you will need to have Unreal Engine 5.2 installed (please refer to *Chapter 1* if you have not done so), and the project file downloaded and ready to go (see the *Technical requirements* section for the link).

Opening the project

To open the project, do the following:

1. Download the `VirtualFilmmaking.zip` project file, then move it to the largest and fastest hard drive on your system (Unreal Engine files tend to take up large amounts of hard drive space).

2. Then create a folder called `Unreal Projects`, which you will use to create all other Unreal Engine projects. Move the project file into this folder and unarchive it by right-clicking on the files and choosing **Extract to "VirtualFlimmaking\"**.

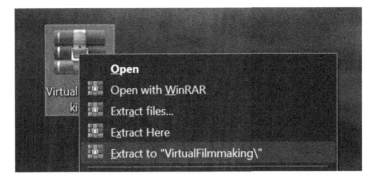

Figure 2.13: Extracting a project file

> **Note**
>
> The project file is a ZIP file. You can use the default Microsoft unarchiver utility to extract it or you can download and use the open source 7-Zip (`https://www.7-zip.org/download.html`).

Once you have unarchived the project file, you will find three items in the folder: **Config** and **Content** folders, along with a file named **VirtualFilmmaking**:

Figure 2.14: Opening the project

3. Double-click on the **VirtualFilmmaking** file to open the project in Unreal Engine 5.2.

Depending on your computer hardware specifications, it might take a while to open, because Unreal Engine will need to compile the shaders. This usually happens only when opening a project for the first time. Just sit back and relax while Unreal Engine does its job.

Setting up the UI and navigating the Level

Once you have the project opened, you will see the following screen:

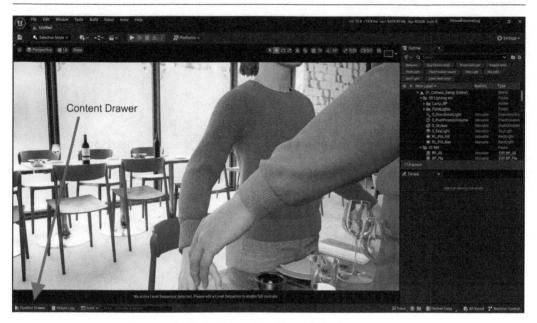

Figure 2.15: Locating the content drawer

In this scene, we have our two metahuman characters, Pia and Ali, in a beautiful virtual bistro. The two metahuman characters will be standing upright. Let's get them to sit down:

1. Access **Content Drawer** in the bottom left of the interface:

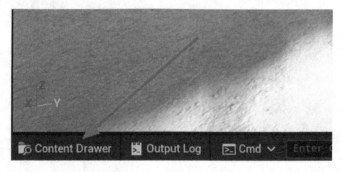

Figure 2.16: Opening Content Drawer

2. Once **Content Drawer** is open, you can click on the **Dock in Layout** button (at the top right of the **Content Browser** panel) to keep it open permanently:

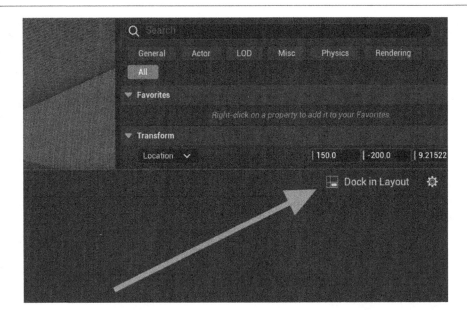

Figure 2.17: Docking Content Drawer in the layout

3. In the Content Browser, you'll find a **Sequences** folder. Select the folder and double-click on the **01_Camera_Setup** sequence. The **Sequencer** panel will open and now our two MetaHuman characters will be seated. Leave the **Sequencer** panel open for now.

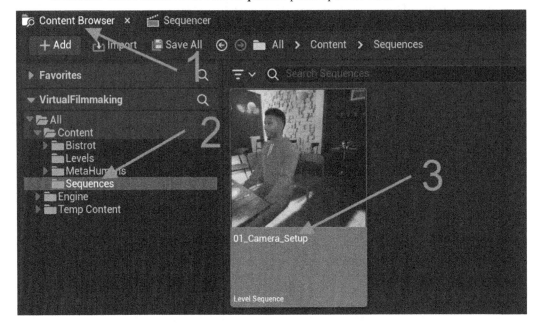

Figure 2.18: Opening the Level Sequence

> **Note**
>
> If for some reason your view is not located in the bistro, press the number *1* key on your keyboard (the number keys across your keyboard, not the numeric pad). This action will reset the view to focus on Pia inside the bistro.

Quite often an Unreal project can consist of hundreds, if not thousands, of 3D objects, and you will eventually experience sluggishness when navigating in the **Viewport**. One way to overcome this is to change **Engine Scalability Settings**. Click on the settings gear icon on the top-right corner of the interface and choose **Engine Scalability Settings**. Instead of a higher setting such as **Cinematic** or **Epic**, you can choose one of the lower settings such as **High** or **Medium**.

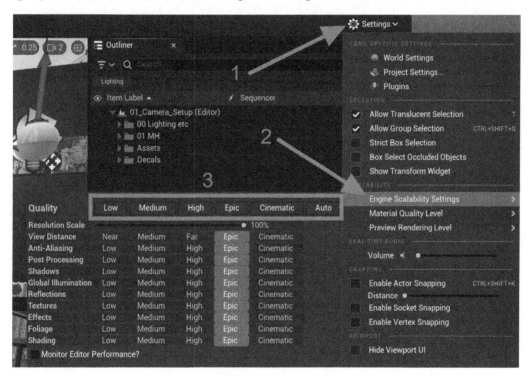

Figure 2.19: Opening Engine Scalability Settings

This will reduce the resolution, but you will have a better/faster experience when navigating the scene.

Creating bookmarks

Before we start creating cameras, I'd like to show you how to create **bookmarks**, so we can always come back to them if we get lost navigating around the scene:

1. In the **Viewport** window, pressing the *G* key will toggle the overlay icons. This will toggle the visibility of lights, cameras, and other Actors placed in the level.

2. Now, if you click once in the **Viewport** and press *1* and *2* (the numeric keys across your keyboard), you can see that I have already made two bookmarks.

3. Let's make a third; using the **Viewport** controls, frame a shot (like the one in *Figure 2.20*) and press *Ctrl + 3*.

Figure 2.20: Creating a bookmark

4. Now use the numbers *1*, *2*, and *3* to jump between the three bookmarks created in the scene. You can create more if you want to, up to a maximum of 10 bookmarks.

5. You can also clear all bookmarks by going to the **Viewport menu | Bookmarks | Clear All Bookmarks**:

Figure 2.21: Clearing bookmarks

Let's now save the project before we continue – to do so, go to **File | Save All**, or use the keyboard shortcut *Ctrl + Shift + S*.

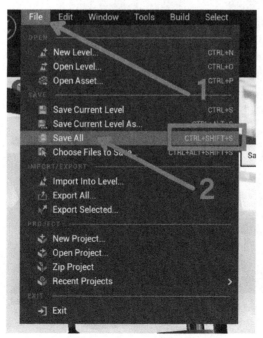

Figure 2.22: Saving the project

> **Note**
>
> Using the **Save Current Level** option or *Ctrl + S* shortcut will not save changes you make to meshes, Materials, Textures, and so on. To completely save your project, you'll need to use the **Save All** or *Ctrl + Shift + S* command. Get into the habit of saving your project occasionally; the keyboard shortcut is helpful for this.

Creating your first camera

In our bistro scene, we would like to create a few cameras, focusing on the two characters. Let's create the first camera focusing on Pia. There are two types of cameras in Unreal Engine: **Camera Actor**, a more typical type of camera, and **Cine Camera Actor**, a more specialized camera that attempts to replicate a real-life camera. We will use the latter in these instructions:

1. Move closer to Pia by using the **Viewport** controls (*WASD*) that you learned about in *Chapter 1*, or any of the bookmarks you created earlier.

2. Then create a Cine Camera Actor. There are a few ways of doing so:

    A. Using the **Viewport** menu, select **Create Camera Here | Cine Camera Actor**:

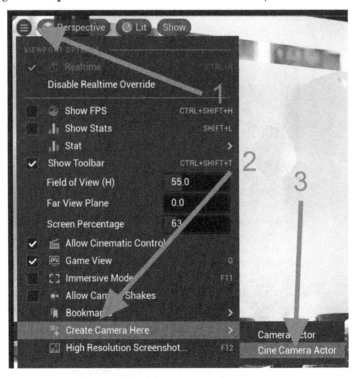

Figure 2.23: First method of creating a camera

B.   Using the **Place Actor** button (the green plus), select **Cinematic | Cine Camera Actor**:

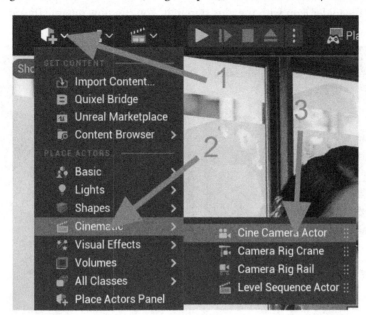

Figure 2.24: Second method of creating a camera

C.   Use **Sequencer** (we will try this method when we jump into creating a sequence later in *Chapter 10*).

3.   Once you've created your first camera, you'll see it listed in **Outliner**. It is always a good habit to rename items and organize **Outliner** appropriately; so, select the camera in **Outliner** (if it is not already selected), press the *F2* key, and rename it CAM_01:

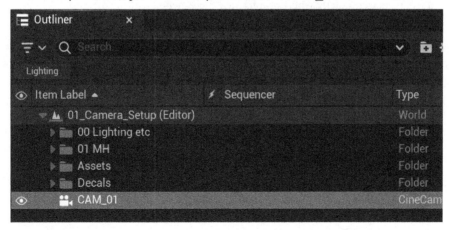

Figure 2.25: Renaming the camera

4. Let's also create a folder for it. Select **CAM_01** and, at the top right of the **Outliner** window, click on the folder icon with the plus sign in it. You can now rename the new folder, which we'll now call **Cameras**:

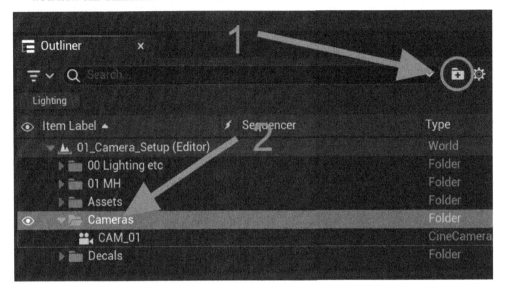

Figure 2.26: Creating folders in Outliner

Because we selected the camera first and then clicked on the folder icon, the camera was automatically included in the folder.

> **Note**
>
> My favorite workflow to create a camera is by using the previously provided method A, as the camera will be placed exactly where you framed the viewport.

You'll also notice that a camera view popped up in the **Viewport** window; this is the **Picture-In-Picture (PIP)** camera view shown in *Figure 2.27*. This is a handy way to always view your camera's POV while you move around in the **Viewport** window.

Figure 2.27: PIP view

But if it gets in the way and you'd like to remove it, select **Edit** (in the top application menu) and choose **Editor Preferences**. The **Editor Preferences** panel will pop up. In the search window, type `Preview camera`, and under the **Look and Feel** section, uncheck **Preview Selected Cameras**:

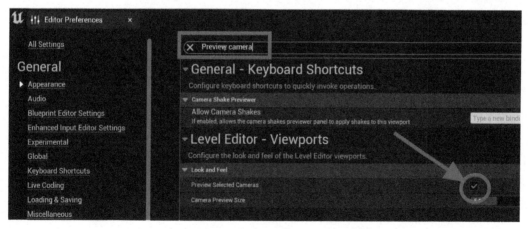

Figure 2.28: Removing the PIP view

Congratulations, you've just created your first camera in Unreal Engine! Now you can go ahead and create one focusing on Ali or both of the characters. You can also try the camera angle techniques mentioned earlier in the chapter.

Summary

In this chapter, you learned about the history of filmmaking, explored the three stages of the filmmaking process, got to know some types of camera lenses, and understood the importance of key camera properties, movements, and angles. You also successfully downloaded and opened a project and created your first camera in Unreal Engine.

All these are building blocks of creating your virtual film. We will dive into each topic a little deeper moving forward.

In the next chapter, we will be learning some universal patterns of stories and narratives used in today's movies, and the three-act structure of storytelling. You will also create storyboards and understand why storyboards are important in filmmaking.

3
Understanding the Art of Storytelling and Creating Your Storyboard

Storytelling has been an essential part of human culture for thousands of years and can take many forms, including verbal, written, visual, and digital storytelling. Regardless of form, it mainly involves creating a connection between the storyteller and the audience by sharing a common experience or emotion and using techniques such as characterization and dialogue to create a compelling narrative. Storytelling can be used to educate, inspire, and influence people's behavior, making it a powerful tool for building relationships and creating a lasting impact on people's lives.

This chapter emphasizes the importance of storytelling by exploring narratives, references, and storyboards. We will also look at the short film idea that we will be working on together throughout this book (though you can create your own short film if you wish).

In this chapter, you will learn about the following topics:

- The universal pattern of narratives
- Implementing the three-act structure of storytelling
- Collecting ideas and references for a short film
- Creating a storyboard

Technical requirements

This is a theoretical chapter. We won't need the project files until the next chapter.

Learning the universal patterns of narratives

The universal patterns of narratives are the common structural elements that can be found in stories across cultures and throughout history. These patterns were first identified by Joseph Campbell, a mythologist and writer, in his book *The Hero with a Thousand Faces*. Campbell's work explored the idea of a "monomyth" or a single-story pattern that could be found in myths and stories from around the world.

Many contemporary writers and artists have intentionally integrated Campbell's theory into their work, including the filmmaker George Lucas, who recognized the impact of Campbell's mythological theory and incorporated it into the *Star Wars* films.

Let's take a look at some of these universal patterns of stories and narratives.

The hero's journey

This is the most well-known pattern, which involves a hero leaving their ordinary world, going on a journey to overcome challenges and obstacles, and returning home transformed.

One example of the hero's journey narrative can be seen in *Star Wars (1977)*:

Figure 3.1: A hero's journey – Star Wars

Star Wars is a perfect illustration of the hero's journey because it follows the classic pattern of a hero's quest: a call to adventure, trials and tribulations, and a return with newfound knowledge and understanding. Luke Skywalker's character embodies the archetype of a hero who undergoes a transformative journey through challenges, mentorship, and self-discovery.

Saying that, the hero's journey narrative doesn't exactly follow a checklist, but is more of a framework. It provides a description of a narrative that works but doesn't dictate what actions the main character takes.

Other examples of the hero's journey can be found in *Back to the Future (1985)*, *Toy Story (1995)*, *The Matrix (1999)*, *The Lord of the Rings (2001)*, and *The Hunger Games (2012)*.

The quest

Similar to the hero's journey, this pattern involves a protagonist seeking out a specific object or goal and facing challenges and obstacles along the way.

Figure 3.2: The quest – The Wizard of Oz

The Wizard of Oz is a classic example of the quest narrative because it follows a similar structure to the hero's journey. The hero, Dorothy, is called to adventure when she is swept away from her home in Kansas by a tornado and finds herself in the magical land of Oz. Dorothy crosses the threshold into the new world of Oz when she steps out of her house and into the technicolor landscape. Along the way, Dorothy makes allies with the Scarecrow, the Tin Man, and the Cowardly Lion, and faces many challenges and tests, such as the Wicked Witch of the West, the Winged Monkeys, and the poppy field. Throughout her journey, Dorothy transforms from a scared and helpless girl into a brave and resourceful hero. Dorothy's ultimate goal is to find the Wizard of Oz who she believes can help her return home to Kansas.

Other examples of quest movies include *Raiders of the Lost Ark (1981), The Lord of the Rings (2001-2003),* and *Pirates of the Caribbean (2003).*

Overcoming the monster

This pattern involves a protagonist facing and defeating a powerful antagonist or monster.

Figure 3.3: Overcoming the monster – Predator

Predator (1987) is a classic example of the overcoming a monster archetype. In this movie, the Predator (the monster) is a highly advanced alien creature hunting down members of the elite military in a jungle. It is presented as an unstoppable and terrifying force that seems impossible to defeat. Major Alan "Dutch" Schaefer (the hero), the leader of the military team, is a highly skilled and experienced soldier who is tasked with taking down the Predator and saving his team. Much of the movie revolves around Dutch and his team trying to outsmart and defeat the Predator (the battle). To defeat the Predator, Dutch uses his knowledge of the jungle and his military skills to create a trap for the Predator, but in the process, he loses most of his team (the sacrifice). In the end, Dutch is able to defeat the Predator by outsmarting the creature and delivering a fatal blow (the triumph). Throughout the movie, Dutch transforms from a confident and experienced soldier to a desperate survivor. He must use all his skills and knowledge to outsmart the Predator and save his team (the transformation).

Other examples of overcoming the monster movies include *King Kong (1933, 1976, 2005)*, *Godzilla (1954)*, *Jaws (1975)*, and *Alien (1979)*.

Rags to riches

This pattern involves a character who rises from a lowly or disadvantaged position to achieve great success or wealth.

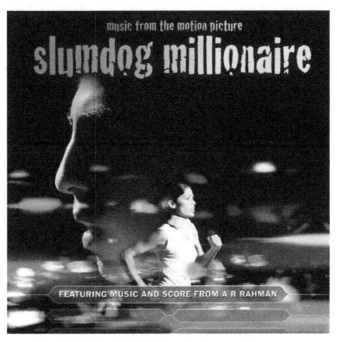

Figure 3.4: Rags to riches – Slumdog Millionaire

The movie *Slumdog Millionaire (2008)* follows Jamal Malik, a poor orphan (the rags) who lives in the slums of Mumbai. Jamal wants to be reunited with his childhood friend and love interest, Latika, and escape from the poverty and violence of the slums (the desire). When Jamal gets an opportunity to appear on the Indian version of *Who Wants to Be a Millionaire?*, he sees this as his chance to reunite with Latika and change his life (the opportunity). Jamal faces many obstacles throughout the movie, including poverty, violence, discrimination, the skepticism of the game show host, and the police (the obstacles), but he finds Prem Kumar, who serves as a mentor to him, challenging him and pushing him to reveal the truth about his past (the mentor). Throughout the movie, Jamal transforms from a poor and uneducated orphan to a confident and successful game show contestant. He uses his street smarts and life experience to answer the questions correctly (the transformation) and, in the end, Jamal wins the grand prize on the game show, which is a substantial amount of money. He is also reunited with Latika and is able to escape from the slums (the riches).

Other examples of rags to riches movies include *Cinderella (1950)*, *Pretty Woman (1990)*, and *The Pursuit of Happiness (2006)*.

Tragedy

This pattern involves a protagonist who faces a tragic fate or downfall, often due to their own flaws or mistakes.

Figure 3.5: Tragedy – The Godfather

In *The Godfather (1972)*, the protagonist, Michael Corleone (the hero), is the youngest son of a powerful mafia family. He initially wants nothing to do with his family's business but is drawn into the world of organized crime when his father is shot. Michael's flaw is his loyalty to his family – he is willing to do whatever it takes to protect them, even if it means engaging in violent and illegal activities (the flaw). Michael faces many obstacles throughout the movie, including rival mafia families, corrupt law enforcement, and the disapproval of his family members (the obstacles). His father, Vito Corleone, who is a powerful and respected mafia boss, teaches Michael about the family business and the importance of loyalty and respect (the mentor). Throughout the movie, Michael transforms from a reluctant outsider to a ruthless and powerful mafia boss (the transformation). Michael's downfall is his descent into violence and corruption. He becomes consumed by his desire for power and control and loses sight of his original intentions (the downfall). In the end, Michael loses his family and his humanity (the catharsis).

Other examples of tragedy movies include *Titanic (1997), Selena (1997), The Perfect Storm (2000),* and *Hotel Rwanda (2004).*

Comedy

In this pattern, a movie may start with a scene that establishes the main character's personality or flaw in a humorous way and usually concludes with a happy ending.

Figure 3.6: Comedy – Kung Fu Hustle

Set in 1940s Shanghai, *Kung Fu Hustle (2004)* follows Sing, a small-time criminal who dreams of joining the notorious Axe Gang. He is initially presented as a bumbling, inept character who is easily intimidated by others. Sing faces many obstacles throughout the movie, including the Axe Gang, a group of highly skilled and ruthless fighters who terrorize the inhabitants of a run-down apartment complex. Sing must also confront his own fears and weaknesses as he learns to harness his own kung fu abilities. The movie features a cast of quirky and memorable supporting characters, including the landlady and her husband, who are skilled kung fu fighters, and the harpist, a musician who uses her instrument as a deadly weapon. The movie is full of slapstick humor, witty one-liners, and over-the-top action sequences. The humor is often absurd and surreal, adding to the overall comedic tone of the film. In the end, Sing learns to overcome his fears and weaknesses and transforms into a hero who saves the inhabitants of the apartment complex from the Axe Gang. This resolution is both satisfying and humorous, as Sing uses his kung fu abilities to defeat the villains in a comedic way.

Other examples of comedy movies include *The Blues Brothers (1980)*, *Home Alone (1990)*, *Shaolin Soccer (2001)*, *Guardians of the Galaxy (2014)*, and *Deadpool (2016)*.

These universal patterns of stories and narratives provide a framework for understanding and analyzing stories across cultures and time periods. While not every story fits neatly into one of these patterns, they can be helpful in identifying common themes and structures that can be found in many stories. Most of these stories are also comprised of structures, and the most common structure used in movies is the three-act structure.

Implementing the three-act structure of storytelling

The acts of storytelling refer to the structural elements that make up a narrative, and there are different theories on how many acts there are in a story. One common theory is the **three-act structure**, which divides a story into three parts: the setup, the confrontation, and the resolution.

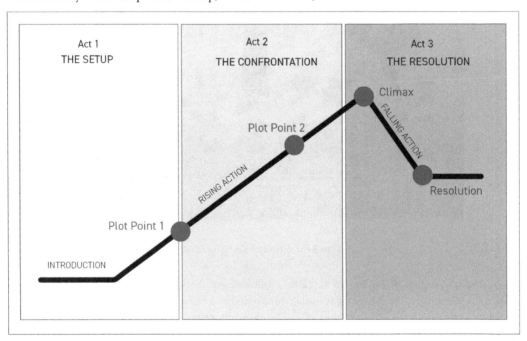

Figure 3.7: The three-act structure of storytelling

Here is a brief overview of each act:

- *Act 1 – the setup*: In this act, the audience is introduced to the characters, the setting, and the conflict that drives the story. This act establishes the protagonist's ordinary world before the inciting incident that disrupts their life and sets the story in motion.

- *Act 2 – the confrontation*: This act is where the majority of the action takes place, as the protagonist faces challenges and obstacles that test their resolve and force them to confront their flaws and weaknesses. This act culminates in a turning point, often referred to as the midpoint, where the protagonist's goals or motivations shift, and the stakes of the story are raised.

- *Act 3 – the resolution*: In this act, the protagonist faces the climax, the highest point of tension in the story, where they confront the primary antagonist or obstacle. After the climax, the story begins to wind down, and the resolution ties up loose ends, resolves conflicts, and provides closure for the audience.

A good example of a three-act story is *The Matrix (1999)*. The movie portrays a future society where people are trapped in a simulated reality called the Matrix, created by intelligent machines to exploit humans as a source of energy. The protagonist, Thomas Anderson, also known as Neo, discovers this truth and joins a group of rebels fighting against the machines, along with others who have also been freed from the Matrix.

The following diagram shows the movie's plot broken down into three acts:

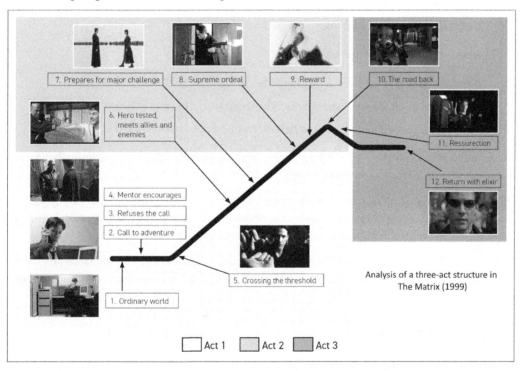

Figure 3.8: Three-act story – The Matrix

Act 1 includes the following sequence of events:

1. Neo has an ordinary life, working in his office cubicle.

2. He then gets a phone call from his mentor, Morpheus, telling him that he can help Neo to get answers.

3. Neo changes his mind on the building ledge and refuses to jump to escape from the agents coming after him.

4. Later when they meet, Morpheus encourages Neo, who then swallows the red pill.

5. Neo is ejected from the Matrix and is brought into the real, machine-controlled, war-torn world.

Act 2 includes the following sequence of events:

1. Neo is then tested by Morpheus and meets the ship's crew and his archnemesis, Agent Smith.

2. When Morpheus gets caught, Trinity and Neo prepare for a rescue. They go back into the Matrix.

3. They endure supreme ordeals but…

4. …manage to rescue Morpheus.

Act 3 includes the following sequence of events:

1. Agent Smith stops Neo from returning to his world, they fight, and Neo is killed.

2. Neo returns to his world, realizes he is "The One," and fights more agents.

3. Neo uses his powers and sets out to free everyone trapped in the Matrix.

Take a moment to study the previous information and see whether you can relate it to other movies that you have watched. Can you name a few?

Other theories suggest there may be more than three acts, such as the five-act structure commonly used in Shakespearean plays. However, regardless of the number of acts, the goals of a story's structure are to engage the audience, build tension, and create a satisfying narrative arc.

In this section, we have understood the three-act structure of storytelling and have seen an example of one such story. In the next section, we will start collecting ideas for our own film and create our storyboard.

Collecting ideas and references for a short film

Now that you have an idea of what a story structure is, let us start collecting ideas and references for your short film. The duration of the short film can be anything from 1 to 20 minutes but for the purpose of this book I suggest you keep your story short, to between 1 and 2 minutes.

Collecting references and ideas is important in filmmaking because it helps filmmakers develop a clear vision for their project and provides them with inspiration and guidance. References and ideas can come from a variety of sources, such as other films, books, paintings, photographs, or personal experiences. By studying and gathering these references and ideas, you can develop a visual language, style, and tone for your project and communicate your vision effectively.

I came across an interesting website that will give you story prompts or story ideas you can use as inspiration for your virtual film: `https://screencraft.org/blog/101-epic-sci-fi-story-prompts/`. These are mainly science fiction-based prompts but there are many other such websites. I encourage you to do some research for your own stories.

There are also Writing Prompt Generator by ServiceScape (`https://www.servicescape.com/writing-prompt-generator`) and Plot Generator (`https://www.plot-generator.org.uk/`), which can be used to get plot or story ideas.

Once you have found your story, we will begin collecting references in the form of images. Google is probably the best place to start finding these, along with Pinterest (`https://www.pinterest.com/`).

Then you can use PureRef (`https://www.pureref.com/`), a great free tool that I use all the time to gather my images together.

Figure 3.9: PureRef reference images

It is as simple as right-clicking on any images you find and then copying/pasting them into PureRef. You can also use the *Ctrl + C* and *Ctrl + V* keyboard shortcuts.

As an example, our story is based in a sci-fi setting, which includes an interior of a spaceship, some sleeping cryogenic pods, an external view of the spaceship, and a large Earth-like planet with lush vegetation and water bodies. Based on this, I would start looking for images related to spaceship interiors and exteriors, planets, landscapes, forests, oceans, rivers, and so on.

Other examples could include collecting images based on the following suggestions:

- The time of day – dawn, noon, the golden hour, twilight, or night
- Specific color palletes – black and white, sepia-toned, duo-toned, tri-toned, or photographic

Collect as many images as you can, make notes, and categorize them as you go. You may or may not use most of them but the more reference images you have, the more ideas will come to mind. Once you have collected your images, it is time to start creating your storyboard.

> **Note**
>
> If you are unsure of the story you would like to create, just follow along; we will create a story together throughout the book.

Creating your storyboard

A storyboard is a visual representation of a film or video production that illustrates the sequence of shots, scenes, and events in a series of drawings or sketches. It serves as a roadmap for the director, cinematographer, and other members of the production team, providing a clear and concise visual plan for the film or video project.

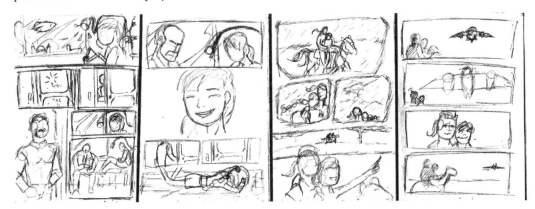

Figure 3.10: A simple storyboard

There are several reasons why storyboarding is important in filmmaking:

- **Visualization**: Storyboarding allows the director and the production team to visualize and plan the shots and scenes in advance, helping to avoid costly mistakes and re-shoots during production

- **Communication**: Storyboarding helps to communicate the vision of the director and the creative team to the crew, actors, and other stakeholders involved in the project

- **Planning**: Storyboarding helps to plan the logistics of the shoot, including camera placement, lighting, and sound, allowing for a smoother and more efficient production process

- **Budgeting**: Storyboarding can help to identify potential budgetary constraints and challenges in advance, allowing for more accurate budgeting and planning

Developing a storyboard

Creating a storyboard can be a fun and creative process. Here are some general steps to follow when creating a storyboard:

1. **Define your project**: Start by defining the purpose of your project, whether it is a film, video, or animation. This will help you determine the story you want to tell and the scenes that need to be included in your storyboard.

2. **Sketch out your scenes**: Use a pencil and paper, or a digital drawing tool, to sketch out your scenes. You can use stick figures or rough drawings to illustrate the action and camera angles. Try to keep your drawings simple and clear, focusing on the composition and framing of each shot.

3. **Add notes and dialogue**: Once you have your scene sketches, add notes and dialogue to indicate important details such as camera movements, lighting, sound effects, and dialogue. This will help you communicate your vision to the rest of your team.

4. **Organize your scenes**: Arrange your scenes in the order you want them to appear in your final project. This will help you determine the pacing and flow of your project.

5. **Revise and refine**: Review your storyboard and make any necessary revisions or refinements. This may include adding or removing scenes, adjusting camera angles or lighting, or refining dialogue or sound effects.

You can download storyboard templates from sites such as StudioBinder (`https://www.studiobinder.com/blog/downloads/storyboard-template/`). StoryBinder also provides sample storyboards you can use for inspiration, which you can find here: `https://www.studiobinder.com/blog/storyboard-examples-film/#Science-Fiction-Movie-Storyboards`.

If you are unable to find the images you're looking for or are unable to draw, there are AI tools that can help you generate storyboard images, such as Adobe Firefly (`https://firefly.adobe.com/`). At the point of writing this book, Adobe Firefly is in beta, and you will have to request access using a free Adobe ID.

There are also sites such as Midjourney (`https://www.midjourney.com/`) and DALL-E 2 (`https://openai.com/product/dall-e-2`) that allow you to generate images to add to your storyboard. You could type in something such as *image of a spaceship landing on Mars* and you'll be presented with several images you can then save and use.

Our narrative and storyboard

For the purpose of this book, here is a storyboard we will work on together:

Figure 3.11: Our storyboard

Our upcoming story, *A New Beginning*, is a straightforward tale with a grand finale. The opening shot features a black screen with a subtle humming sound that emanates from within a spaceship. Soon, we observe an image emerging on the screen, revealing a flight deck with a planet visible in the distance. As the camera moves closer to the front of the spaceship, we learn from the holographic screen that the planet visible through the spaceship viewport is both safe and habitable.

Two cryogenics pods containing two human-like figures are situated at the back of the spaceship. The onboard computer commands the spaceship to initiate the landing procedure, and a space shuttle is then launched toward the planet.

As the space shuttle enters the planet's atmosphere, it traverses a beautiful and vibrant landscape, indicating that the planet is perfect for habitation. As the shuttle lands and the door opens, the two beings disembark and walk toward the edge of the water body.

At this moment, the identities of the two humans are unveiled, with the big reveal of their names being Adam and Eve. The screen fades to black, and the title **A NEW BEGINNING** appears.

So now that we have a storyboard and the narrative, we can begin to work on our virtual film in Unreal Engine!

Summary

In this chapter, you learned about the universal patterns of story and narratives and understood how to implement the three-act structure of storytelling. You also learned the importance of collecting ideas and references for a short film and how to create a storyboard.

In the next chapter, we will jump into Unreal Engine and start creating our project, adding the spaceship interior environment, adding bookmarks, and importing 3D objects.

Part 2:
Production: Creating the Environment

In this part, you will learn essential skills to elevate your Unreal Engine world-building proficiency. *Chapter 4* guides you through the process of importing 3D objects and crafting levels, enhancing your ability to shape virtual worlds. *Chapter 5* introduces the powerful tool Quixel Megascans, demonstrating how to create photorealistic environments using photogrammetry 3D objects. Delve into *Chapter 6* to harness the art of crafting and applying materials to 3D objects, refining your ability to bring realism and detail to your virtual creations. This segment equips you with key techniques to create dynamic and visually stunning environments within Unreal Engine.

This part includes the following chapters:

- *Chapter 4, Importing 3D Objects and Creating Levels*
- *Chapter 5, Creating Environments with Quixel Megascans*
- *Chapter 6, Creating and Applying Materials to 3D Meshes*

4

Importing 3D Objects and Creating Levels

In the last two chapters, we learned the importance of understanding the filmmaker's main tool, the camera, and its properties, as well as collecting references and creating storyboards. In this chapter, we will start working on our virtual film in Unreal Engine.

First, we will start to understand the terminology used in film and in Unreal Engine. This knowledge will aid in the creation of a master sequence, which will outline the specific shots and camera angles needed for the scene.

Then we will create an Unreal Engine project, which will serve as the framework for the scene. Once this is done, it will enable us to add and use projects from the Unreal Engine Marketplace, which can include pre-made assets such as environments, props, and characters. After selecting the necessary assets, the next step is to add Levels and create bookmarks to aid in navigating the scene. Finally, we will import 3D objects into the project to flesh out our first two scenes and bring them to life.

By following these steps, it is possible to create a dynamic and visually stunning 3D scene using Unreal Engine.

In this chapter, we will cover the following topics:

- Understanding Unreal Engine terminology
- Reviewing our film's shot list and structure
- Creating the Unreal Engine project
- Importing Marketplace projects
- Organizing the Outliner
- Removing Lightmaps
- Creating Levels

- Adding Bookmarks
- Importing 3D objects
- Building the space scene

Technical requirements

All of the project files required for this book can be found through the following link: `https://packt.link/gbz/9781801813808`.

It contains the following:

- The shot list, which shows exactly how and when we will be using the provided assets
- The assets list, which consists of download links for the assets we will be using in the film
- The 3D models, Textures, images, sound effects, and music we will be using in the film

Understanding Unreal Engine terminology

Unreal Engine is a game engine and has been since the beginning. Only recently, filmmakers started using Unreal Engine to create virtual films, and as such, there is certain terminology that differs between the two. Let us have a closer look:

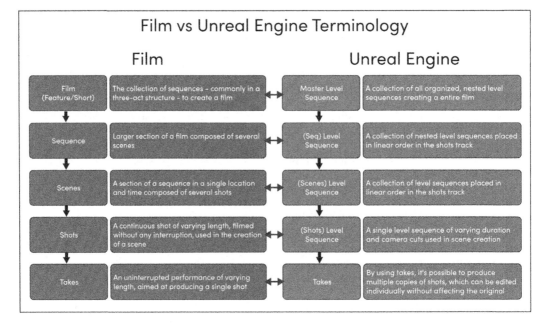

Figure 4.1: Film versus Unreal Engine terminology

A typical feature film is made by shooting **takes**. The best takes are then chosen as the final **shots**, which are grouped into **scenes**. The scenes then become part of a **sequence** and sequences become the complete **film**. In Unreal Engine, we will be using a feature called **Level Sequencer** to achieve this.

In our short film, we will be creating a **master sequence** (the complete film), which will consist of several scenes, which will in turn be made up of several shots and takes. It is important for us to plan this right at the beginning, so we have clear direction and clarity for production.

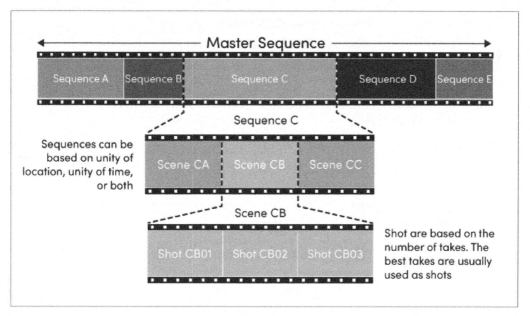

Figure 4.2: A typical film structure

I will be explaining more terminology used in Unreal Engine compared to filmmaking in the coming sections, but for now, it is important that you understand these terms and structures in Unreal Engine as we need to create nested Levels with proper naming conventions to ease the process of the narrative.

Now that we are familiar with the film structure and how it will relate to our film in Unreal Engine, let us look at the shot list I have provided (which you can download from the link in the *Technical requirements* section) so we can begin creating our Unreal Engine project.

Reviewing our film's shot list and structure

The shot list provided contains very detailed information about each shot—the location, cast members, visual effects needed, set dressing, sound effects, and music required. It's good practice to have a shot list handy, especially when working in a team, so each team member has a specific task to carry out. However, the shot list is not set in stone; it is a guide and may change as we progress.

Let's have a look at our virtual film structure:

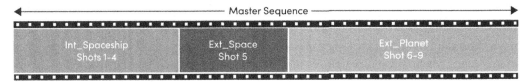

Figure 4.3: "A New Beginning" film structure

We have a total of three sequences:

- **The spaceship interior sequence** (shots 1 through 4): These are comprised of shots entirely done in the spaceship, which includes the flight deck area and the cargo area, where the cryo-pods will be placed

- **The space sequence** (shot 5): This is the external shot of the space shuttle launching toward the planet after receiving instructions from the onboard computer

- **The planet sequence** (shots 6 through 9): This sequence will comprise all the shots taking place on the planet, which includes the shuttle flyby, the shuttle landing, the two characters walking toward the water body, and the big reveal

In this chapter, we will create the first and second sequences. We will tackle the third sequence in *Chapter 5*.

> **Note**
>
> The downloadable file (from the link in the *Technical requirements* section) has all the 3D assets, images, sound effects, and music you will need to create the short film.

Now that you have an understanding of our film's structure, let's jump into Unreal Engine to start creating our short film.

Creating the Unreal Engine project

By now, you should be familiar with running Unreal Engine and creating a project. Here, we are going to recap the process, so the next few steps are a repeat of *Chapter 1*.

First, open up the Epic Games Launcher. Then go to the **Library** section and click the **Launch** button for Unreal Engine version 5.2. This will open the Unreal Project Browser:

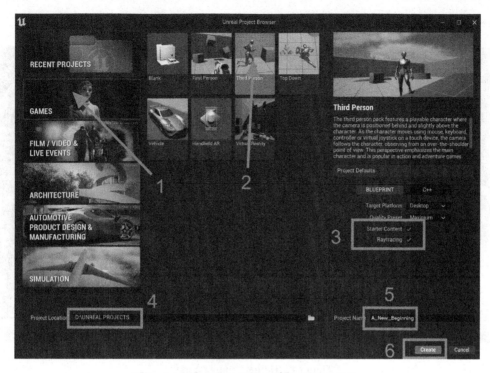

Figure 4.4: Creating an Unreal Engine project

Here, do the following:

1. Click on the **GAMES** category.

2. Choose the **Third Person** template.

3. Enable **Starter Content** (this will add additional content to your project so you can use it in your project) and **Raytracing**.

4. Choose the project location.

5. Fill in **Project Name** – like the name of our film, I will call the project A_New_Beginning. (Remember that Unreal Engine project names cannot be more than 20 characters, nor can they start with numbers, and they certainly can't have spaces in between the words. However, you can make use of underscores or hyphens to separate words.)

6. Click the **Create** button.

After a few seconds, you will be presented with the following screen:

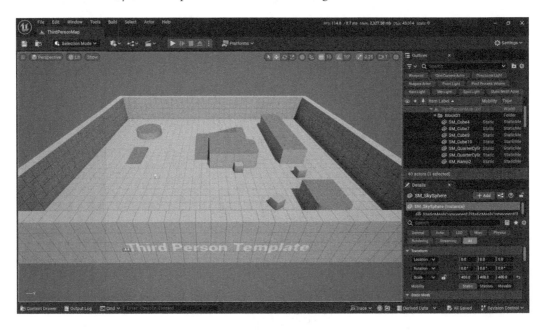

Figure 4.5: Unreal Engine interface

Now you have successfully created the project. In the next section, we will import a free Unreal Engine Marketplace project to create our first scene.

Importing Marketplace projects

As mentioned earlier, the first scene we're going to work on is the internal part of the spaceship. To do this, we are going to use a free project available in the Unreal Engine Marketplace. The best way to get this project is by using the Epic Games Launcher.

> **Note**
>
> The Unreal Engine Marketplace is an excellent resource to buy and sell digital assets, including 3D models, Textures, animations, music, sound effects, and more, for use in games, films, and other digital projects. In this project, we will be using assets that are available for free.

Here's how to do this:

1. Open the Epic Games Launcher and select the **Marketplace** tab.

2. In the search window, type Spaceship and press *Enter*.

3. You'll be presented with lots of options, so on the right of the screen, filter for free content by selecting **Free** under **Max Price**.

Figure 4.6: Choosing the Free option

4. Select **Spaceship Interior Environment Set** (the following screenshot will help you find the asset you're looking for) and click on the **Add To Project** button.

Figure 4.7: Add To Project

5. In the pop-up panel, select **Show all projects**, then scroll down and look for our project. You'll get a notification that the project file is not compatible with Unreal Engine 5.2. To fix this, in the **Select Version** list, pick **5.0** and click the **Add to Project** button.

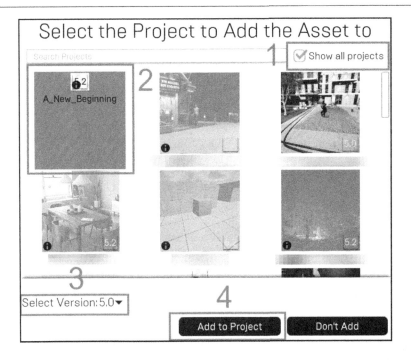

Figure 4.8: Choosing the compatible version

> **Note**
>
> This **Add to Project** button will not be active until you change the Unreal Engine version to 5.0. Now that we have changed to a compatible version (version 5.0), it will not cause any issues in our project.

6. Back in Unreal Engine, you will notice that there is a new folder called **SpaceshipInterior** in the Content Browser. This means that the project has been successfully imported.

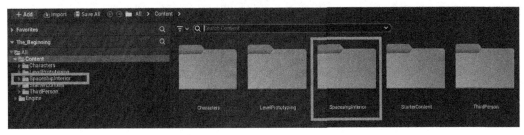

Figure 4.9: The added project in the Content Browser

7. Open the **Spaceship Interior** folder and select the **Maps** folder, then double-click on the **Demonstration** Level. The project will open, and you'll find yourself in the spaceship.

You can navigate around to check out the spaceship.

Figure 4.10: The spaceship interior

> **Note**
>
> In Unreal Engine, coming from game terminology, the terms Maps and Levels are used interchangeably. These refer to the levels and sub-levels that can be created in a project. From a filmmaker's perspective, we will refer to them as sequences, scenes, and shots.

8. To hide the overlay icons in the Viewport, use the **Viewport** menu and check the **Game View** option (or simply press the G key on your keyboard) to toggle them on or off.

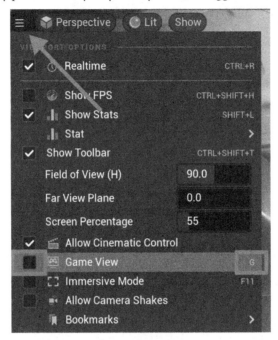

Figure 4.11: Toggling game mode

Great, you have managed to import the interior of the spaceship into your current project. Next, we will start organizing the Outliner.

Organizing the Outliner

In the **Outliner** panel (at the top right of the screen), you can see the list of items currently populating the scene. These consist of cameras, decals, lights, and 3D static meshes. Currently, there are 1,046 items (or Actors).

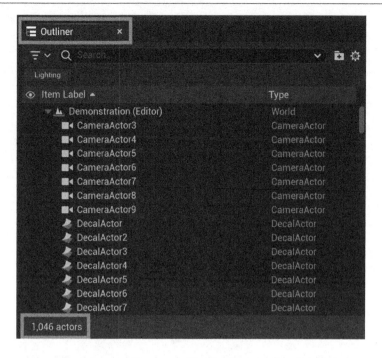

Figure 4.12: The Outliner

> **Note**
>
> All the items in the Content Browser are referred to as assets, but once they are used in the Level (scene), they are known as Actors.

Let's start by removing Actors we don't need and moving similar Actors into their respective folders:

1. Select all the cameras in the Outliner and press the *Delete* key on your keyboard.

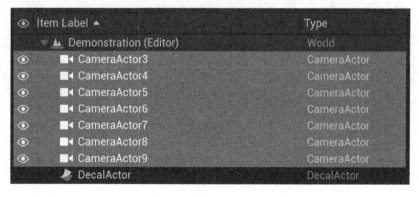

Figure 4.13: Deleting the cameras

2. We also need to delete all the **SphereReflectionCapture** Actors and the **LightmassImportanceVolume** Actors too.

3. Next, select all the **Decal** Actors and click the **Create Folder** icon at the top right of the panel.

Figure 4.14: Creating folders

This will automatically populate the **Decal** Actors into their own folder. Rename the folder to Decals so it is clear what the folder contains.

4. Now make folders for all the lights and Static Meshes.

5. Next, delete the remaining three Actors – **ExponentialHeightFog**, **PostProcessVolume**, and **SkyLight** – as we won't be needing these for now.

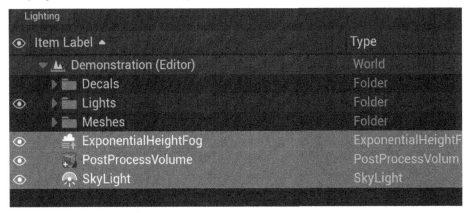

Figure 4.15: Deleting the remaining Actors

6. Finally, save the project by going to **File**, then **Save All** (or using the *Ctrl + Shift + S* keyboard shortcut).

In the next section, we will remove Lightmaps (baked lights) that are in the project.

Removing Lightmaps

In Unreal Engine 5, Epic Games introduced **Lumen**, a fully dynamic global illumination and reflection system. Prior to this, the precomputed (or "baked") lighting method was used, where the light and shadow information was permanently "baked" onto the surface of 3D objects, thus moving the lights or changing their color and intensity would not have any effect. The only way was to re-bake the lights, which would usually take anything from minutes to hours, depending on the complexity of the scene. With **Lumen**, all light properties and positions are changeable in real time. This is an absolute game-changer!

To take advantage of the **Lumen** real-time lighting, we will need to ensure that we remove all remnants (if any) of baked lights in the scene. Here's how to do so:

1. Go to the **Window** drop-down menu and select **World Settings**.

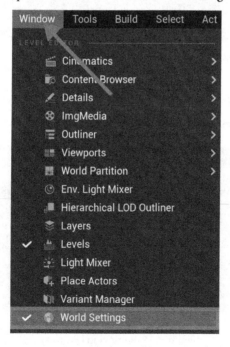

Figure 4.16: Opening the World Settings panel

2. In the **World Settings** panel, type `Lightmaps`.

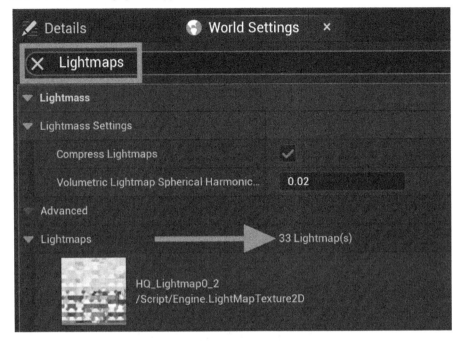

Figure 4.17: Found 33 Lightmaps

You will notice that there are currently 33 Lightmaps in the project. Let's remove them.

3. In the same **World Settings** panel, replace the word **Lightmaps** with `force`.

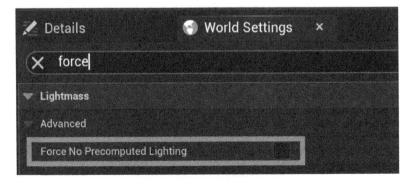

Figure 4.18: Removing Lightmaps

4. Check the **Force No Precomputed Lighting** option, and you will receive the following message. Click **OK**. This action will not remove the Lightmaps just yet; it is just an instruction letting you know what to do next.

Figure 4.19: Warning message

5. To permanently remove all Lightmaps, access the **Build** drop-down menu and select the **Build All Levels** option.

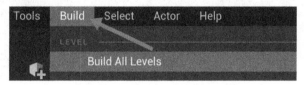

Figure 4.20: Building the lights

6. In the **World Settings** panel, type Lightmaps again, and you will now find that it's unavailable. This means the Lightmaps have now been successfully removed (you may need to do this twice to ensure the Lightmaps are completely removed).

There is one last thing we need to do to ensure we are using dynamic lighting (real-time lighting), and that is to change the mobility mode of all our lights to **Moveable**. The advantage of setting the lights to **Moveable** is that it gives you the ability to change their color, intensity, and other properties in real time. The disadvantage is that it is a CPU-intensive process, but since we're working on a virtual film and not a game, we can take advantage of the real-time lighting and shadows.

7. Select all the **PointLight** Actors in the Outliner, then in the **Details** panel, under the **Mobility** section, select the **Movable** option.

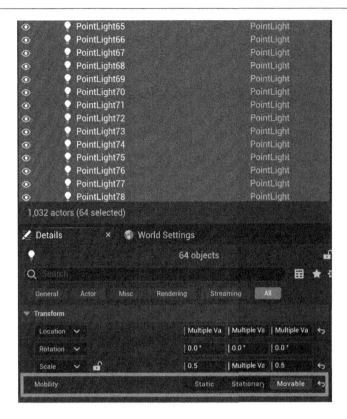

Figure 4.21: Changing lights to Movable

8.   Repeat the previous step for all the **SpotLight** Actors.

And with that, the scene is now completely lit by dynamic lights. It's a good idea to save your project again now.

So, in this section, we successfully removed baked lights in the project to take advantage of real-time global illumination. In the next section, we will start creating our Levels.

Creating Levels

Referring to the storyboard, in our first Level (sequence), we have five shots in the spaceship. Here is the breakdown:

- **Shot 1**: Fade-in and spaceship console lighting up
- **Shot 2**: Close-up of console displaying a message indicating that the planet is habitable
- **Shot 3**: Showing the cryo-pods
- **Shot 4**: Showing the computer's landing instructions screen

You can see the four shots that will make up the first sequence here:

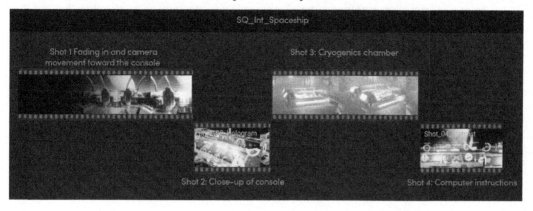

Figure 4.22: Spaceship internal shots

Now that we've established our four shots, let's go ahead and create our first Level/sequence:

1. Select the **Content** folder in the Content Browser, then right-click and choose **New Folder**. Name the new folder A_New_Beginning. Then, open the folder and create another folder inside it named Levels.

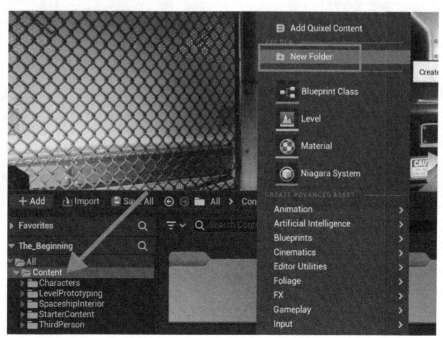

Figure 4.23: Creating a new Levels folder

We will use **Demonstration** as our first Level, but we will have to rename it first. Unreal Engine will not allow you to rename a Level while it is currently open, so follow the next step to complete this correctly.

2. In the Content Browser, find the **StarterContent** folder, then open the **Maps** folder, and double-click on **StarterMap**. When prompted to save, choose **Save Selected**. This will remove the **Demonstration** project from the PC's memory, so we can rename it (if prompted with **Save Content**, click **Save Selected**).

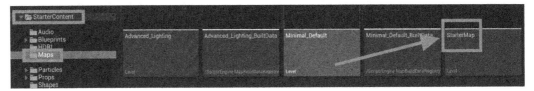

Figure 4.24 – Opening a temporary Level

3. Locate the **Demonstration** Level inside **Content | SpaceshipInterior | Maps**. Right-click on it and choose **Rename** (or press *F2*). Let's rename it to INT_Spaceship.

4. For organizational purposes, drag and drop the **INT_Spaceship** Level into the newly created **Levels** folder. When prompted, choose **Move**.

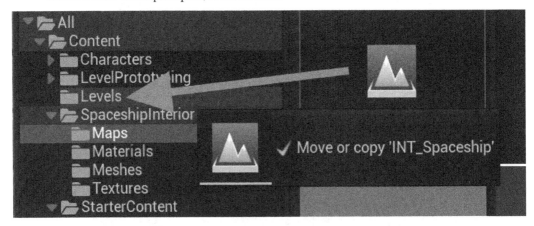

Figure 4.25: Moving the Level

5. If you are prompted with any warning messages when executing the move action, like the one in the following screenshot, just click **OK**.

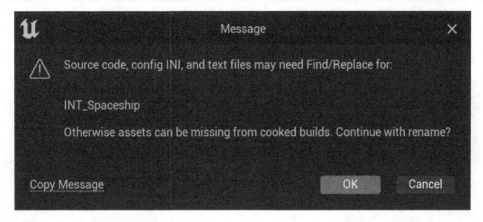

Figure 4.26: Message when moving the Level

6.   Open the **INT_Spaceship** Level by double-clicking on it, so we can continue working on it.

We have successfully created a **Levels** folder where will keep all our Levels and have moved the spaceship scene inside it. Next, we will add Bookmarks for our planned camera shots.

Adding Bookmarks

We initially discussed Bookmarks in *Chapter 2*. Now, it is time to create Bookmarks for our planned shots so that when we revisit this Level later, in *Chapter 10*, we can add cameras and animate them. Here's how to create Bookmarks for planned shots:

1.   Move the current view closer to the bridge of the spaceship, then press *Ctrl + 1* on the keyboard to create **Bookmark 1**. We will use this Bookmark for shot 1.

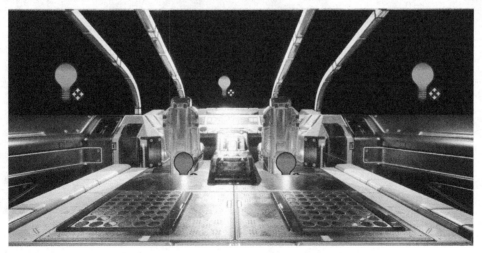

Figure 4.27: Bookmark 1 for shot 1

2. Since shot 2 and shot 4 will be in the same vicinity, we will create a Bookmark for both shots here. Move closer to the console and set it in such a way that the whole console can be seen, as shown in *Figure 4.28*. Press *Ctrl + 2* to create **Bookmark 2.**

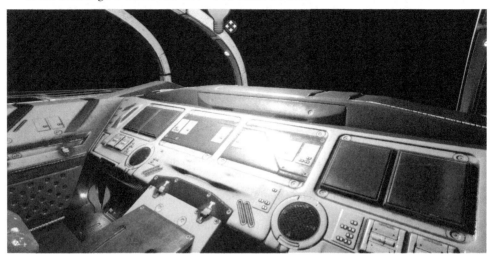

Figure 4.28: Bookmark 2 for shots 2 and 4

3. To create Bookmarks for the cryo-pods area shot (shot 3), we will move to the back of the spaceship. Go past the two doors and you will come to an area that is large enough to place the two pods. Then press *Ctrl + 3* to create **Bookmark 3**.

Figure 4.29: Bookmark 3 for the cryo-pods

You may now test the Bookmarks by pressing *1*, *2*, and *3* across the top of your keyboard. While we are here, let's import the cryo-pod.

Importing 3D objects

To import the cryo-pod, we will be using a 3D model downloaded from Sketchfab (you can find the exact link in the provided assets list). I have made some modifications to the downloaded 3D model, including adding Material IDs in Blender, which will allow us to add custom Materials to the different parts of the cryo-pods (we will learn about creating custom Materials in *Chapter 6*).

> **Note**
>
> **Material IDs** are pre-defined surfaces created in a 3D application. This means surfaces of a 3D object can be isolated and textured differently. You'll find the full instructions on how to create Material IDs using Blender in the *Appendix* of this book. Saying that, it's good to have some basic skills with DCC software such as Blender (https://www.blender.org/), in case you need to augment the downloaded 3D assets before importing them into Unreal Engine.
>
> It is also worth noting that Sketchfab, a great repository for buying and selling 3D assets, will likely be called just Fab (https://www.fab.com/) by the time you read this book.

To import the cryo-pod, follow these instructions:

1. In the Content Browser, select the **Content** folder, then in the **A_New_Beginning** folder, create a folder named `3D_Models` (it is good practice to use an underscore to separate the two words for legibility purposes). Inside that folder, create another folder and name it `Cryo_Pod`.

Figure 4.30: Create the Cryo_Pod folder

2. Locate the **3D Models** folder in the downloaded project file. The 3D model is named `Cryo-Pod.fbx`.

> **Note**
>
> Among all the 3D model filesystems available out there, Autodesk FBX is probably the most flexible and most used in the industry. The FBX filesystem is preferred by Unreal Engine as it supports Static Meshes, Skeletal Meshes, animations, Materials (basic support – may not match original Material in your content creation app), Textures, Rigid Meshes, Morph Targets, cameras (no animation), and lights.

3.   Drag the Cryo-Pod.fbx file into the new **Cryo_Pod** folder. In the panel that appears, ensure the Material import method is set to **Create New Materials** and click on **Import All** (if you get a **Message Log** popup, just close it).

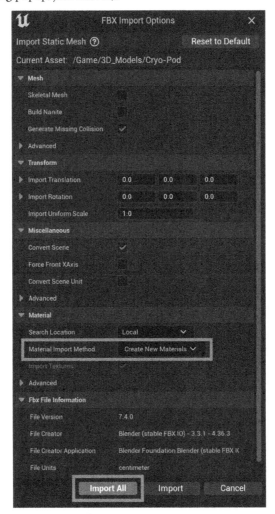

Figure 4.31: FBX Import Options panel

The **Cryo_Pod** folder will now be populated with a few items:

- The static meshes, including **Cryo-Pod_Bed**, **Cryo-Pod_Glass**, **Cryo-Pod_Human**, and **Cryo-Pod_Main_Body**

- The Materials (colored spheres) that were automatically generated by Unreal Engine, using the Material IDs created in Blender (see the *Appendix* for full instructions on creating Material IDs)

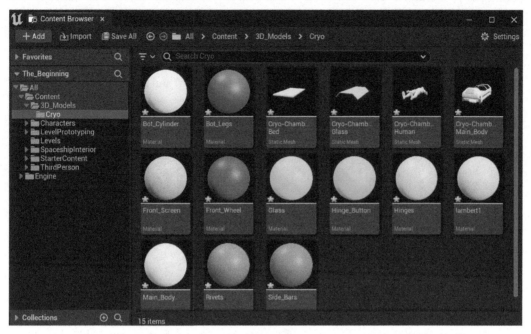

Figure 4.32: The newly imported static meshes and Materials

> **Note**
>
> You will notice little asterisks (*) at the bottom left of every imported item in this folder. This is Unreal Engine's way of telling you that these assets are still unsaved in the project. Use the *Ctrl + Shift + S* shortcut to save them all. Once you do that, the asterisks will disappear.

4. To ease the addition of the cryo-pod into the scene, use the **Dock in Layout** mode for the Content Browser and change **Thumbnail Size** for the items to **Small**, so you have more space available in the Viewport.

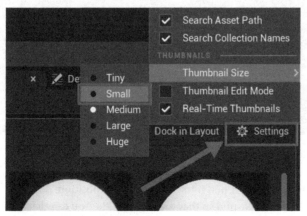

Figure 4.33: Changing the icon size

5. Select all four static meshes and drag them into the area where you need to place the cryo-pod.

6. As you drag and drop the four objects into the scene, they will also be listed in the Outliner. Since they are still selected, this is a good time to put them into their own folder. Click the top-right folder icon (as we did in the *Organizing the Outliner* section) and name the folder Cryo.

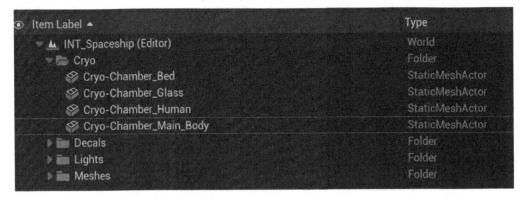

Figure 4.34: Cryo items in a folder

7. You may also notice that the objects in the scene are smaller than we would like them to be. Let's enlarge them by selecting all four objects in the **Cryo** folder, then in the **Details** panel, scale them up to 8 units. Instead of typing 8 into the **X**, **Y**, and **Z** slots separately, use the padlock icon to scale them all at once. While here, we can also change the mobility mode of all four objects to **Movable**.

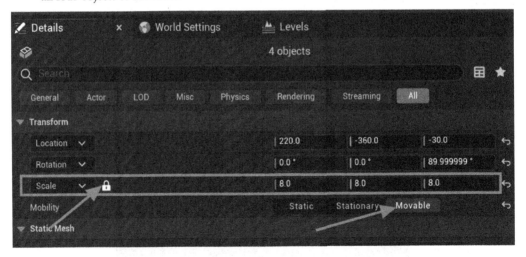

Figure 4.35: Scaling up the cryo-pod

8. You can now rotate the cryo-pod into the appropriate position, duplicate it using *Ctrl + D*, and then drag the second cryo-pod so they are side by side. You can delete the crate on the far side so that the cryo-pods can be positioned correctly.

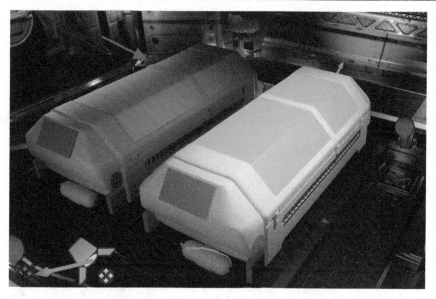

Figure 4.36: Duplicating the cryo-pods and deleting the crate

And with that, you can save your project. Later, in *Chapter 6*, we will revisit this sequence to edit and apply Materials and Textures to the objects. Our spaceship interior sequence is done for now; let's now create the second sequence – the space sequence.

Building the space scene

In the previous sections, we successfully created the first sequence of the film by adding the internal scene of the spaceship to the project, adding Bookmarks, and importing the cryo-pods. In this section, we will be creating the second sequence, which you can see here:

Figure 4.37: The completed space scene

By now, you probably already have an idea that we are separating our sequences into different Levels. This will become very handy when we assemble our master sequence in *Chapter 10*.

This new sequence will contain the following Actors:

- **The Earth, moon, and stars**: These are created using the Unreal Engine **Modeling** tool

- **The spaceship**: This is imported into Unreal Engine from the downloaded project file

To get started, we will need to create a new Level.

Creating an empty Level

Here's how to create an empty Level for our second sequence:

1. Go to **File** and select **New Level** (*Ctrl + N*). In the **New Level** pop-up panel, choose **Empty Level** and click **Create**.

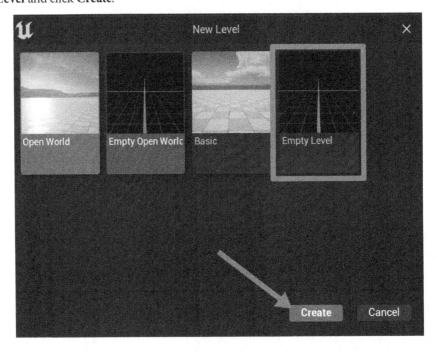

Figure 4.38: Creating a new empty Level

An empty Level is the most appropriate here for our space scene. You'll get an empty black screen. Don't worry, we're on the right track.

2. Now go to **File**, choose **Save Current Level As…**, name the Level EXT_Space, and ensure you save it in the **Levels** folder we created earlier.

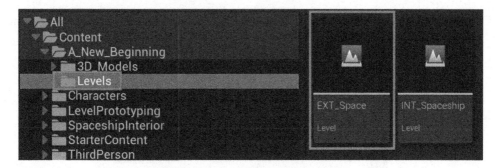

Figure 4.39: New Level in the Levels folder

Great! Now that our Level has been created, let's start creating the planet, the moon, and the stars.

Creating the planet

The first thing we will create is the Earth object, and we will use the Unreal Engine **Modeling** tool plugin to do so. Follow these steps to utilize the **Modeling** tool plugin:

1. Click the **Selection Mode** drop-down menu – if you can't see the **Modeling** mode, simply proceed to *step 2*, but if you can see the mode, you can skip to *step 5*.

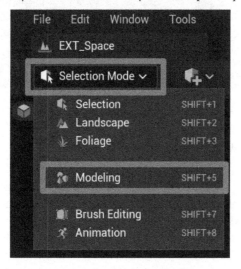

Figure 4.40: Accessing the Modeling mode

Unreal Engine 5 comes with an assortment of plugins, which includes the **Modeling** tool, which allows you to create both simple and complex 3D models right in the engine. If the **Modeling** mode is not present, then that means it has not been enabled in the **Plugins** panel. Let's enable it.

2. In the top-right corner of the Unreal Engine interface, open the **Settings** drop-down menu and select **Plugins**.

Figure 4.41: Accessing Plugins

3. When the **Plugins** panel opens, in the search window, type **Modeling** and you'll see a list of plugins. Enable the **Modeling Tools Editor Mode** plugin.

Figure 4.42: Enabling the Modeling Tools Editor Mode plugin

4. Select the **Modeling** mode from the **Selection Mode** dropdown.

> **Note**
>
> After enabling the **Modeling** mode, Unreal Engine will prompt you to restart. If you have not saved the project, you will be prompted to do so. Once Unreal Engine has restarted, proceed to the next steps.

Two new panels will pop up on the left side of the interface – the **Mode Toolbar** and the **Modeling** panels.

5. Now, in the **Mode Toolbar** panel, under the **Shapes** category, select the **Sphere** icon. As soon as you do that, in the **Modeling** panel, you'll be presented with the **Sphere** properties.

6. In the **Sphere** properties, do the following:

    *   Set **Radius** to 1,000,000

    *   Set **Subdivision Type** to **LatLong**

    *   Set both **Horizontal Slices** and **Vertical Slices** to 200

    *   Change **Pivot Location** to **Centered**

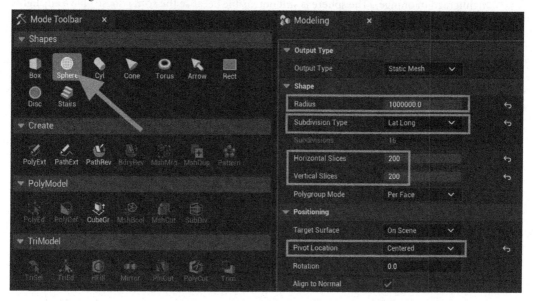

Figure 4.43: Properties to create the planet

7. Once you have set these values, in the Viewport, click **Accept**.

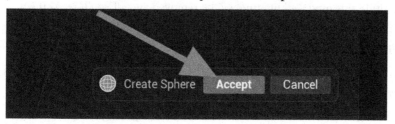

Figure 4.44: Click Accept to create the sphere

You can only confirm whether you've completed the previous steps correctly if you see the **Sphere** Static Mesh Actor in the Outliner.

8. With **Sphere** listed, go back to **Selection** mode, by going to the **Mode** selection dropdown and choosing the **Selection** mode (or hitting *Shift + 1*).

9. You'll notice that the Viewport is still black. The reason for this is that the sphere you just created is huge (around 1 million units!) and we're basically right inside it. To zoom out, double-click on the **Sphere** Static Mesh in the Outliner.

10. Now we will need to scale the **Earth** Actor by **10** units (similar to what we did earlier, in *Figure 4.35*) and zoom out by double-clicking on the **Earth** Actor again.

11. You'll now see an orange outline of the sphere (in Unreal Engine, selected Actors are always highlighted in orange). The sphere is still not visible because the scene doesn't have any lights (yet). For now, in the **Viewport** menu, change **View Mode** from **Lit** to **Unlit**.

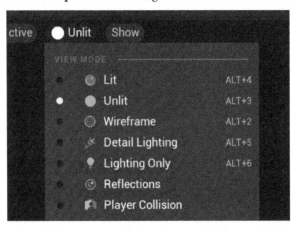

Figure 4.45: The first five visualization modes in Unreal Engine

While we're here, let's have a quick look at some of the main options under **View Mode**:

- **Lit**: This is the final result of all Materials and lighting applied in the Level. We will be in this mode 99% of the time.

- **Unlit**: In this mode, all lighting will be removed and all you'll see is the base color of the objects in the Level. This is useful for scenes with no lights.

- **Wireframe**: This mode will reveal the polygon edges of the objects in the scene.

- **Detailed Lighting**: This mode is used as a diagnostic when checking the effects of the base color of the object on the Materials' normal map.

- **Lighting Only**: This mode is similar to **Detailed Lighting** except that it will not show the Normal Map effects (we will learn what Normal Maps are in *Chapter 6*).

12. Now that the sphere is visible, let's rename the **Sphere** Actor to Earth by selecting the sphere in the Outliner and pressing *F2*.

13. Ensure that the Earth's location is set to **X = 0**, **Y = 0**, and **Z = 0** in the **Details** panel.

14. Then, save the project (*Ctrl + Shift + S*).

With the planet added, let's add the moon to our scene.

Creating the moon

To create the moon, we will be duplicating the **Earth** actor, scaling it down to two units, and moving it beside the **Earth** Actor. To do this, follow these steps:

1. Select the **Earth** Actor in the Outliner (or by clicking on it in the Viewport) and press *Ctrl + D*.
2. You'll now have a copy of the **Earth** Actor (the default name will be **Earth2**). Press *F2* and rename it to Moon.
3. In the **Details** panel, scale the **Moon** Actor down to **2** units (remember to enable the padlock icon to scale uniformly).
4. Now use the X or Y (red or green) axis gizmo to move the moon out of the **Earth** Actor.

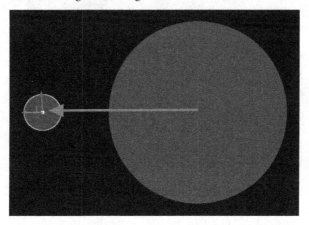

Figure 4.46: Moving the moon using the axis gizmo

5. With the moon completed, save your project again.

Obviously, any space scene is not complete without stars! So, let's create the stars as a background to our space scene.

Creating the stars

Now it's time to create the stars; however, this time, we will be using a custom Material. Materials will be covered in depth in *Chapter 6*, but for now, just follow these steps to create the stars:

1. Select the **Earth** Actor, press *Ctrl + D* to duplicate it, and rename the duplicate Stars.
2. Scale the **Stars** Actor to **1000** units – the **Earth** and the **Moon** Actors are now located inside the **Stars** sphere.

In the next steps, adding the **Stars** texture to the inside surface of the **Stars** sphere will create the illusion that we're in space – neat!

3. In the Content Browser, select the **A_New_Beginning** folder and create two new folders called `Materials` and `Textures`.

4. Locate the **Textures** folder in the downloaded project file (which you can download from the *Technical requirements* section). Then drag the `8k_stars_milky_way.jpg` file into the newly created **Textures** folder in the Content Browser. This is the file we're going to use as our background image.

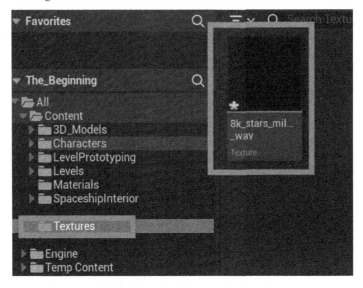

Figure 4.47: Importing the Stars texture into Unreal Engine

5. Now, to create a custom Material for the stars, open the **Materials** folder, right-click inside of it, and choose **Material**.

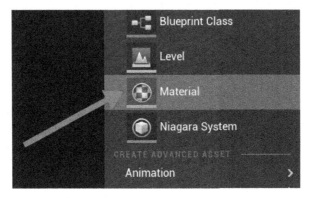

Figure 4.48: Creating a new custom Material

6. You'll be prompted to give it a name – let's go with M_Stars (here, *M* denotes we're creating a Material).

> **Note**
>
> Naming conventions are used throughout Unreal Engine to differentiate between generated assets. They help in organizing the assets and when searching for them in the Content Browser. You can find the recommended naming conventions at https://docs.unrealengine.com/5.1/en-US/recommended-asset-naming-conventions-in-unreal-engine-projects/. We will also go over the suggested naming conventions in Unreal Engine for assets as and when we create them in our project.

7. Once the **M_Stars** Material has been created, double-click to open it up. The Material Editor will appear – don't be intimidated by the interface; it will be covered in depth in *Chapter 6*.

8. For now, click on the **Textures** folder in the Content Browser, then drag the **8k_stars_milky_way** texture into the Material Editor.

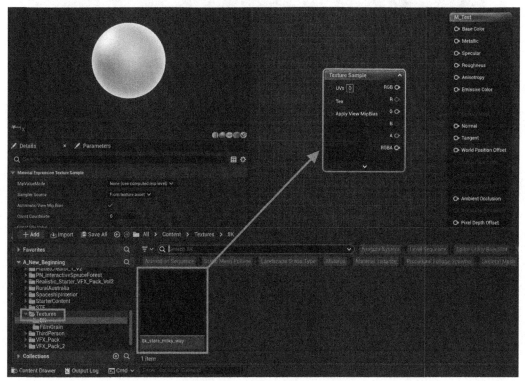

Figure 4.49: Dragging the stars texture into the Material Editor

When you drag the **M_Stars** Material from the Content Browser into the Material Editor, Unreal Engine creates a **Texture Sample** node. The **Texture Sample** node contains the 8k_stars_milky_way.jpg image, which needs to be connected to the **M_Stars** output/result node. This will then make the **Stars** texture show on the inside of the **Stars** Actor.

9. Now connect the **RGB** pin to the **Emissive Color** pin by clicking on the **RGB** pin and dragging it to the **Emissive Color** pin.

10. Click the **M_Stars** result node (the node on the right of the **Texture Sample** node) and open the **Details** tab. Remember that the node must be selected to reveal its properties.

11. Change **Blend Mode** to **Translucent** and enable **Two Sided**.

12. Click on **Apply**, then **Save**.

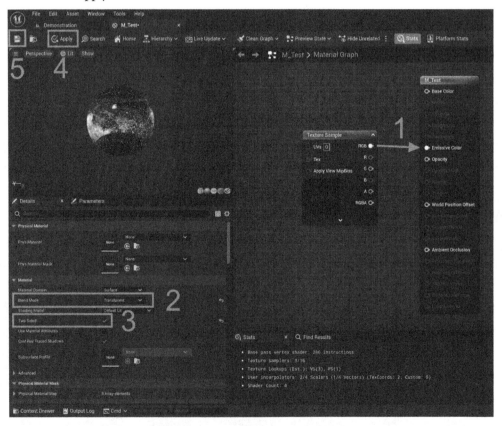

Figure 4.50: Creating the Stars Material

13. You can now close the Material Editor by clicking the **X** in the top-right corner.

And with that, you've just created your very first Material (again, we will revisit this Material in *Chapter 6* to add a few more enhancements to it).

14. Next, in **View Mode**, uncheck **Game Settings** and re-select the **Lit** mode.

15. Now select the **Stars** Actor in the Outliner. Next, in the **Details** panel, scroll down till you see the **Materials** section. Then drag the **M_Stars** Material into the **Element 0** Material slot, then switch back to the **Lit** mode.

Figure 4.51: Applying the Material to the Stars Actor

Now, because Unreal Engine is a game engine, the **Auto Exposure** feature is on by default. This feature automatically adjusts the scene exposure to simulate eye adaptation to changes in brightness. It's all well and good if we are developing a game, but we're not. For this project, the exposure level in our film needs to be locked. There are several ways of doing this in Unreal Engine, but our approach will be by using an Actor called the **Post Process Volume (PPV)**. The PPV comes with many other features, but we will cover those in greater depth in *Chapter 12*.

16. So, to fix our dark scene situation, let's add a PPV to our scene to lock the exposure. So, click **Place Actor** (the green + button) | **Visual Effects** | **Post Process Volume**.

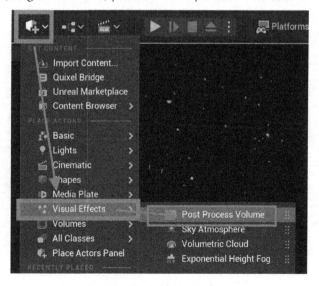

Figure 4.52: Adding a PPV

17. In the Outliner, select the **Post Process Volume** Actor. Then in its **Details** panel, in the search window, type `inf`, and enable **Infinite Extent (Unbound)**. This will allow any settings that we change in this Volume to affect the whole Level/scene and not just be restricted to the bounds of the Volume.

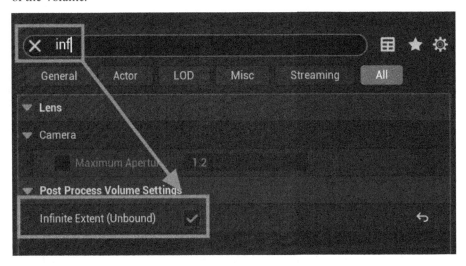

Figure 4.53: Setting Infinite Extent (Unbound)

18. Next, clear the search window, and type `exp` into the **Exposure** category, enable **Metering Mode** and set it to **Manual**, then enable **Exposure Compensation** and set it to `12.0`. This will lock the exposure of the Level.

Figure 4.54: Locking the exposure

> **Note**
>
> Detailed information about **Metering Mode** and **Exposure Compensation** can be found here: `https://docs.unrealengine.com/5.2/en-US/auto-exposure-in-unreal-engine/`

19. Now, in the **View** mode, re-check **Game Settings**.

20. Select the Earth, moon, and stars, and add them to a new folder named **Planet**.

Voilà – you now have a stars background! Feel free to right click in the Viewport to look around and explore the scene so far. Now, save the project, and when you're ready, let's add Materials to our Earth and moon.

Positioning and adding Materials to the Earth and Moon

We successfully created a very basic custom **Stars** Material and applied it to the stars background. It would be a shame if we left the **Earth** and **Moon** Actors in their current condition, without any Material, though. Instead of creating another custom Material, let's use some of the ready-made Materials that come with Unreal Engine.

However, before we start adding their Materials, we'll have to position the planet and the moon so they will be in view from the spaceship flight deck. Here's how to do this:

1. In the Outliner, select the planet and the moon, and press *Ctrl + G* to group them.

2. Then, to reposition them, enter the following **Location** values:

    - **X = 1129096.0**

    - **Y = 44116311.0**

    - **Z = 2363257.0**

3. Select the Earth's Static Mesh and press the *F* key to frame the view.

4. Now, ungroup the planet and moon (*Shift + G*) and move the moon to your desired location.

> **Note**
>
> These values are just guidelines. We may need to tweak them when we start creating the individual shots in *Chapter 10*.

Now, here's how to add Materials:

1. We will start by adding **Directional Light** to the scene, using the **Place Actor** green + icon at the top of the interface:

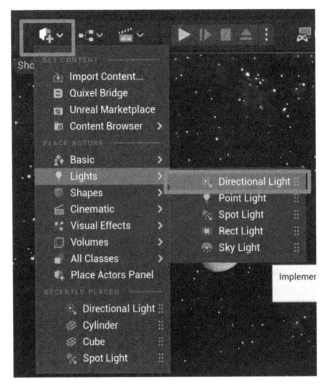

Figure 4.55: Adding Directional Light

We finally have light in our scene. In Unreal Engine, **Directional Light** is mainly used to replicate sunlight. The position of **Directional Light** is not important; what is important is its rotational value. Now, to make the scene look how we want it to be, let's tweak the **Directional Light** settings.

2. Select **DirectionalLight** in the Outliner list.

3. Then, in the **Details** panel, do the following:

    *   Set all of the **Location** values to **0.0**

    *   Under **Rotation**, set **X** to **0**, **Y** to **-26**, and **Z** to **30**

    *   Change **Mobility** to **Moveable**

    *   Under **Light**, change **Intensity** to **0.8 lux**

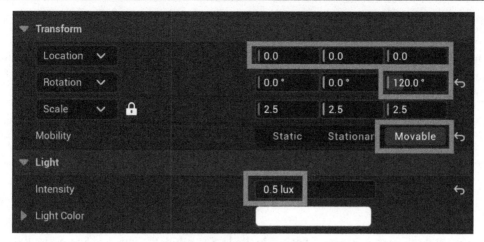

Figure 4.56: Tweaking the Directional Light settings

4. In the Content Browser, select the **StarterContent** folder, then open the **Materials** folder. You now have a collection of ready-made Materials that you can drag and drop onto the **Earth** and **Moon** Actors.

> **Note**
>
> The **Starter Content** folder exists in the Content Browser because we enabled it when we first created the project. It consists of ready-made assets we can use in any project. We will customize some of these assets to use them in our project in the coming chapters.

5. Drag the **M_Rock_Slate** Material onto the **Earth** and **Moon** Actors.

You may drag and drop different Materials onto the **Earth** and **Moon** Actors – go ahead and try it.

Now you should have a more convincing-looking scene, but we're not quite there yet. We will add a photorealistic planet and moon texture in *Chapter 6*.

> **Note**
>
> I can't stress enough the importance of saving the project often, especially when you import new assets into the Content Browser. If Unreal Engine decides to crash, the imported items will not be saved, and you'll have to re-import them.

Finally, let's work on the final piece – adding the spaceship.

Adding the spaceship

In the previous section, we managed to create a space scene by creating spheres and adding Textures to them. Though simplistic, the scene is taking shape. The final bit is to add the spaceship. To do that, follow these steps:

1. In **Content Browser | A_New_Beginning | 3D Models**, create a new folder and name it Spaceship.

2. Locate the **3D Models** folder in the downloaded project file. Then drag Spaceship.fbx into the **Spaceship** folder in Unreal Engine.

3. In the **FBX Import Options** popup, click **Import All**. If there is a **Message Log** pop-up, you can just close it.

4. Select the three static meshes – **Spaceship_Body**, **Spaceship_Engines**, and **Spaceship_Railguns** – and drag them into the Level.

5. As soon as you do that, they will populate the Outliner. As we have done before, we will need to create a folder and name the folder Spaceship (organization is key!).

6. Let's group all three meshes so we can move them as one. Select all three meshes in the Outliner and press *Ctrl + G*.

7. Now, position the spaceship using the following values:

    *   **Location**: X = -7706, Y = -8735, Z = 205.0

    *   **Rotation**: X = 0, Y = 0, Z = 0

    *   **Scale**: X = 20, Y = 20, Z = 20

8. Now, create a Bookmark here (*Ctrl + 1*). Position the view so it resembles *Figure 4.57*.

    Here is the result of the instructions:

Figure 4.57: Semi-completed space scene

We will revisit this scene in *Chapter 6* to add some believable Textures and Materials to the spaceship, the Earth, and the moon. But for now, save your project. And we're done!

Summary

In this chapter, you have started to understand some Unreal Engine terminology and created your first Unreal Engine project. With that, you now know how to add free (or paid) Marketplace content to your Unreal Engine projects, and have learned why organizing the Outliner and the Content Browser using folders is an important workflow for any Unreal Engine project. Furthermore, you have also gained the knowledge of how easy it is to import 3D objects and Textures into Unreal Engine and how to create a simple custom **Stars** Material.

In the upcoming chapters, we will be revisiting this Level to add Textures, Materials, and camera animation. Specifically, in the next chapter, we will learn about the Quixel Bridge library and Quixel Megascans assets to enhance the planet's environment.

5

Creating Environments with Quixel Megascans

In the preceding chapter, you learned how to initiate your initial Unreal Engine project for your virtual film. We commenced by generating Levels for both the internal and external space scenes. After, we imported 3D objects, fashioned basic shapes using the **Modeling** tool, and incorporated a rudimentary Material.

In this chapter, we will pick up where we left off and focus on fabricating the planet environment. Our objective is to create a vibrant landscape comprising trees, rocks, a lake, clouds, and fog. To achieve this, we will search the Unreal Engine Marketplace for complimentary environments and utilize Megascans asset packs, which can be made available for Unreal Engine 5 through Quixel Bridge.

The primary aim of this chapter is to familiarize you with the functionality of Quixel Bridge, which serves as your portal to Megascans and MetaHumans (the topic of MetaHumans will be explored in detail in *Chapter 7*).

We will be covering the following topics:

- Understanding compositions
- Getting started with Quixel Bridge
- Downloading and using Megascans assets
- Creating a landscape environment

Technical requirements

Here is a link to this book's project files: https://packt.link/gbz/9781801813808. If you downloaded the project files in the previous chapter, you already have all the files you'll need for this chapter.

Understanding compositions

As I mentioned in *Chapter 2*, the camera is a powerful storytelling tool, so when used creatively, you can convey the exact message of the narrative.

For example, in this film, I wanted to convey a feeling of everything being mysterious – what's happening? Who are these two characters in the cryogenics chambers? Where did they come from? It is not until the end that the answers will be revealed, and even after that, I still want the audience to be asking questions – are these characters the original Adam and Eve? Or are the names just a coincidence?

This leads us nicely to composition.

In a nutshell, **composition** is the arrangement and placement of visual elements within the frame of the image being captured by the camera. It is a crucial aspect of visual storytelling as it helps create the desired mood, convey emotions, and direct the viewer's attention to specific elements of the scene. Every shot is carefully planned, and every element in the shot tells a story. Nothing in the shot is there by chance, so before setting up a shot, you need to ask yourself – what am I trying to visualize? What feeling or experience am I trying to convey to the audience? What message am I trying to present?

Let's learn about a few composition techniques and then apply them to our film:

- **Framing**: This refers to the size and position of the subject or objects within the frame. A close-up shot, for example, may be used to emphasize a character's emotional state, while a full shot may be used to show the setting and environment:

Figure 5.1: Framing shots

- **Rule of thirds**: This is a guideline for composition that suggests dividing the frame into thirds both horizontally and vertically, and placing important elements at the intersections of these lines. This creates a sense of balance and visual interest. This is a very popular framing method that's used heavily in films and animation:

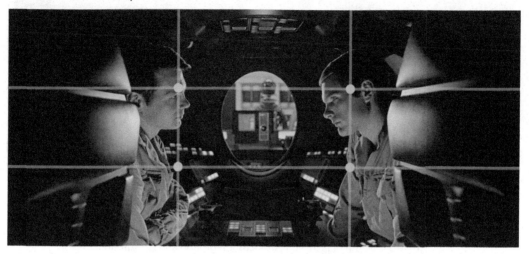

Figure 5.2: Rule of thirds (2001: A Space Odyssey, 1968)

- **Leading lines**: This refers to the use of lines within the frame to guide the viewer's eye to a particular part of the image. For example, a road or hallway may be used to lead the viewer's eye to a character or object:

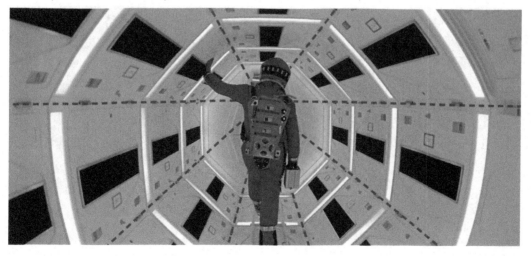

Figure 5.3: Leading lines (2001: A Space Odyssey, 1968)

- **Depth of field**: This refers to the range of distances in the scene that are in focus. By adjusting the depth of field, filmmakers can draw attention to specific elements within the scene and create a sense of depth and dimensionality:

Figure 5.4: Depth of field – out-of-focus foreground and background

- **Color schemes**: This refers to the use of specific colors and combinations of colors to create a desired visual effect, mood, or atmosphere within a scene or the entire film. Different colors and color combinations can convey different emotions, themes, and motifs, and can be used to support the storytelling and visual style of the film:

Figure 5.5: The popular teal and orange color scheme (Tron Legacy, 2010)

These are only a few techniques that can be used when you're telling your story, but you can see that overall, composition is a powerful tool for filmmakers to create engaging and visually compelling images that support the narrative of their story. We will be using several of these composition techniques in our film, and I will point them out as we go along.

Build only what you see

One other critical concept to keep in mind is that you should only build what is necessary to achieve the desired shot.

In contrast to building a game or other interactive media, where the player may need to explore a vast and detailed environment, our focus is on creating visually compelling shots from a single-camera point of view. This is akin to constructing a real-life movie set, where only the elements visible within the camera frame need to be built.

I bring this up now because as we proceed with building the planet environment, we will be working with a large number of high-polygon and photorealistic assets. Without careful planning and optimization, this can lead to unnecessary system lag and even cause Unreal Engine to crash unexpectedly. By adopting a *"build only what you see"* mindset, we can avoid these issues and ensure that our workflow is as efficient as possible.

With that in mind, let's return to Unreal Engine and pick up where we left off in our project.

Getting started with Quixel Bridge

Throughout this section, our focus will be on familiarizing ourselves with the **Quixel Bridge** feature that was introduced in Unreal Engine 5. This feature grants access to a vast collection of photorealistic, photogrammetry Megascans assets that can be easily accessed and downloaded directly into your Unreal Engine project. Thanks to the built-in Quixel Bridge feature, incorporating these assets into your workflow has never been simpler.

It is worth noting that, at the time of writing, over **14,000 assets** are available through Quixel Bridge for free. This provides an unparalleled Level of variety and flexibility, allowing creators to fully realize their artistic visions without the limitations of asset availability.

To get started with Quixel Bridge, follow these steps:

1. Open the project we are working on (if you're following along, it's **A_New_Beginning**).

2. Create a new Level (*Ctrl + N*), choose the **Basic** template, and click **Create**:

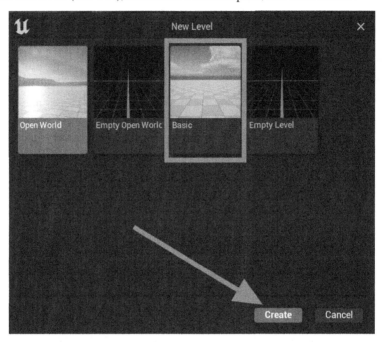

Figure 5.6: Creating a new basic Level

3. You will be presented with a new Level. Save it by pressing *Ctrl + Alt + S* and naming it QuixelBridgeDemo (be sure to save it in the **Levels** folder).

    Though we have created this Level, we won't be using it in the project; we're just using it to learn about Quixel Bridge and its features.

4. Now, in the application menu, click on **Window**, then select **Quixel Bridge**:

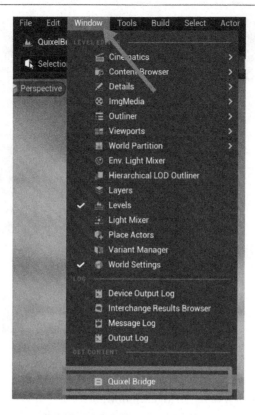

Figure 5.7: Accessing Quixel Bridge

If for any reason Quixel Bridge is not listed in the **Window** drop-down menu, ensure you are using Unreal Engine 5.2. If you are using an older version, you'll need to enable it in the **Plugins** browser, as shown here:

Figure 5.8: Enabling the Quixel Bridge plugin

5.   Once you've selected Quixel Bridge from the menu, you will get a login prompt – log in using your Epic ID, which you created in *Chapter 1*.

6.   You'll now have a floating **Bridge** window. Let's dock it so that we can have a closer look at its features. To do so, drag the **Bridge** tab beside the **QuixelBridgeDemo** Level tab, as shown in *Figure 5.9*:

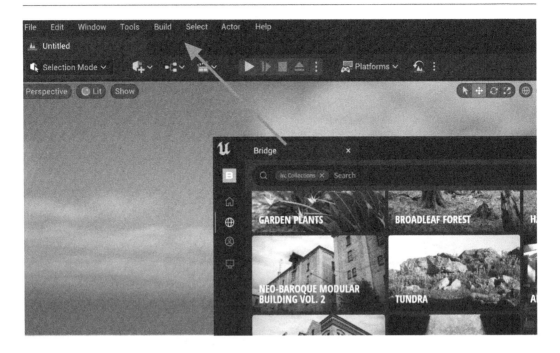

Figure 5.9: Docking the Bridge window

Now, we will have a larger view of the **Bridge** window:

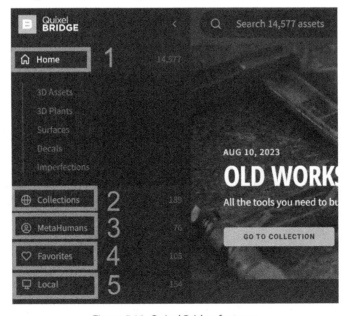

Figure 5.10: Quixel Bridge features

On the left of the screen, you'll see a list of Quixel Bridge features. This includes the following:

- **Home** (**1**): This option reveals the latest collection, trending assets, and newest assets in every category

- **Collections** (**2**): Here, you will have curated content with references and samples of renders for the **Environment**, **Essentials**, **Vegetation**, **ArchViz**, **Community**, and **Tutorials** categories

- **MetaHumans** (**3**): This option allows you to access the MetaHumans that you created using the MetaHuman Creator (more on this in *Chapter 7*, where we will create customized MetaHuman Actors)

- **Favorites** (**4**): This option shows the items you have favorited for quick access

- **Local** (**5**): This option allows you to access all the Megascans and MetaHuman assets that have been downloaded onto your computer

Now that we have an understanding of the Quixel Bridge interface, let's dive a little deeper into it and start using an asset in our Level.

Downloading and using Megascans assets

To download and use Megascans assets, follow these steps:

1. From Quixel Bridge's **Home** tab, on the left of the screen, select the **3D Assets** category, then the **Building** category, and then the **Wall** category:

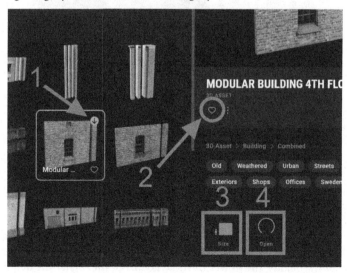

Figure 5.11: Quixel Bridge – 3D Assets

2. From the list of assets, select **Modular Building Ground Floor Kit**. The details panel of the asset will be revealed. There are several important features here that you need to know about:

- **Download Assets (1)**: Clicking this button will download the asset onto your computer disk.

- **Favorite (2)**: This button will favorite the asset, after which it will be available in the **Favorite** tab for future use.

- **Size (3)**: This option will show the size of the 3D asset relative to the height of a human being (which is around 1.8 meters).

- **Open (4)**: This option indicates that the 3D asset is one-sided – that is, the assets were created with polygons facing only in one direction for optimization purposes. This will become clearer shortly, once we have added the 3D asset to our scene.

On the lower right of the Bridge interface, you will see additional features:

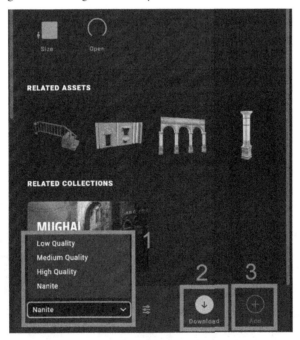

Figure 5.12: Quixel Bridge – additional features

These features include the following:

- A pop-up list (1) that allows you to choose the **quality of the asset** you are going to download. The higher the quality, the slower the download, but the higher the definition of the assets when viewed up close.

- Another **Download** button (**2**) that allows you to download the asset.

- An **Add** button (**3**) that allows you to add the asset to your project (once you download the asset, the button will turn green, enabling it).

3. Choose the **Nanite** version and download the 3D asset. Once you're done, click the **Add** button.

    Once added, the asset will be listed in the **Megascans** folder in the Content Browser:

Figure 5.13: The Megascans asset added to the Content Browser

---

Note

Nanite is undoubtedly the optimal choice when using Quixel Megascans. This revolutionary technology enables the real-time rendering of highly detailed scenes consisting of millions of triangles, even on less powerful hardware, and is a major step forward from the days of painstaking polygon counting, which was a notorious headache for 3D modelers. Before the advent of Nanite, 3D meshes that were created in applications such as Maya or Blender had to undergo a time-consuming optimization process to ensure that they were "light" enough to be used in games or films.

Nanite also supports a variety of advanced rendering features, including dynamic global illumination and ray tracing. This allows for more realistic and immersive environments that are truly breathtaking to behold. By utilizing this cutting-edge technology, we can create scenes that are both visually stunning and efficient to work with.

The **Megascans** folder will consist of three **Static Mesh** assets, three **texture files**, and a **Material Instance** asset. Static meshes are 3D models that are associated with the asset, while the Texture files are the "paint" for the walls; they are applied to the meshes using a **Material Instance** asset (we will do a deep dive into Materials in *Chapter 6*).

4. Select each of the Static Meshes and drag them into the Viewport.

5. Reset their position by zeroing their location. The best way to do this is by clicking on the **Reset to Default** button in the details panel:

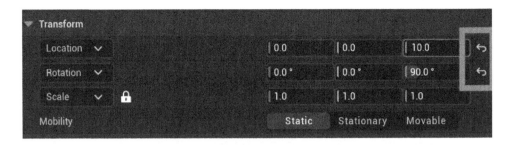

Figure 5.14: The Reset to Default buttons

6. The Static Meshes you've just added from Bridge are modular. They can be arranged to make a larger construction if you duplicate (*Ctrl + D*) and arrange them as you like.

7. Using the object snapping feature (which is enabled by default) enables the Static Meshes to be snapped together to help with arranging them:

Figure 5.15: The snapping feature in Unreal Engine

The snapping feature, located at the top right of the Viewport, enables the Actors to be snapped in the following ways:

-   **Position grid**: In this case, the snapping is set to every 10 units. Click on the number to change its snap size. When highlighted in blue, the snapping feature is turned on. Click on it to disable it.

-   **Rotation grid**: This allows rotation snapping and is measured in degrees. When highlighted in blue, the snapping feature is turned on. Click on it to disable it.

-   **Scale grid**: This allows snapping to occur when you're scaling the Actor. When highlighted in blue, the snapping feature is turned on. Click on it to disable it.

Go ahead and zoom into the 3D object to inspect how detailed they are close up. Take note that they are one-sided – you can look through them if you rotate them.

8. Now, switch to **Wireframe** mode (*Alt + 2*) to see how dense the meshes are. Then, switch back to the **Lit** view (*Alt + 4*):

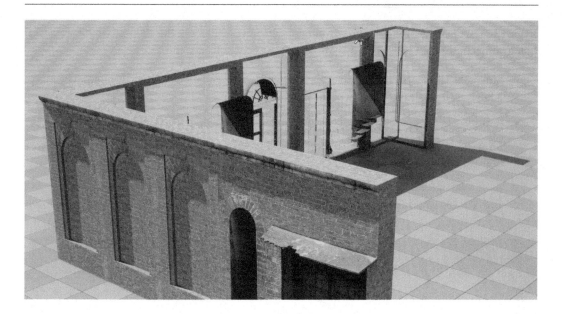

Figure 5.16: The one-sided objects for optimization

In this section, you employed the Quixel Bridge functionality within Unreal Engine. By utilizing this feature, you were able to peruse a collection of Quixel Megascans 3D assets and select and download those that suited your needs. Additionally, you discovered the benefits of incorporating Nanite meshes into your workflow, recognizing their superiority over other quality options.

Now that you have gained a fundamental understanding of Quixel Bridge, we can put this knowledge to use and start creating a landscape for our planet.

Creating the landscape environment

Earlier in this chapter, you understood the crucial role that composition plays in the art of storytelling. To craft a compelling narrative through visual media, a variety of composition techniques can be employed. As we continue to develop our film, we will be implementing these techniques to achieve a polished and professional look.

To take our production to the next Level, we are fortunate to have access to a vast array of high-quality assets. Thanks to Quixel Bridge, these assets can be easily integrated into our project without us needing to sacrifice visual fidelity. This allows us to create a production-quality film with ease, ensuring that our audience is fully immersed in the world that we have created.

Before we start building the planet environment, let's have a glance at the shot list. There are a total of four shots in the third sequence:

- **Shot_06**: The space shuttle traverses the surface of the planet and flies through a beautiful landscape to indicate the planet is habitable.

- **Shot_07**: The space shuttle starts descending to the surface, particles flying as it lands.

- **Shot_08**: The two occupants – a male and a female – disembark and walk toward the water body to admire the beautiful sight.

- **Shot_09**: The camera focuses on the two humans. On their chest are their names, Adam and Eve. The camera zooms out and the scene fades to black, after which the title *A New Beginning* is revealed:

Figure 5.17: Shots 06 to 09 in the third sequence

Now, let's jump back into Unreal Engine and start creating a landscape for the planet.

Creating a landscape using free asset packs

Creating a landscape in Unreal Engine is tedious and can take hours. To ease the process of building the landscape for our planet, we'll search for some free landscape asset packs available from the Unreal Engine Marketplace. If we need to, we will add additional assets via Quixel Bridge to further customize the scene. This process is very intuitive and loads of fun, so let's get started:

1. Open the Epic Launcher and go to the **Marketplace** tab. In the **Search Products** window, type Landscape and, in the **Max Price** category, choose **Free**.

2. From the list of assets, choose **Landscape Pro 2.0 Auto Generated Material** and click on the **Add To Project** button.

3. In the search bar that pops up, search for A_New_Beginning. Once our current project is visible, click on the project thumbnail and select **Add to Project**. This is shown in *Figure 5.18*:

Figure 5.18: Adding the landscape asset pack

Once the project has been added, it will be listed as **STF** in the Content Browser. This folder contains pre-made Levels that we can use in our shots.

4. In the **STF | Pack03-LandscapePro | Maps** folder, select the **open_world_LSP_v2** Level and press *Ctrl + D* to duplicate it.

5. Rename the duplicated Level by selecting it and pressing *F2*. Then, name it EXT_Planet.

6. For organizational purposes, move the **EXT_Planet** Level to the **Levels** folder in the Content Browser.

7. Open the **EXT_Planet** Level by double-clicking on it. Once open, using the right mouse button, look around the scene.

The environment we want will need to be Earth-like with luscious green trees, a lake or a river, and perhaps some rock features. This scene has all of that – a hilly landscape with foliage and clouds. This is a good start.

Referring to the storyboard, we will be able to utilize this Level for all four shots in this sequence, each slightly tweaked to meet the narrative. For Shot_07, the space shuttle will fly across the landscape. To give a sense of depth to the scene, we will aim for the following:

- **Foreground trees**: We will have trees (and some rock formations) on the left and right of the screen, making the audience focus on the space shuttle.

- **Midground hills and a water body**: This gives the illusion that the planet is vast and luscious.

- **Background**: The blue sky and fluffy clouds give the feeling of a clean environment:

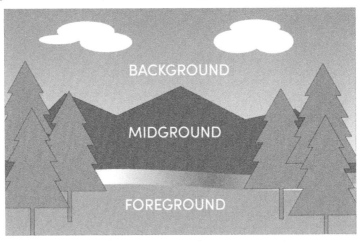

Figure 5.19: Adding depth to the scene

This is a large landscape, so finding a suitable spot is going to be time-consuming. However, I have found the perfect spot. Let's take a look.

8. Click the green + icon, as shown in the following screenshot, choose **Basic**, and then select **Actor**:

Figure 5.20: Adding an Actor to position our shot

An Actor icon will pop up in the middle of the Viewport. An Actor is an empty object – in 3D applications, it is known as a null object. It has its various usages but, in our case, we will use it to position our view.

9. In the **Details** panel, select the Actor and enter these values for the **Location** properties:

    - **X** = -43105

    - **Y** = -90502

    - **X** = -2395

    Then, press *Enter*; the Actor will move to the exact location of our shot.

10. Now, double-click on the Actor in the **Outliner** area to move your view to the same location as the Actor. You may need to rotate your view and frame the shot, as shown in *Figure 5.21*:

Figure 5.21: Landscape view for Shot_06

Don't worry if your shot doesn't look exactly like this. I've done a bit of color correction to the image for the sake of clarity. We still have a few tasks to carry out in this scene before we move on to the next shot.

11. Now, create a bookmark (*Ctrl + 1*) and save our project (*Ctrl + Shift + S*).

    Let's go ahead and remove the Actors we won't be needing in this scene.

12. In the **Outliner** area, delete the following Actors:

    - All of the **SphereReflectionCapture** Actors

    - The **TextRenderActor** Actor

    - The **PlayerStart** Actor

13. Now, select the **Atmospheric Fog**, **DirectionalLight**, **ExponentialHeightFog**, **PostProcessVolume**, **Sky Sphere**, and **SkyLight** Actors, and add them to a new folder named **Environment**. You can hold the *Ctrl* key while selecting the Actors to add to the selection.

14. Then, select the rest of the Actors and add them to another folder named **Landscape**:

Figure 5.22: A well-organized Outliner area

This scene has all we need to create **Shot_06**, fulfilling the foreground, midground, and background elements as we planned. Before we continue further, though, let's quickly look at a potential issue that you may encounter at this stage.

Dealing with the TEXTURE STREAMING POOL OVER... error

At this stage, you may start seeing an error in the top-left corner of the Viewport saying **TEXTURE STREAMING POOL OVER...**. This is shown in *Figure 5.23*:

Figure 5.23: The TEXTURE STREAMING POOL OVER... warning message

This is a very common warning that is simply telling you that the Textures in your scene are using more memory than you have allocated for them and as a result, Unreal Engine has started decreasing the quality of your Textures to compensate.

To rectify this problem, press the tilde key on your keyboard (~) and type r.streaming.poolsize ?, as shown in *Figure 5.24*. Then, press *Enter*:

Figure 5.24: Checking the current streaming.poolsize memory allocation

Now, click the **Output Log** button on the lower left of the interface. This will reveal the current memory allocation. In this case, it is **1000** MB:

```
Cmd: r.streaming.poolsize ?
HELP for 'r.Streaming.PoolSize':
-1: Default texture pool size, otherwise the size in MB
r.Streaming.PoolSize = "1000"    2  LastSetBy: Scalability

Cmd v   Enter Console Command

Content Drawer   Output Log  1  Cmd v   Enter Console Command
```

Figure 5.25: Current memory allocation

Depending on your installed graphics card's memory capacity, you can increase the memory allocation by typing r.streaming.poolsize 2000 in the console command window. This will allow Unreal Engine to allocate 2,000 MB of your graphics card's memory for Texture streaming and make the warning disappear.

> **Note**
>
> For more detailed information on the streaming pool, go to https://www.techarthub.com/fixing-texture-streaming-pool-over-budget-in-unreal/.

Adding rocks

As mentioned previously, adding foreground, midground, and background elements is a good composition technique to add a sense of depth to the scene. We've already finished **Shot_06**. However, for the sake of learning, we will add a few more elements to the scene.

In this section, we will add some rocks, turning to the Unreal Engine Marketplace for help:

1. In the Unreal Engine Marketplace, search for Sci Fi and set **Max Price** to **Free**.

2. You will come across the **Megascans – Sci-Fi Landscape** asset. Follow the same process as shown in the *Downloading and using Megascans assets* section to add it to your project.

3. In the Content Browser, you will find the **MS_SciFiLand** folder. This folder will consist of a plethora of Megascans assets, from rock formation to plants to decals – exactly what we need!

   Browsing and looking for exactly what you need is going to be time-consuming since this package has tons of folders! I want to show you how you can take advantage of the filter system in the Content Browser to view certain assets all at once.

4. Let's say you want to view all the Static Meshes that are available in the package. In the Content Browser, select the **MS_SciFiLand** folder.

5. Then, click the **Add Filter** menu icon and choose **Static Mesh**:

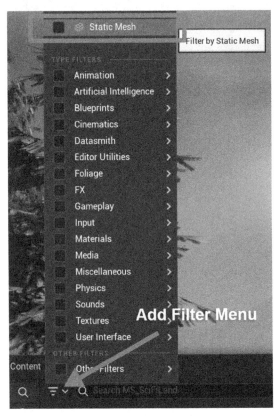

Figure 5.26: Using the Add Filter menu

Voilà! The Content Browser will now display all of the Static Meshes in the **MS_SciFiLand** folder:

Figure 5.27: Using the Static Mesh filter

6.   Choose a few **Rock** assets and drag and drop them into the scene.

7.   This is where the fun begins. Be as creative as you want with the scene. Instead of adding many different assets to the scene, you can duplicate and use the same assets over and over. This is a good way to optimize the scene. Also, a pro tip: to cycle between **Translate**, **Rotate**, and **Size** faster, tap the spacebar instead of using the *W*, *E*, and *R* keyboard shortcuts, and remember to use *Ctrl + Z* to undo.

Here is what I have done:

Figure 5.28: Adding additional rocks to the scene

> **Note**
>
> In Unreal Engine, the action of dragging an asset from the Content Browser into the scene creates an instance of the asset, which means that even if you duplicate the assets many times over, the engine only needs to process it once. Hence, it is a good idea to reuse the same assets in your scene by changing their position, rotation, and scale to reduce lag. This also keeps your project small in size and easier to manage. This is especially true for Nanite meshes, which will seamlessly "blend" with each other when overlapped. This is another reason why Nanite meshes are the way to go.

In this section, we added the rock Static Meshes to the foreground of the scene. In my case, I kept it minimal. You can always come back and tweak the scene to your heart's content, but for now, we will keep it like this. In the next section, we will add more trees to our scene.

Adding trees

You may have noticed that the **MS_SciFiLand** package came with tons of Static Meshes, but none are suitable to be used as trees. Once again, let's browse the Unreal Engine Marketplace to find some more suitable assets:

1. Similar to what we did earlier, search for Trees in the Unreal Engine Marketplace and ensure you select **Free** in the **Max Price** category. Browse the results and select **temperate Vegetation: Spruce Forest**:

Figure 5.29: The temperate Vegetation: Spruce Forest package

2. Once you're done, in the Content Browser, look for the **PN_interactiveSpriceForest** folder.

    Since the filter is still set to **Static Mesh**, when you select the folder, you'll be presented with all the trees available in the package.

3. Add a few trees to the scene as per *Figure 5.30*, and move and scale them as appropriate:

Figure 5.30: Trees added to the scene

4. Finally, organize the **Outliner** area by putting the rocks and trees in a folder called **Foliage**, and save your project.

With the rocks and trees in the shot, we are forcing the audience's eyes into the distance, where our space shuttle will be flying across the landscape. In the next section, we will add distant mountains to the scene.

Adding mountains

In this section, we will add a mountain range in the distance to show how vast this planet is. We will achieve this using another free asset pack:

1. In the Unreal Engine Marketplace, search for Landscape Backgrounds and add the asset to the project.

2. When prompted for the version, select the **5.0EA** version; this has the closest compatibility to Unreal Engine 5.2:

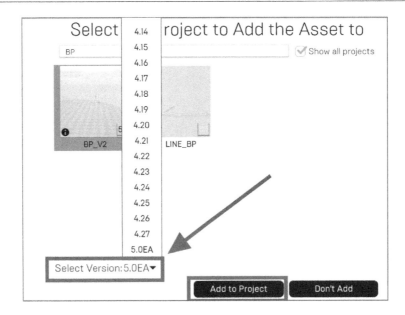

Figure 5.31: Selecting the compatible version of the asset for Unreal Engine

3. Once added, you'll find the **PhotoR_Backgrounds** folder. In that folder, use the Content Browser filter system to view only the Static Meshes.

4. Add the **pr_background_mountain_d_2_spring** asset to the scene, as shown in *Figure 5.32*:

Figure 5.32: Background mountains added to the scene

5. Now, duplicate the mountain twice and place them using the following coordinates:

- For **pr_background_mountain_d_2_spring**, use the following coordinates:

  - **Location**: X = -593715, Y = -197309, X = 23474
  - **Rotation**: X = 3.5, Y = 7.0, X = -150
  - **Scale**: X = 5.0, Y = 5.0, Z = 5.0

- For **pr_background_mountain_d_2_spring2**, use the following coordinates:

  - **Location**: X = -593715, Y = -294043, X = 15234
  - **Rotation**: X = 7.0, Y = 6.0, X = -90
  - **Scale**: X = 5.0, Y = 5.0, Z = 5.0

- For **pr_background_mountain_d_2_spring3**, use the following coordinates:

  - **Location**: X = -593715, Y = -811021, X = 24019
  - **Rotation**: X = 7.0, Y = 6.0, X = -70
  - **Scale**: X = 6.0, Y = 6.0, Z = 9.0

  Though I have provided these values, it's not important to have the mountains in the same locations; you can arrange them as you like, so long as they look believable (that is why the reference photos you collected in *Chapter 2* are helpful).

6. Now, organize the **Outliner** area – I suggest that you place the **Mountain** object in the **Landscape** folder – and save your project.

Wow, our scene looks good! We will return to this shot for further enhancements in *Chapter 12*.

You now understand how you can utilize Quixel Bridge to import Megascans into the project, and you also accumulated useful asset packs that you can reuse in future chapters and projects.

In the next section, we will identify the location for **Shot_07**, where the space shuttle will commence its descent to the surface of the planet.

Setting the space shuttle landing area

In the previous section, we successfully created **Shot_06**, where the space shuttle will traverse the landscape. In this section, we will continue using the same environment to create our next shot, **Shot_07** – this shot requires us to have a large open area where we can land a space shuttle.

So, complete the following steps:

1. In the Content Browser, create a new folder in the **3D_Models** folder and name it `Shuttle`.

2. From the downloaded project files, drag `Shuttle.fbx` from the **3D Models** folder into the new **Shuttle** folder.

3. In the **FBX Import Options** dialog box, ensure **Import Animations** is enabled and **Create New Materials** is selected in the **Material Import Method** drop-down menu:

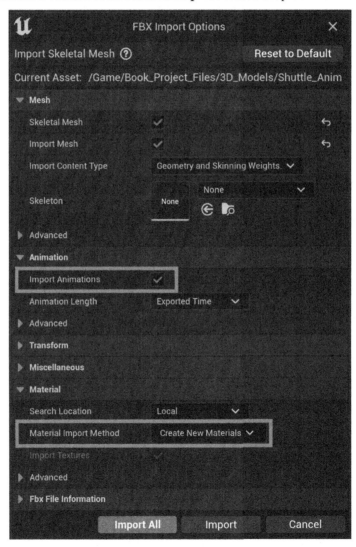

Figure 5.33: Shuttle import dialog options

4. From the **3D_Models | Shuttle** folder, drag and drop the **Shuttle** (Skeletal Mesh) asset from the Content Browser into the scene.

5. Then, in the **Shuttle** asset's **Details** panel, change the following values:

    •   **Position**: **X** = -57153, **Y** = -69823, **Z** = -2463

    •   **Rotation**: **X** = 0, **Y** = 0, **Z** = 180

    •   **Scale**: **X** = 2.0, **Y** = 2.0, **Z** = 2.0

Figure 5.34: The shuttle added to the scene

6. Double-click the **Shuttle** Actor in the **Outliner** area so that you're closer to it, reframe the view, as shown in *Figure 5.34*, and create a bookmark (*Ctrl + 2*).

7. We will leave this scene as is for now and save the project (*Ctrl + Shift + S*).

In this section, we managed to add the space shuttle to the scene, which we will be using for the landing sequence for **Shot_07**. In the next section, we will work on creating the last two shots, where the two characters walk toward the water body and then reveal their identities.

Setting up the final shot

For our final shot, I have identified the perfect location. However, for now, we will only be placing placeholder characters in the scene (we will create and add customized MetaHuman characters to this scene later in *Chapter 7*).

So, to set up the final shot, complete the following steps:

1. In the Content Browser, open the **Characters | Mannequins | Meshes** folder and drag **SKM_Manny_Simple** into the Level.

2. With the asset still selected, in the **Details** panel, change the following values:

   - **Location**: **X** = -58507, **Y** = -78409, **Z** = -3403

   - **Rotation**: **X** = 0.0, **Y** = 0.0, **Z** = -185

3. In the **Details** panel, double-click on **SKM_Manny_Simple** to move the camera view to the asset's position.

4. Duplicate **SKM_Manny_Simple** using *Ctrl + D*, then move the duplicated character so that the two characters stand side by side.

5. Now, create a bookmark here (*Ctrl + 3*).

   Here is the result:

Figure 5.35: The final shot with the two placeholder characters

6. Finally, save the project (*Ctrl + Shift + S*).

You should now have the two characters with the space shuttle in the background. We will use this location as the final shot in the film before we fade to black and reveal the end title, but we still have lots of work to do.

Summary

This chapter taught you how to access a vast collection of high-quality Quixel Megascans assets through the Quixel Bridge feature. You can now easily access various assets, such as 3D buildings, 3D plants, surfaces, and decals, more directly within Unreal Engine.

Additionally, you were introduced to a selection of free asset packs from the Unreal Engine Marketplace via the Epic Games Launcher, which allows you to quickly build environments. The possibilities are limitless.

In the upcoming chapter, we will delve into how to create Textures and Materials – these will enable you to control the visual appearance of the 3D meshes present in your scenes, and empower you to adjust attributes such as color, reflectivity, bumpiness, and transparency, creating the desired visual effects.

6

Creating and Applying Materials to 3D Meshes

Previously, in *Chapter 4*, you were briefly introduced to how to create custom Materials. Materials are vital to learn about in Unreal Engine as they determine the visual quality and realism of objects in a scene. They allow for artistic control over Textures, colors, and lighting effects, enabling you to create visually stunning environments. Additionally, understanding Materials helps optimize performance and enables interactive gameplay mechanics.

The primary aim of this chapter is to familiarize you with creating basic Textures and Materials and applying them to 3D meshes. However, it's important to note that we won't be doing a deep dive into learning and creating complex Materials – that's a book by itself, and we've got a film to finish!

In this chapter, you will be exposed to Unreal Engine's real-time Material and Texture capabilities, the **physically based rendering** (**PBR**) workflow, and working in the Material Editor, and with Master Materials, and Material Instances.

We will be covering the following topics:

- Understanding Materials and Textures
- Creating Master Materials and Material Instances
- Working with Materials with image-based Textures
- Applying Materials to scenes

Technical requirements

Here is a link to the book's project files: `https://packt.link/gbz/9781801813808`. If you downloaded the project files in the previous chapter, you already have all the files you'll need for this chapter.

Understanding Materials and Textures

Before we start creating and applying Textures and Materials to our 3D meshes for the current project, let us first understand the concept behind them in Unreal Engine 5. This will give us a good understanding of how Materials and Textures work in Unreal Engine and how we can customize them for our use.

Understanding Materials

Materials (also known as **shaders** in other 3D applications) are essentially assets created in Unreal Engine that are applied to a 3D mesh to control its appearance. In its simplest form, think of Materials as paint with various properties such as color, Texture, transparency, and other visual characteristics. Materials can be applied to individual parts of an object or whole surfaces such as a landscape, wall, or floor.

Figure 6.1: A library of Materials available in Unreal Engine 5

On a basic level, in Unreal Engine, you can create two types of Materials:

- **Procedural-based Materials**: These Materials can be generated using built-in nodes such as the **Noise** node. Some examples of procedural Materials are tiles, granite, water, marble, stone, and so on. Procedurally generated Materials are expensive to generate in Unreal Engine, but the advantage of this approach is that they are almost always *seamless in nature*, meaning, when applied to surfaces, there will not be any visible seams.

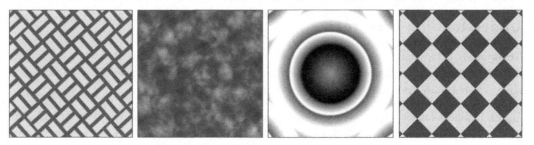

Figure 6.2: Procedurally generated Textures

> **Note**
>
> When a certain operation is considered expensive, it means that it consumes a considerable amount of processing power, memory, or other system resources, potentially resulting in slower frame rates, longer loading times, or reduced responsiveness. Developers strive to optimize these expensive operations to improve overall performance and ensure smooth gameplay experiences.

> **Note**
>
> There is a web-based procedural Texture generator you can use to create procedural-based Textures. You can find it here: `https://cpetry.github.io/TextureGenerator-Online/`.

- **Image-based Materials**: These Materials are created using images, which are referred to as **Texture maps**. Texture maps can be created in several ways – using a camera or scanner, or they can be hand-drawn in a digital application such as GIMP or Adobe Photoshop. The advantage of Texture maps is that they look photorealistic, but at the expense of taking up more disk space and requiring higher processing power (expensive) if not optimized correctly. In Unreal Engine, Texture maps are the preferred method of creating Materials due to the unique optimization capabilities of the engine.

Figure 6.3: Image-based Materials

Understanding Textures

Textures are 2D images that are created outside of Unreal Engine and imported when needed. As discussed, these images can be created in any image editing application or downloaded from sites such as Poly Haven (`https://polyhaven.com/`), and many more.

Unreal Engine is capable of processing images with the following formats and file types: `bmp`, `float`, `jpeg`, `jpg`, `pcx`, `png`, `psd`, `tga`, `dds`, `exr`, `tif`, and `tiff`. It is important to note that regarding sizes, Texture images created for Unreal Engine adhere to the power of two, from 1 x 1 pixels and up to 8,192 x 8,192 pixels (see *Figure 6.4*).

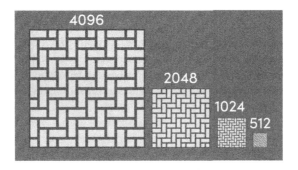

Figure 6.4: Images adhering to the power of two in pixels

You can find more information about Texture formats here: `https://docs.unrealengine.com/5.1/en-US/Texture-format-support-and-settings-in-unreal-engine/`

Understanding PBR Materials

Before we start creating any Materials, you need to understand how Unreal Engine generates photorealistic, real-time Materials using a method called physically based rendering.

PBR is a shading and rendering technique used in computer graphics to create highly realistic and physically accurate Materials and lighting in 3D scenes.

PBR is based on the principles of physics and how light interacts with different Materials in the real world, considering factors such as surface reflectivity, roughness, metallic properties, and so on. Just like in the real world, the interaction of light hitting a surface will depend on the surface itself – smooth surfaces will have better reflections of their surroundings and rough surfaces will have a blurry (diffused) effect, as seen in *Figure 6.5*:

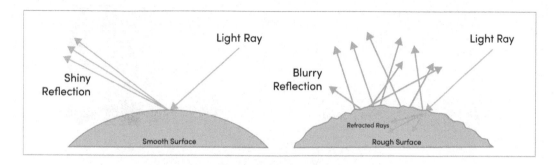

Figure 6.5: How light interacts with different surfaces

The core concept of PBR revolves around the use of a standardized set of Material properties, often referred to as the **PBR workflow** or **PBR pipeline**. These properties typically include the following:

- **Albedo** or **Base Color**: This represents the surface color of the Material under direct lighting conditions.

- **Metallic**: This specifies whether a Material is metallic or non-metallic. Metallic Materials have reflections that resemble metals such as gold or copper, while non-metallic Materials have diffused reflections such as plastic or wood.

- **Roughness**: This determines the surface smoothness or roughness of a Material. Rough surfaces scatter light in more random directions, while smooth surfaces provide sharper reflections.

- **Normal Map**: This property adds small-scale surface details such as bumps or crevices to simulate intricate surface geometry without changing the underlying mesh.

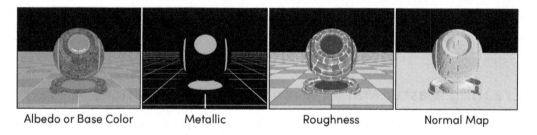

Figure 6.6: The standard PBR Material properties

Figure 6.6 shows these properties separately, while *Figure 6.7* shows the result of combining the Material properties in Unreal Engine (this is achieved in the Material Editor, which we will learn about in the next section):

Figure 6.7: The result of combining all PBR Material properties

By using these standardized Material properties, PBR allows artists and developers to *create Materials that are physically accurate and consistent across different lighting conditions*. PBR Materials respond realistically to different types of lighting, such as direct light sources, environment maps, and even reflections from other objects in the scene.

PBR has become widely adopted in the game development and visual effects industries because it provides a more intuitive and predictable workflow for creating realistic Materials. It helps artists achieve greater visual fidelity and consistency in their renderings, making virtual objects look more like their real-world counterparts.

Now that you have a basic concept of the Textures and Materials used in Unreal Engine, let's start creating some.

Creating Master Materials and Material Instances

In this section, you will learn how to create basic PBR Materials from scratch using the Unreal Engine Material Editor, which we briefly looked at in *Chapter 4*, and then you will learn the significance of **Material Instances** and why we use them.

Remember, we are making a film, so I will not dabble too much in the nitty gritty of creating complex Materials for our use – I'm going to keep it simple. There are tons of ready-made Materials accessible to us through **Quixel Bridge** and the **Unreal Engine Marketplace** that we will utilize in our project, which I will cover later in this chapter.

Creating plastic, rubber, and metal Master Materials

To learn how to create Master Materials, we will start by creating some basic Materials that will be the building blocks for creating any other Materials. Let's start by creating some common Materials: plastic, rubber, and metal-looking Materials. Let's get started:

1. Open the current project we're working on – **A_New_Beginning** – and create a new Level. Choose the **Basic** Level from the popup and click **Create**:

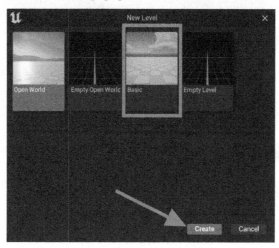

Figure 6.8: Creating a new blank Level

2. Add a sphere to the Level by clicking the + **Place Actor** button, then choosing **Shapes | Sphere**:

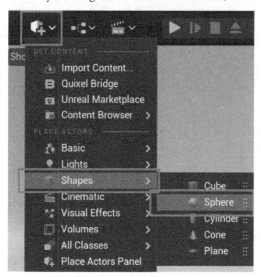

Figure 6.9: Creating a sphere

3. Duplicate the sphere twice, using *Ctrl + D*, and then drag the duplicates beside each other, as shown in *Figure 6.10*:

Figure 6.10: The duplicated spheres

4. In the Content Browser, create a new folder and call it Demo_Materials. Open the folder and right-click inside it. Then, in the pop-up panel, choose **Material**:

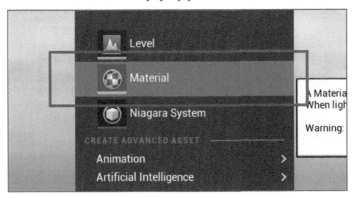

Figure 6.11: Creating a new Material

5. When prompted, give the Material a name, such as M_Plastic (remember, the M denotes it's a Material). Double-click the Material to open the Material Editor.

> **Note**
>
> As I mentioned in *Chapter 4*, we will be adopting the Unreal Engine naming conventions when creating assets. As a refresher, you can find the details here: `https://docs.unrealengine.com/5.1/en-US/recommended-asset-naming-conventions-in-unreal-engine-projects/`

Although the Material Editor has many panels, we will only be working with the three most used for our project.

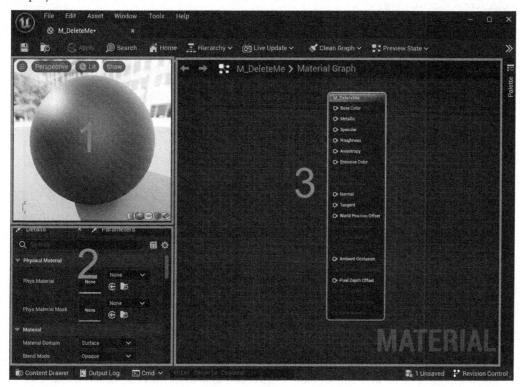

Figure 6.12: The Material Editor panels

Here are the panels we will be working on:

1. **The Viewport panel**: This panel gives you a real-time preview of the Material as it is generated

2. **The details panel**: This panel will display the properties of the selected functions and nodes in the **Material Graph** panel

3. **The Material Graph panel**: This is where you will be spending 99% of your time creating nodes and functions for your Material

Now we are ready to create our Materials – as you may have guessed from the Material name, we will start with creating a plastic Material.

Creating a plastic Material

Our first attempt will be to create a plastic Material. The one object that comes to mind is a snooker ball. A snooker ball is a very shiny, polished object, and often comes in various bright colors. We'll make ours bright red.

So, let's create our Material:

1. In **Material Graph**, right-click and type Constant. In the list that pops up, choose **Constant3Vector**:

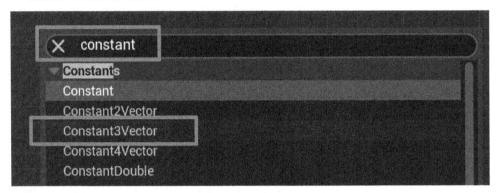

Figure 6.13: Creating a Constant3Vector node

> **Note**
>
> **Constants** (also known as **Constant Material Expressions**) are the most commonly used nodes that can hold a float value. There are constants that hold one float value, **Constant2Vector** holds two float values, **Constant3Vector** holds three float values, and **Constant4Vector** holds four float values. Here, we are using **Constant3Vector** to hold the three **R**, **G**, and **B** values for the color of the sphere.

2. The **Constant3Vector** node will now be placed in **Material Graph**. Next, double-click on the node swatch (the black square) to open the **Color Picker** pop-up panel. From there, slide the **Saturation** and **Value** sliders to the very top to get the bright red color.

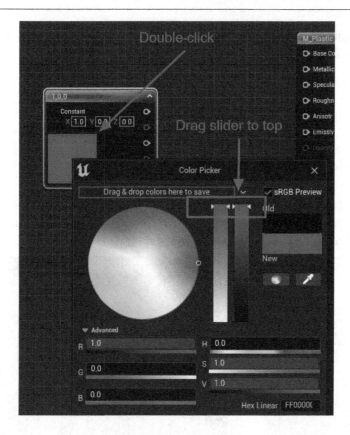

Figure 6.14: Changing the Constant3Vector node color

3. Click on the topmost white pin on the **Constant3Vector** node, then drag and attach it to the
    Base Color pin of the **Result** node of the Material.

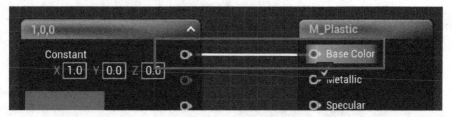

Figure 6.15: Connecting the RGB pin to the base color pin

The **Viewport** panel will now show the result of the process you just completed. We have a red
ball, but it's not plasticky enough – it needs more shininess. We have three properties we can
adjust, **Metallic**, **Specular**, and **Roughness**, to give us the look we are after. Which of these
options do you think we need to use?

Hint: **Metallic** is used for metal objects, **Specular** has been set by default to **0.5** by the engine, and **Roughness** is the opposite of smoothness/shininess.

You got it – it's **Roughness**!

Note

Unreal Engine uses a default **Specular** value of **0.5**. This is an accurate value and works for the vast majority of Materials. To create diffused or shiny Materials, you should really use the **Roughness** value and not the **Specular** value.

---

4. In **Material Graph**, right-click and type `Constant` again, but this time, from the list, choose **Constant**. A green-colored node with a single pin will now be available. Drag the white pin to the **Roughness** pin. Voilà – you get a shiny red sphere!

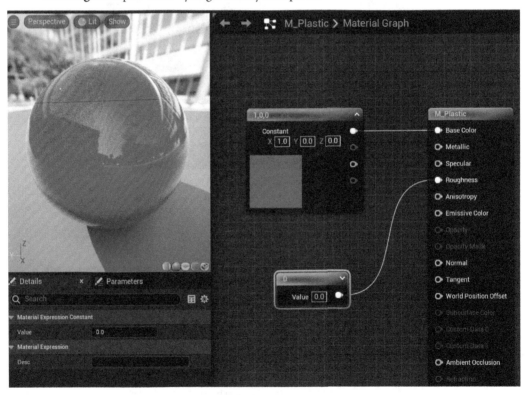

Figure 6.16: Shiny red sphere created using two nodes

> **Note**
>
> The constant value is at **0.0**, meaning there is no roughness, which is exactly what we need in this scenario.

5. Now, click the **Apply** and **Save** buttons at the top left of the Material Editor, then close the panel:

Figure 6.17: Click the Apply and Save buttons every time you make changes

6. Drag the **M_Plastic** Material from the Content Browser onto the left-most sphere.

Congratulations! You just created your first Material. How easy was that?

Creating a rubber Material

Let's now attempt to make a rubber ball – a red rubber ball, to be exact. I think you already know how to do this, but let's do it together anyway:

1. Duplicate **M_Plastic** with *Ctrl + D* and rename it to M_Rubber.
2. Double-click the Material to open the Material Editor.
3. Change the value of the **Constant** node connected to the **Roughness** pin to 1.0.
4. Click **Apply** and **Save**, then drag the **M_Rubber** Material to the middle sphere.

Figure 6.18: The newly created red rubber Material

> **Note**
>
> In Unreal Engine, the values we key into the nodes range from 0 to 1 only. 0 means 0% and 1 means 100%. To get 50%, you need to key in 0.5, and so on.

With the rubber Material completed, let's create a metal one.

Creating a metal Material

For our third Material, let's aim for a chrome ball:

1. Duplicate the **M_Plastic** Material and rename it M_Chrome.

2. Double-click the Material to open the Material Editor.

3. Double-click the **Constant3Vector** node swatch (the red box) and change the **Saturation** value to **White** (drag the vertical slider toward the bottom). Then click **OK**.

4. Then create a new **Constant** node – this time by holding the *1* key across the top of the keyboard (not the numpad) and left-clicking anywhere in **Material Graph**. To create the **Constant2Vector** node, hold the number *2*, and you can do the same for **Constant3Vector** and **Constant4Vector**.

5. Attach the **Constant** pin to the **Metallic** pin and change the **Constant** value to 1.

    The preview panel shows the chrome Material we just created.

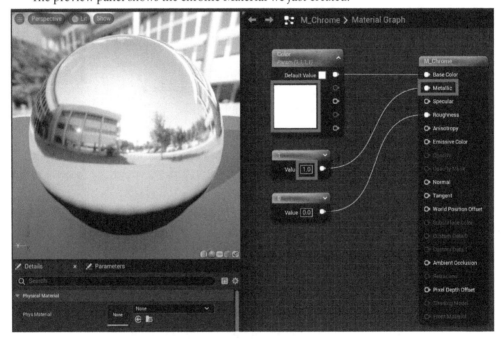

Figure 6.19: Chrome Material created with just a few tweaks

Note

When setting the **Metallic** property in the Material Editor, the settings are either 1 (it being metal) or 0 (it being non-metal); there are no in betweens.

6. Click **Apply** and **Save**, then close the Material Editor.

7. Drag **M_Chrome** onto the third sphere and save the project.

Figure 6.20: The completed plastic, rubber, and metal Materials

As you can see, it is not that complicated to create basic Materials in Unreal Engine. These are the basic building blocks of generating Unreal Engine Materials.

> **Note**
>
> There is very comprehensive documentation by Epic Games available at the following link that gives you real-world values to generate photorealistic-looking Materials: `https://docs.unrealengine.com/5.2/en-US/physically-based-Materials-in-unreal-engine/`. I suggest you keep this as a reference for your projects.

In the next section, we will be looking at another workflow of creating Materials, using Material Instances.

Creating and using Material Instances

In the previous section, you created some simple Materials using the Material Editor. Although we used very simple nodes, we had to click on **Apply** and **Save** every time we changed any properties for it to take effect – not exactly real-time, is it? It is okay to do this if you have a few Materials, but it becomes a chore if you have a few hundred to tweak in a hurry. What if there was a way to update the Materials on the fly, and what if you're able to change one property that will change all others at the same time? This is where **Material Instances** come into play.

Say we want to have a variation of the chrome sphere, perhaps one in red and another in blue. It'll be easy to duplicate and change the RGB properties every time you duplicate the Material, but that is not a good workflow, because every time you duplicate a Material, Unreal Engine is forced to allocate memory for it. Just imagine if you had hundreds or thousands of these Materials in your project – you'd run out of video memory before you know it!

Instead, let's do an experiment:

1. In the Content Browser, select the **M_Chrome** Material, right-click, and choose **Create Material Instance**.

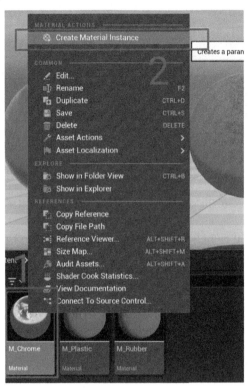

Figure 6.21: Right-click on M_Chrome to make a Material Instance

2. For a Material Instance, we use `MI_` as the naming convention. So, let's name the Material Instance `MI_Chrome_Red`.

Note

From now on, I will refer to Master Materials using **M_** and Material Instances with **MI_**. What this means is that the Master Materials (parents) will retain their properties and the Material Instances will inherit their properties from their parent.

---

3. Select the chrome sphere in the Viewport. Then, in its **Details** panel, double-click the Material thumbnail under the **Materials** section – this is the fastest way to open the Material assigned to the selected object. (Hey, it's all about productivity!)

Figure 6.22: Double-click to open the Material Editor

4. Select the **Constant3Vector** node, right-click on it, and choose **Convert to Parameter**. You will be prompted to give it a name – let's name it `Color`.

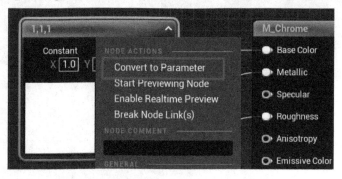

Figure 6.23: Right-click to convert to parameter

5. Do the same for the **Metallic** and **Roughness** constants, right-clicking and naming them `Metalness` and `Roughness`, respectively.

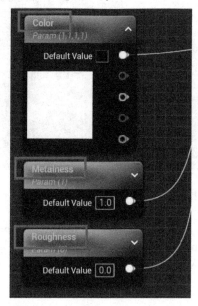

Figure 6.24: Converting the nodes into parameters

6. Click on **Apply** and **Save**, then close the Material Editor.

7. Duplicate the chrome sphere (*Ctrl + D*) and apply **MI_Chrome** to it. Nothing changes.

8. Now open the **MI_Chrome** Material (double-click on its thumbnail).

9. You will notice that the Material Editor looks different – it's more simplified, and you'll notice the three parameters we assigned in the **Details** panel (**Metalness**, **Roughness**, and **Color**). Enable all three by clicking their respective checkboxes.

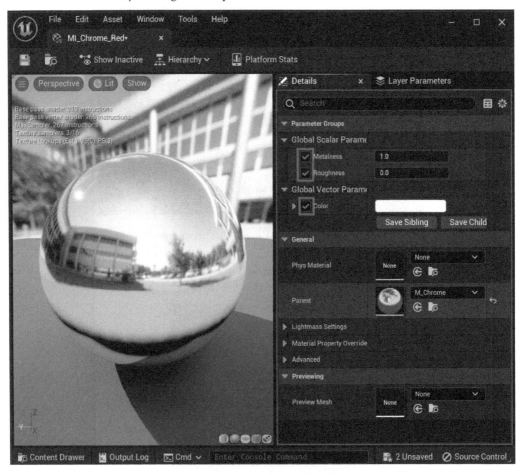

Figure 6.25: The Material Instance editor

10. Once the parameters are enabled, they can be tweaked, and the changes are updated instantly in the Viewport. Click the color swatch and drag the mouse inside the color wheel to get an on the fly, color change. Wow!

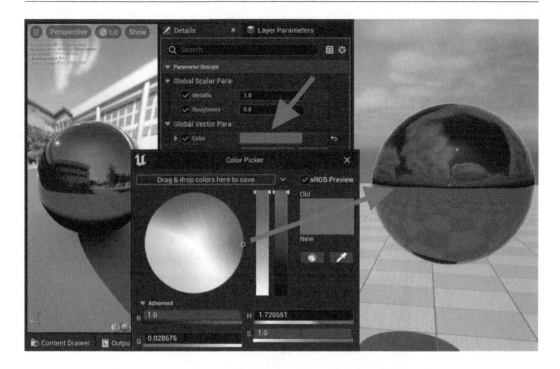

Figure 6.26: Using the Color parameter to get an instant color update

You also can tweak the **Metalness** and **Roughness** values to achieve the desired look.

11. Now duplicate **MI_Chrome_Red** and name it MI_Chrome_Blue. Open its editor and change its color value to **Blue**. Then, duplicate the red sphere and apply the **MI_Chrome_Blue** Material to it.

Figure 6.27: The completed chrome spheres with different variations

It will be useful for you to know that changing the parameters of the Master Material (parent) will influence all the Material Instances (children), as long as the child parameters are not overridden. Furthermore, this workflow minimizes draw calls (less processing power) as the red and blue spheres are instances (children) of the Master Material.

You now have a good understanding of how to generate basic Materials and Material Instances and why Material Instances are useful and an important workflow. In the next section, we will be diving into creating Materials with image-based Textures.

Working with Materials with image-based Textures

In the preceding section, you successfully generated elementary Materials employing straightforward constant nodes. In this section, we shall progress to the next level by crafting PBR Materials, employing images known as Texture maps. This progression is not significantly more intricate than the techniques you have previously employed; it merely entails the incorporation of a few additional nodes.

We will continue from the previous Level (**Material_Demo**), and we are going to be creating a simple wooden Textured box. Let's go:

1. Create a cube from the **Place Actor (+)** drop-down menu and press the *F* key to frame it.

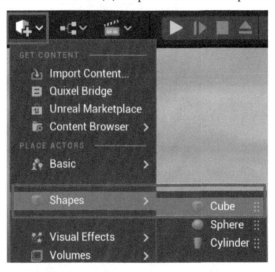

Figure 6.28: Creating a new cube

2. In the Content Browser, open the **Demo_Materials** folder. Then right-click and make a new Material. Let's call it M_Wood_Box.

3. Double-click to open the **M_Wood_Box** Material.

    To create this Material, we will be using three Texture maps:

    - **T_Wood_Floor_Walnut_D**

    - **T_Wood_Floor_Walnut_M**

    - **T_Wood_Floor_Walnut_N**

> **Note**
>
> It's common practice for Texture artists to give a prefix and suffix to filenames for easy identification or when searching for the appropriate Textures in the Content Browser. In this case, the prefix *T* means it is a **Texture**, and the suffixes *D*, *M,* and *N*, mean **Diffuse**, **Metallic**, and **Normal** respectively.

4. While the Texture Editor is open, press *Ctrl + spacebar* to open the Content Brower in the editor itself.

5. From here, select the **StarterContent** folder (*1*), then select the **Textures** folder (*2*), and then type `Floor` in the **Search** window (*3*). You'll be presented with the three Textures shown in *Figure 6.29*:

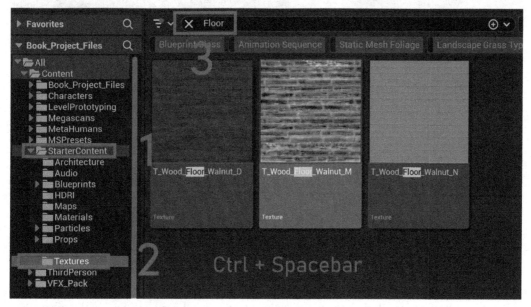

Figure 6.29: Creating a new cube

6. Select the three Textures and drag them into **Material Graph**. Then arrange them and connect the **RGB** pin of each **Texture Sample** node to its appropriate pins on the **M_Wood_Box** node, as shown in *Figure 6.30*:

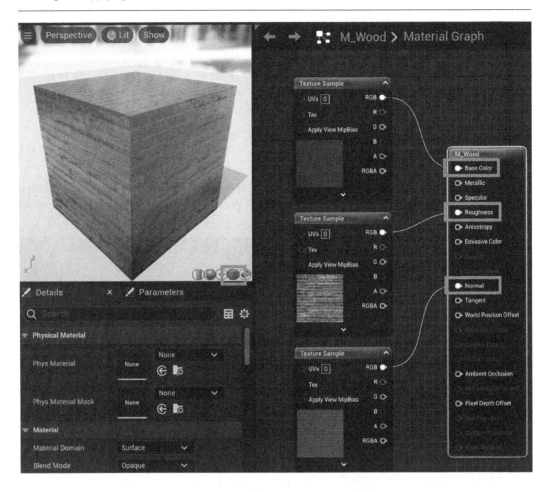

Figure 6.30: Texture Sample node connectivity

7.   In the **Preview** panel, click the tiny cube icon to preview the cube instead of the sphere. You can spin the cube around to inspect the Texture you just applied. Click on **Apply** and **Save**, then close the Texture Editor window.

8.   Drag the **M_Wood_Box** Material onto the cube in the Viewport and save the project.

Congratulations, you just created your first image-based Material!

> **Note**
>
> When you dragged the Texture maps into **Material Graph**, you did two processes at the same time – first, you created three **Texture Sample** nodes, and second, you automatically assigned the appropriate Texture maps to them. I find this the fastest way to create a Texture-based Material.

There are loads more things we can do with this Material and things can become more involved, but we're not going to go any further. At this point, you now have the fundamental knowledge of creating Materials in Unreal Engine.

To speed things up, throughout the rest of the book, we will be using ready-made Materials found in **Starter Content** or on Quixel Bridge (`https://quixel.com/bridge`), or free Materials we will look for in the Unreal Engine Marketplace.

> **Note**
>
> If you find that 3D objects you procured from third-party sites such as **Sketchfab** (`https://sketchfab.com/`) or **CGTrader** (`https://www.cgtrader.com/`) lack surfaces that you can assign Materials to, you will find a step-by-step guide in the *Appendix* on how to add additional surfaces using the concept of Material ID using Blender.

Now that you have a good understanding of Master Materials and Material Instances in Unreal Engine, let's use that knowledge to continue working on our project.

Applying Materials to scenes

Earlier, you acquired knowledge on generating fundamental Materials through the Material Editor. Understanding the creation of Master Materials and Material Instances is crucial, as they serve as the foundation for developing Materials in Unreal Engine.

In this final section, let's delve into expediting the process of generating and applying Materials to your scenes without starting from scratch. You have the advantage of accessing numerous pre-made Materials already available for use in Unreal Engine. These Materials can be found on the Unreal Engine Marketplace and can also be accessed through Quixel Bridge.

Downloading Material packs from the Unreal Engine Marketplace

Let's first browse the Unreal Engine Marketplace to identify and download Materials that might be useful for our virtual film:

1. Open the Epic Games Launcher and select the **Marketplace** tab.
2. In the **Search Product...** window, type `Automotive Materials`.

    Automotive Materials is a collection of high-quality automotive-themed Materials and Textures that have been set up for use in Unreal Engine. You will find **Interior** and **Exterior** categories containing folders for car paint, metals, lights, reflectors, leather, textiles, wood, and carbon fiber – perfect for our use!

Figure 6.31 shows the product that you're looking for:

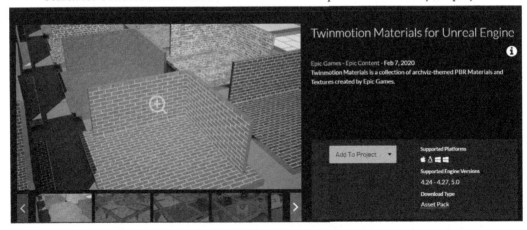

Figure 6.31: The useful automotive Materials

3. Click on the **Add To Project** button and add it to the **A_New_Beginning** project. (You may need to choose the closest alternative version, which is **Version 5.1**.)

4. Another free Texture pack is **Twinmotion Materials**. This package has over 497 Materials; however, this makes it a large download (8 GB). The initial loading of these assets will require shaders to be compiled and could take some time.

    Search for `Twinmotion Materials` in the Marketplace and add it to your project.

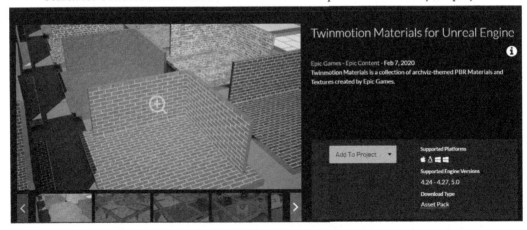

Figure 6.32: Twinmotion Materials pack

These are some of the Material packs I found to be useful. There is much more you can find in the Marketplace, but this should suffice for our project. In the next section, we will return to our project and apply Materials to the required objects in our scenes.

Applying Materials to the cryo-pod

We are finally doing it – applying Materials to the 3D meshes in our scenes! In *Chapter 4*, we left some of the 3D meshes without any Materials and I promised we would return to them to do so. So, let us start working on it:

1. Open the **A_New_Beginning** project if you have not done so. Then, in the **Levels** folder, double-click to open the **INT_Spaceship** Level.

2. Press the number *3* on your keyboard to jump to **Bookmark 3**.

    In this scene, we added the two cryo-pods but left them without any Materials applied to them. The cryo-pods we added in *Chapter 4* were pre-made with Material IDs. If you'd like to replace them with the one you made from the *Appendix*, then you can do so now. You can import the FBX file and replace the one we have added; otherwise, just use the one that is already added to the scene.

3. Since we're going to be applying the same Materials to both pods, completely delete the one in the rear (using **Outliner**) and we will duplicate the one in the front once we've finished applying the Materials.

4. In the previous section, we added the **Automotive Materials** pack, and it is listed in the Content Browser. Select the **Automotive Materials** folder; then, in the **Filters** panel, select **Materials | Material Instances**. All the Material Instances in this folder will be displayed.

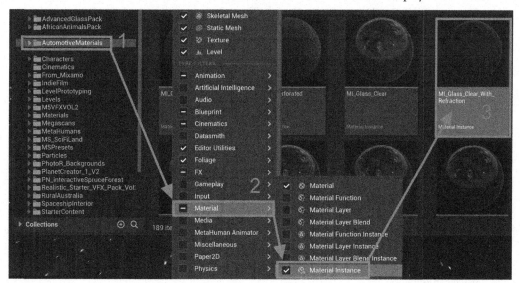

Figure 6.33: Adding the glass Material Instance

5.   Drag **MI_Glass_Clear_With_Refraction** onto the **Glass** (green) surface of the cryo-pod. Now you'll be able to see through the cryo-pod's glass surface.

6.   With the filter still enabled, in the Content Browser's search window, type `metal steel`. You will see three Materials – select **MI_Metal_Steel_Brushed** and drag it onto the main body of the cryo-pod.

Figure 6.34: Narrowing down the search using the search window

7.   You can continue adding the Materials to the cryo-pod using the Material IDs you made in the previous section. Remember to clear the filters if you don't see the Materials you're looking for. These are what I used:

Material IDs	Materials	From Folder
Disc, Capsule, Legs	M_Metal_Gold	Starter Content
Front Screen	M_Tech_Hex_Tile_Pulse	Starter Content
Rivets/Hinge	MI_Metal_Silver	Automotive Material
Hinge Button	MI_Lamp_Red	Automotive Material
Vents/Bed	MI_Lamp_Blue	Automotive Material

Table 6.1: Materials to be added the cryo-pod surfaces

All the other Materials are good to go, but you may have noticed that the **M_Tech_Hex_Tile_Pulse** Material does not show the hexagon pattern as shown in the Material thumbnail. The problem we're facing is that the hexagon pattern is too large to fit nicely into the area of **Front Screen**, as we can see here:

Figure 6.35: Problematic front screen

We will need to increase the number of hexagons. So, let's do a bit of tweaking.

8. Select the cryo-pod. Then, in the **Details** panel, scroll down to the **Materials** section and double-click on the **Element 2** thumbnail.

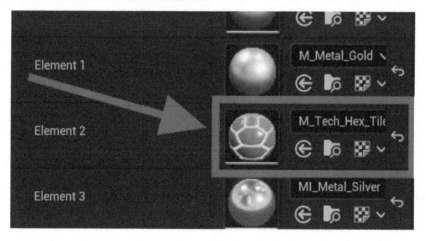

Figure 6.36: Opening the Material Editor for Element 2

9. In the Material Editor, zoom out using the scroll wheel and use the right mouse button to pan around. Look for a comment, as shown in *Figure 6.37*, that indicates **BumpOffset**. Here you'll find a **TexCoord (Texture Coordinate)** node:

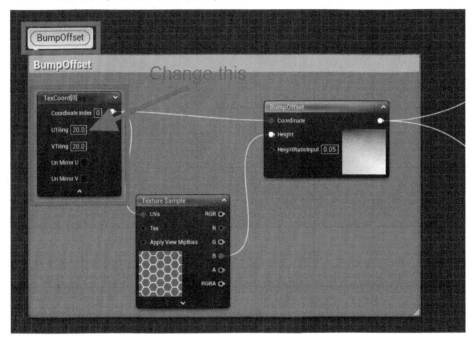

Figure 6.37: Change TexCoord UTiling and VTiling

10. Click the down arrow to reveal the **UTiling** and **VTiling** options, and change both values to 20 units.

11. Click **Apply** and **Save**, then close the Material Editor. The **Front Screen** view now looks much better, and you'll notice that it is pulsating! Could this mean that it is monitoring a living organism?

> **Note**
>
> The **Texture Coordinate** node holds the *U* and *V* information of the Texture it connects to. We use these values to change the **Height** (**U**) and **Width** (**V**) values of the Textures in the Material Editor. In this scenario, we increased both the *U* and *V* values to have more hexagons displayed in the panel.

12. The Material application is complete. Delete the **Cryo-Pod_Human** Actor from the Outliner and duplicate the cryo-pod. Select the object and press *Ctrl + D* to duplicate it and move it into place.

Figure 6.38: The completed cryo-pods

13. Now save the project (*Ctrl + Shift + S*).

In this scene, our only task was to apply Materials to the cryo-pod object. If you have followed the instructions correctly, your scene should look like *Figure 6.38*. The next task we have to do in this scene is adding the two human figures sleeping in the cryo-pods. We will add them in *Chapter 7*, where we will learn how to create **MetaHumans**.

Adding photorealistic Materials to the Earth object

In *Chapter 4*, we added some basic Materials to the Earth and moon objects and left it at that. In this section, we will carry on from where we left off, adding photorealistic Materials to objects:

1. Open the **EXT_Space** Level. We have the spaceship, Earth, moon, and stars objects here. You can check the Outliner to confirm this.

2. In the Content Browser, select the **Materials** folder. You will have the **M_Stars** Material we made in *Chapter 4* listed here.

3. Locate the **Textures** folder in the downloaded project file. Using the following list, drag the Textures into the existing **Textures** folder in the Content Browser:

    · **2k_earth_clouds**

    · **2k_earth_daymap**

    · **2k_earth_normal_map**

    · **2k_earth_specular_map**

    · **2k_moon**

Figure 6.39: The five newly imported Textures

4. Save the project using the **Save All** command (*Ctrl + Shift + S*). This will ensure the imported Textures are saved.

5. Now, select the **Materials** folder. In the folder, right-click and create the following Materials:

    · **M_Earth**

    · **M_Clouds**

    · **M_Moon**

6. Double-click to open the **M_Earth** Material.

7. Press *Ctrl* + spacebar to bring up the Content Browser, then select the same **Texture** folder and drag the **2k_earth_daymap**, **2k_earth_normal**, and **2k_earth_specular_map** Textures into **Material Graph**.

8. Drag the three Textures and arrange and connect the nodes in order, as shown in *Figure 6.40*:

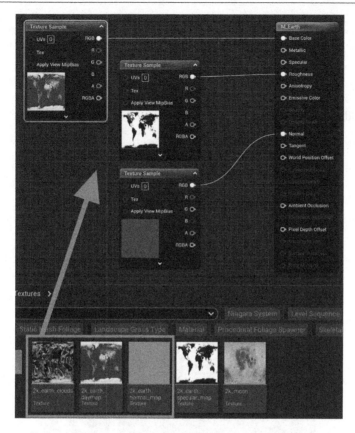

Figure 6.40: Drag the three Earth Textures into Material Graph

9. Click **Apply** and **Save**, close the Material Editor, then drag the **M_Earth** Material onto the Earth object.

Figure 6.41: The completed Earth Material

What we have now is the Earth Texture applied to the Earth mesh. Let's add the clouds Texture for some cloud coverage.

Adding the clouds

Here's how to add the clouds Texture:

1. In the Outliner, select **Earth** (object) and duplicate it. Then rename the duplicate `Earth_Clouds`.

2. In the **Details** panel, in the **Transform** section, scale the **Earth_Clouds** object by **10.2** on each axis:

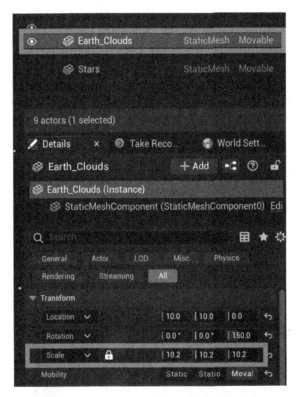

Figure 6.42: Scaling up the Earth_Clouds object

3. Back in the **Materials** folder, double-click the **M_Clouds** Material, then press *Ctrl* + spacebar to bring up the Content Browser. From the **Texture** folder, drag the **2k_earth_clouds** Texture into **Material Graph**. Next, in the **Details** panel, under the **Material** section, change **Blend Mode** from **Opaque** to **Translucent** – this will now enable the **Opacity** pin in the **M_Atmosphere** node. Then connect the **RGB** pin of the **Cloud** node to the **Opacity** pin:

Figure 6.43: Connecting the cloud Texture

In the Material preview window, you will notice that the clouds are dark instead of white. Let's fix them.

4. We will need a **Constant3Vector** node. Do you still remember how to create it? Press and hold the *3* key on your keyboard (not the numpad), then click the left mouse button.

5. Double-click in the node swatch (black box), and change its color to **White**. Connect the node's **RGB** pin to the **Emmissive Color** pin. When you preview the clouds, they are now white.

6. We will also need the following nodes:

    -   **SkyAtmosphereLightDirection**: To create this, right-click in the graph and type the node name.

    -   **VertexNormalWS**: To create this, right-click and type the node name. The combination of the **SkyAtmosphereLightDirection** and **VertexNormalWS** nodes hides the cloud effect on the dark side of the Earth.

- **Multiply**: To create this, press *M* on the keyboard and left-click. We will need *two* of these nodes, so use *Ctrl + D* to duplicate it. The **Multiply** node mathematically multiplies the information from inputs *A* and *B*.

- **DotProduct**: To create this, right-click and type the node name. The **DotProduct** node calculates the falloff generated by the directional light in the scene.

- **Constant**: To create this, press *1* on the keyboard and left-click.

7. Now arrange and connect the nodes as shown in *Figure 6.44*:

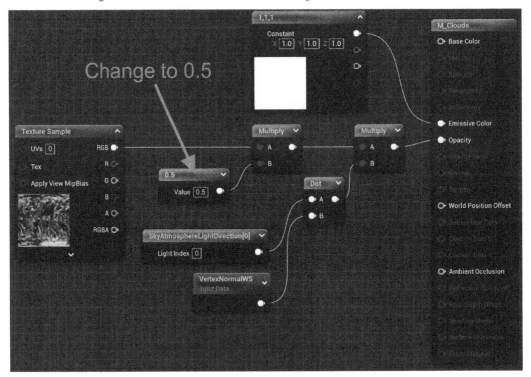

Figure 6.44: Connecting the cloud Material

8. Apply and save the Material. Then drag the **M_Cloud** Material to the **Earth_Cloud** Static Mesh, and you'll see that we've got clouds! Adjust the **Constant** value for denser clouds.

Figure 6.45: Cloud Material applied

> **Note**
>
> To understand more about the nodes (Material expressions) in Unreal Engine, use this link: `https://docs.unrealengine.com/5.2/en-US/unreal-engine-Material-expressions-reference/`

The final Material we will add to the Earth object is the atmosphere Material. This will give the Earth a glowing-bluish edge, mimicking a hazy atmosphere.

Adding the atmosphere Material

Here's how to create the atmosphere Material:

1. In the Outliner, duplicate the **Earth_Cloud** Static Mesh and rename it `Earth_Atmosphere`.
2. In the **Materials** folder, duplicate **M_Clouds** and rename it `M_Atmosphere`. Open it.
3. Delete all the nodes connected to the **Opacity** pin – you can *box select* them and hit the *Delete* key.
4. Change the **Constant3Vector** node color to a bluish color by changing **R** to `0.14`, **G** to `0.47`, and **B** to `0.6`.
5. Connect a **Constant** node to **Vector3Node** using the **Multiply** node (**M**) and pin it to the **Emissive** pin.
6. Change the **Constant** value to `0.2`. Increase or decrease this value if you need more or less of a hazy look.
7. Right-click in the editor and type `Fresnel`, then select it from the list.

> **Note**
>
> **Fresnel** refers to the phenomenon where the visibility of light reflections varies in intensity depending on the viewing angle. For instance, when you stand directly above a pool and gaze downward, you'll observe fewer reflections on the water's surface. However, when you shift your perspective so that the water aligns parallel to your eye level, you'll gradually perceive an increasing number of reflections on the water's surface. A more detailed exploration of the **Fresnel** node can be found here: `https://docs.unrealengine.com/5.2/en-US/using-fresnel-in-your-unreal-engine-Materials`.

8. Right-click again and type `Power`, then select it from the list.

9. Arrange and connect the nodes as shown in *Figure 6.46*:

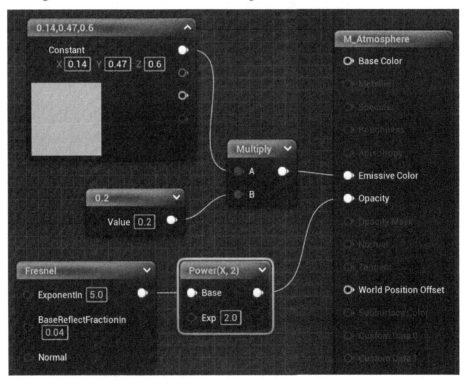

Figure 6.46: Connecting the atmosphere Material

10. Click **Apply** and **Save**, then close the Material Editor. Now drag the **M_Atmosphere** Material to the **Earth_Atmosphere** Static Mesh.

Figure 6.47: The completed Earth with clouds and atmosphere

By now, you should be able to figure out how Materials are generated; as such, I will let you finish the moon Material on your own. Once done, save the project!

> **Note**
>
> The spaceship has some Materials assigned to it. However, you are welcome to inspect and change the Materials as you like. This will allow you to practice what you've learned and apply your own Materials if you wish. Remember to ungroup the spaceship using *Shift + G* first.

There is so much more we can do with Materials, but remember, the more nodes we add to **Material Graph**, the more draw calls will occur. We will revisit this scene in *Chapter 12* to give it a filmic look, but we will leave it as it is for now.

Summary

Learning about and applying Materials in Unreal Engine is crucial for creating realistic and visually captivating environments, objects, and characters. It allows for precise control over properties such as color, Texture, and reflectivity, enabling the realization of diverse artistic visions.

You now have a good grasp of generating basic Materials and the importance of optimizing them. Having acquired a solid understanding of generating basic Materials and recognizing the significance of optimizing them, you are now equipped with this valuable knowledge. Additionally, you have been introduced to a wide array of pre-existing Materials, which offer the advantage of swift application without the requirement of extensive time investment in their creation.

In the upcoming chapter, we will embark on the creation of our two human characters, utilizing the groundbreaking Epic MetaHumans technology. This revolutionary tool within Unreal Engine empowers creators with unparalleled ease to generate remarkably realistic and customizable human characters.

Part 3: Production: Adding and Animating Characters

In this part, you will breathe life into your Unreal Engine projects. *Chapter 7* explores the creation of actors using Unreal Engine MetaHumans, unlocking the potential to craft lifelike characters. You'll then progress to *Chapter 8*, where you'll discover the intricacies of retargeting MetaHumans for animation, ensuring seamless integration into your virtual world. *Chapter 9* takes you further by adding mocap animations and expressive facial features to your MetaHuman characters, enhancing the depth and realism of your digital narratives.

This part includes the following chapters:

- *Chapter 7, Creating Actors with Unreal Engine MetaHumans*

- *Chapter 8, Retargeting the MetaHumans for Unreal Engine 5*

- *Chapter 9, Adding Animations and Facial Expressions to Your MetaHuman Characters*

7

Creating Actors with Unreal Engine MetaHumans

Over the past few chapters, we've accomplished the creation of our world. In the realm of film and animation, this process is commonly referred to as set dressing, encompassing various elements such as the spaceship's interior, cryo-pods, the spaceship itself, planets, the space shuttle, and the surrounding landscape. All these components contribute to the visual storytelling aspects. The term **mise en scène** is frequently employed to describe such scenarios, emphasizing the art of crafting a scene.

In this chapter, our focus will be on the crucial component that has been missing thus far: the Actors themselves, and what better method to achieve this than by utilizing Epic Games remarkable high-fidelity digital humans known as MetaHumans?

The introduction of MetaHumans accompanied the launch of Unreal Engine 5, making the creation of photorealistic digital human characters more accessible than ever before. Using **MetaHuman Creator (MHC)**, you will have the opportunity to fashion our two characters, Adam and Eve, and subsequently import them into Unreal Engine. Then, in *Chapter 8*, we will proceed to incorporate rigs and animate these characters in accordance with our storyboard.

So, in this chapter, we will be covering the following topics:

- Getting started with MetaHuman Creator
- Using MetaHuman Creator
- Downloading and importing your MetaHumans

Technical requirements

There are no files associated with this chapter. However, you will need to open the project file we've been working on from the previous chapters. If necessary, here is the link to them: `https://packt.link/gbz/9781801813808`.

Getting started with MetaHuman Creator

MetaHuman Creator simplifies the process of creating digital humans by offering a web-based, user-friendly interface and intuitive controls. You can easily manipulate and refine characters in real time, adjusting facial expressions, hair, and other features with just a few clicks. The tool also provides an efficient means of importing the created characters into Unreal Engine for further development, animation, and integration into virtual environments.

Let's learn how to access MHC:

1. Open the **A_New_Beginning** project.

2. Then click the **Place Actor** + icon and choose **Quixel Bridge**.

3. Once the **Quixel BRIDGE** panel opens, dock it to have a larger view of the window.

4. Next, sign in using your Epic ID (*1*). Once signed in, click on the **MetaHumans** tab (*2*). You'll now see a list of characters. These are the MetaHuman presets.

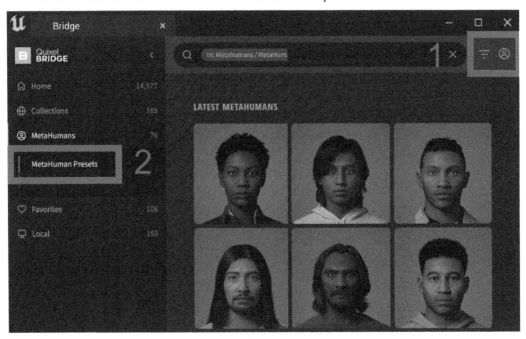

Figure 7.1: Accessing the MetaHumans tab in Quixel Bridge

You might also see a **My MetaHumans** category. Do not worry if you do not have this yet – the MetaHumans you create and download will be listed here once you are done creating your MetaHuman, as seen in the following screenshot:

Figure 7.2: My MetaHumans category

5.   Let's first create the Eve character. I'm going to choose **VIVIAN** from the presets. Then click on the **START MHC** button.

Figure 7.3: Choosing our MetaHuman character

6. On the following screen, from the **Version** drop-down list, choose **Unreal Engine 5.2** and click the **Launch MetaHuman Creator** button:

Figure 7.4: Launching MHC

So, in this section, you logged into the MetaHuman Creator system using the Quixel Bridge interface in Unreal Engine. In the next section, we will continue with creating and customizing the Eve and Adam characters, but before that, you need to familiarize yourself with the MHC interface.

Using MetaHuman Creator

MetaHuman Creator is a web-based character creation tool that allows for the customization of photorealistic CG human actors. Once you build your character, you can then easily transfer the character into Unreal Engine using Quixel Bridge. The following information will allow you to be as creative as you want when creating your version of Adam and Eve; we have a big list of preset characters to choose from, but how they look can be further customized.

A few minutes after launching MetaHuman Creator, the interface will be loaded and our chosen character, Vivian, will be listed as one of the default characters. Let's proceed:

1. Select the **Create** tab.

2. Choose **Vivian** (or your character of choice) from the list.

3. Click on the **Create Selected** button.

Figure 7.5: The MetaHumans Creator interface

4. You will now be in the MetaHumans main editor. Let's first rename the character by clicking on the pencil icon – I'm going to call the character Eve.

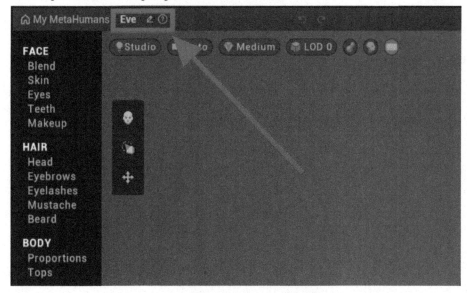

Figure 7.6: Renaming the MetaHuman

Now, let's get familiarized with the main interface.

Understanding the MHC interface

Figure 7.7 shows a labeled image of the MHC interface:

Figure 7.7: The main MHC interface

Let's break the image down:

- **Studio/Select Environment** (*1*): This button reveals a panel that allows you to change the lighting condition in the Viewport. Here, you can find both **Indoor** and **Outdoor** lighting settings, the **Background Color** swatch, and a **Light Rig Rotation** slider. These lighting settings will allow you to view the character in different colors and lighting conditions.

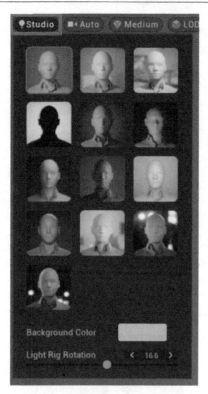

Figure 7.8: The Studio/Select Environment panel

- **Auto/CAMERA SWITCHING** (*2*): This allows you to change the camera position from **Auto** to **Face**, **Body**, **Torso**, **Legs**, **Feet**, and **Far**. Each setting has a keyboard shortcut associated with it, *1* through *6*.

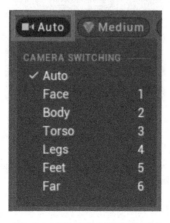

Figure 7.9: Auto/CAMERA SWITCHING panel

- **Medium/Select Render Quality** (*3*): This panel gives you the option of upping the render quality of the MetaHuman display.

Figure 7.10: The render quality setting

- **Auto LOD/Level Of Detail** (*4*): This drop-down menu gives you a preview of the MetaHuman's **Level Of Detail (LOD)** when previewed closer or farther away from the camera in Unreal Engine. This is Unreal Engine's method of optimizing the scene – as the characters move further from the camera, Unreal Engine will decrease the quality of the MetaHuman to optimize the scene.

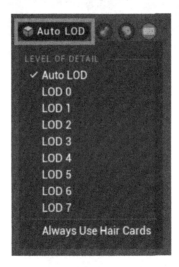

Figure 7.11: LOD settings

- **Clay Material** (*5*): Use this button to toggle to a clay material view, which helps the sculpting process by eliminating visual distractions.

- **Hide Hair** (*6*): Toggle this button to show and hide the character's hair.

- **Hotkey Display** (*7*): This toggles the hotkey display on the right side of the interface.

Figure 7.12: Using the hotkey display

- **Blend Mode** (8): This mode allows you to customize the MetaHuman by dragging any of the MetaHuman presets at the bottom of the mode into the three **PRESETS** slots to further customize the MetaHuman.

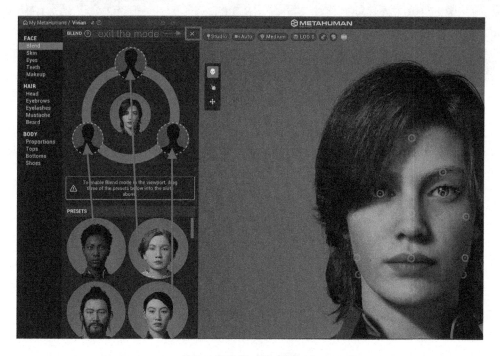

Figure 7.13: The Blend Mode

- **Sculpt Mode** (*9*): By enabling this mode, you can sculpt the MetaHuman by clicking and dragging the feature points on her face. In case you change your mind, the **Undo** and **Redo** buttons are at the top of the interface, or you can press *Ctrl + Z* to undo. Then click the **Sculpt Mode** button again to disable it.

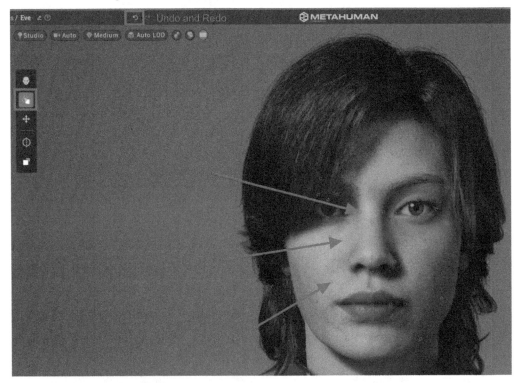

Figure 7.14: The Sculpt Mode feature points

- **Move Mode** (*10*): This mode enables the facial marker controls. You can augment the facial features by moving the curved lines. Click the **Move Mode** icon again to disable this mode.

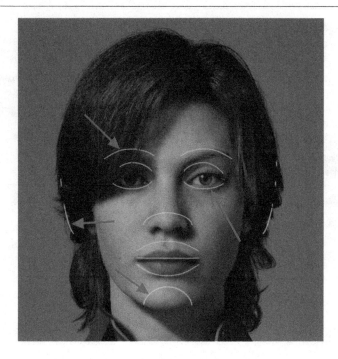

Figure 7.15: The Move Mode facial controls

- **Face, Hair, and Body Controls** (*11*): These options allow you to customize how your character looks. We will explore these options in the following subsections.

- **Animation Toolbar** (*12*): The toolbar at the bottom of the interface controls various animations in the Viewport. You can select **Facial Poses**, **Body Poses**, **Expression Loops**, and **Technical Loops**.

As just mentioned, let's look at the **Face**, **Hair**, and **Body** controls to customize our Eve character.

Reviewing the Face controls

The **Face** controls enable changes to the MetaHuman's facial features such as **Skin**, **Eyes**, **Teeth**, and **Makeup**:

- **Skin**: The **Skin** editor has three tabs – **Skin**, **Freckles**, and **Accents**.

  - In the **Skin** tab, you can change **Color**, **Texture**, **Contrast**, and **Roughness**.

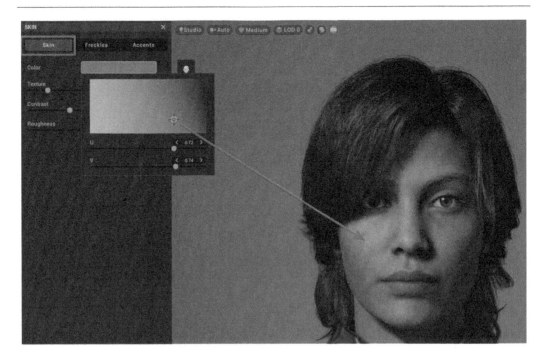

Figure 7.16: Augmenting the skin color

- In the **Freckles** tab, you can control **Strength**, **Density**, **Saturation**, and **Tone Shift**.

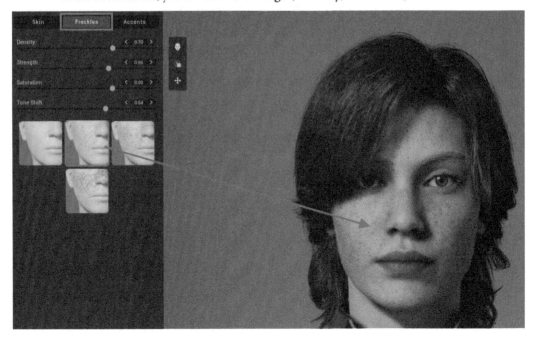

Figure 7.17: Adding and removing freckles

- In the **Accents** tab, you can simulate different skin characteristics such as blushing, suntan, dark circles under the eyes, and so on.

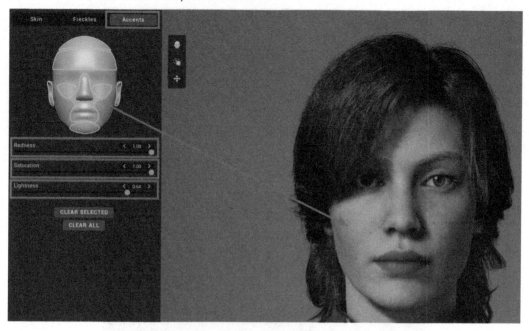

Figure 7.18: Adjusting accents on the cheek area

- **EYES**: MetaHuman Creator has a very powerful eye-editing tool that includes ready-made eyes in the **Presets** tab.

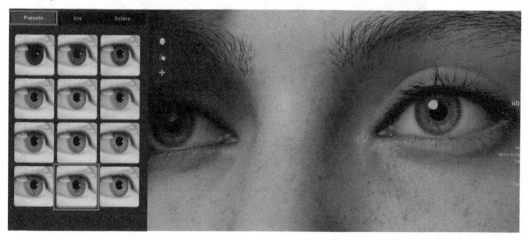

Figure 7.19: Using the eye presets to change the eye color

- In the **Iris** tab, you can further customize properties such as the color and size of the iris. You are also able to change both eyes or each eye separately.

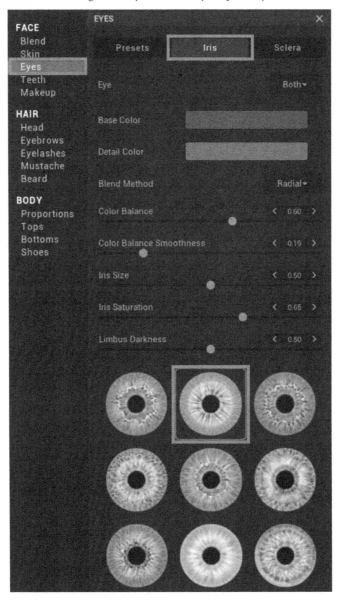

Figure 7.20: Changing the Iris properties

- The **Sclera** tab controls the white part of the eye. Here, you can adjust **Tint**, **Brightness**, **Sclera Rotation**, **Vascularity** (density of veins), and **Veins Rotation**.

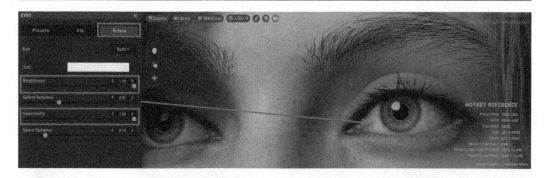

Figure 7.21: Sclera adjusts the white of the eye and adds or removes veins

- **TEETH**: This editor allows for realistic controls for teeth color, gum color, and plaque color, plus sliders for **Plaque Amount** and **Jaw Open**. Clicking on the control points will reveal a drop-down menu, which you can then adjust using sliders.

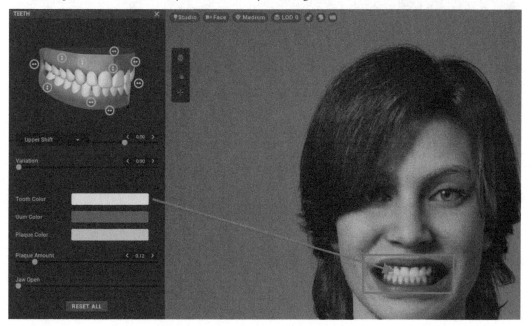

Figure 7.22: Using the TEETH editor

- **MAKEUP**: MHC has some very detailed makeup features that work well with the skin tone of the character, including options for **Foundation**, **Eyes**, **Blush**, and **Lips**.

Figure 7.23: Applying makeup using the MAKEUP editor

Reviewing the hair controls

The **HAIR** controls allow you to edit the MetaHuman's hair features such as **HEAD**, **EYEBROWS**, **EYELASHES**, **MUSTACHE**, and **BEARD**:

- **HEAD**: This section allows you to choose the hair from the presets list, which you can further enhance using the **Color**, **Roughness** (shininess of the hair), and **Salt & Pepper** (the amount of gray hair) properties. The **Details** tab has features such as **Ombre** (shade or shadow) and **Highlights**:

Figure 7.24: Changing the MetaHuman's hairstyle using presets

- **EYEBROWS**: This section contains eyebrow presets, plus controls in the **Details** tab for **Color**, **Roughness**, **Salt & Pepper**, and **Salt & Pepper Lightness**.

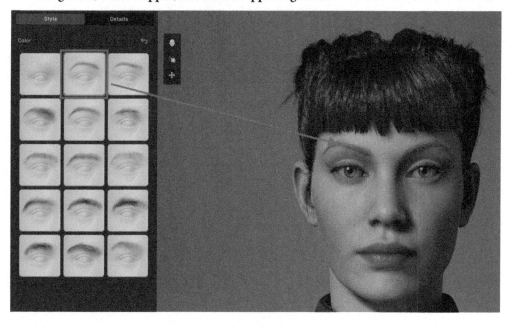

Figure 7.25: Using the EYEBROWS editor

- **EYELASHES**: Similar to the **EYEBROWS** editor, the **EYELASHES** editor has presets for eyelash styles, plus a **Details** tab with controls for **Color**, **Roughness**, **Salt & Pepper**, and **Salt & Pepper Lightness**.

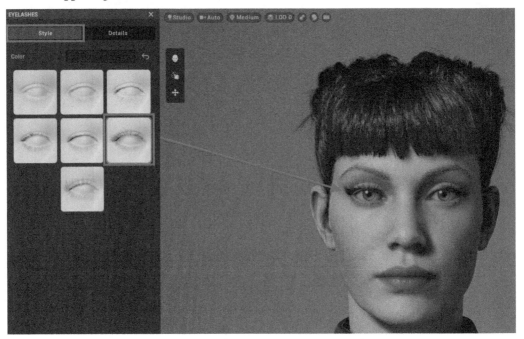

Figure 7.26: Using the EYELASHES editor

- **MUSTACHE** and **BEARD**: The **MUSTACHE** and **BEARD** controls are used to configure the style and color. The **MUSTACHE** controls support the **Salt & Pepper** option just described in the hairstyle controls.

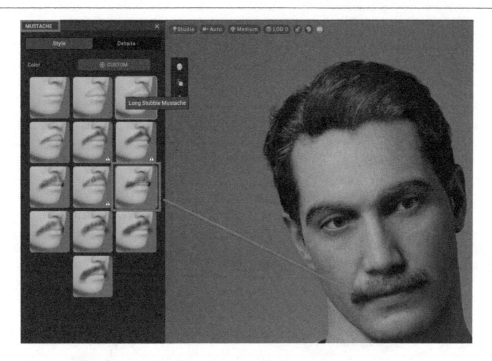

Figure 7.27: The MUSTACHE editor

The **BEARD** controls include **Salt & Pepper** too, but also **Highlights** and **Ombre**.

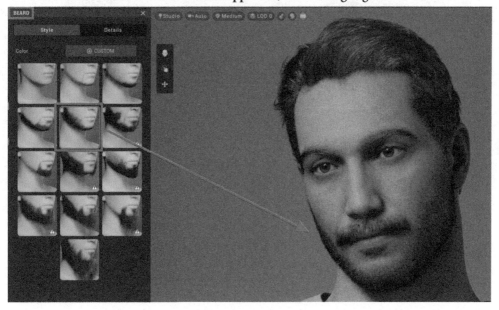

Figure 7.28: The BEARD editor

Reviewing the body controls

This category allows you to customize the body type, body proportions, and clothing:

> **Note**
>
> Just so you know, in our virtual film, we will not be using the body section of the MetaHuman, but for the purpose of familiarizing yourself with MetaHuman Creator, go ahead and customize your MetaHuman as you like.

- **PROPORTIONS**: Select the **PROPORTIONS** panel to set the height and body type of your MetaHuman. You have three tabs to choose from – **Short**, **Average**, and **Tall**.

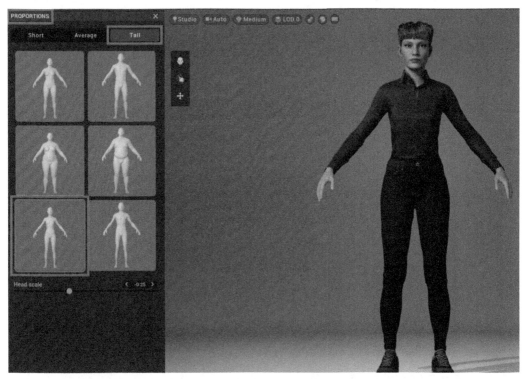

Figure 7.29: Setting the proportions of your MetaHuman

- **Tops, Bottoms, and Shoes**: This section allows you to customize and choose from a variety of tops, bottoms, and shoes for your MetaHuman. Here are some clothing examples:

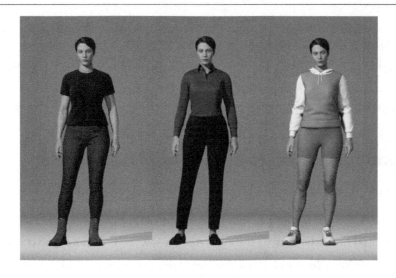

Figure 7.30: Customizing tops, bottoms, and shoes

Creating our MetaHumans

Go ahead and create and customize your version of Adam and Eve.

Creating your MetaHuman characters is so much fun! You can spend as much time as you want creating your character at this stage, however, you can also come back to customize them further at any time because MetaHuman Creator saves changes automatically, and your customized MetaHuman characters are always available through the Quixel Bridge interface inside of Unreal Engine.

I went ahead and gave both my characters a rather simplistic appearance, as shown in *Figure 7.31*.

Figure 7.31: The completed Adam and Eve MetaHumans

I used the standard characters for both Adam and Eve, with a slight tweak of the appearance, and gave them simple black tops and bottoms, and a simple hairdo. Their clothing will not matter as we will not be using their body for the animation, which we will be attempting in the next chapter.

At this point, we have covered a lot in this section regarding how you can use MetaHuman Creator to create unique characters. If you're happy with your character design, in the next section, you will learn how to download and import them into Unreal Engine.

Downloading and importing your Metahumans

To download and import your characters into Unreal Engine, complete the following steps:

1. Open the **A_New_Beginning** project if it is not already open.
2. Open Quixel Bridge by clicking the **Place Actor** + icon and selecting **Quixel Bridge**.
3. Click the **My MetaHumans** tab and you'll find both characters available under the **CURRENT METAHUMANS** category.

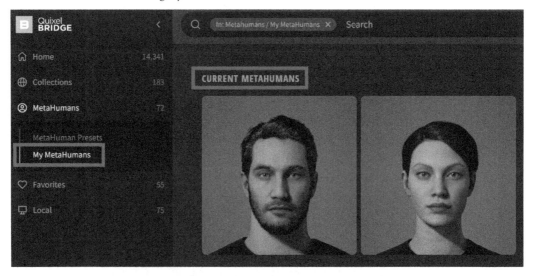

Figure 7.32: Characters now available in Quixel Bridge

> **Note**
>
> If you do not see the characters listed under the **CURRENT METAHUMANS** category, you may have been logged out of the system. You'll know this if you see a blue **Sign In** button at the bottom right of the Quixel Bridge interface. Sign in and both characters will now be available for download.

4. Select the **ADAM** character, and at the bottom right of the interface, ensure **Highest Quality** is selected. Then click the **Download** button (this process will take some time to download).

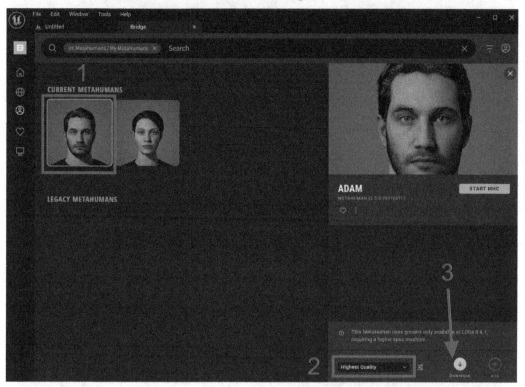

Figure 7.33: Downloading the Adam character

> **Note**
>
> Since we are making a virtual film, and we will have close-ups of the two characters, **Highest Quality** will be the best option here.

5. Once the download is complete, the **Add** button will now be active at the bottom right of the Quixel Bridge interface. Click on it to add the MetaHuman to the Content Browser.

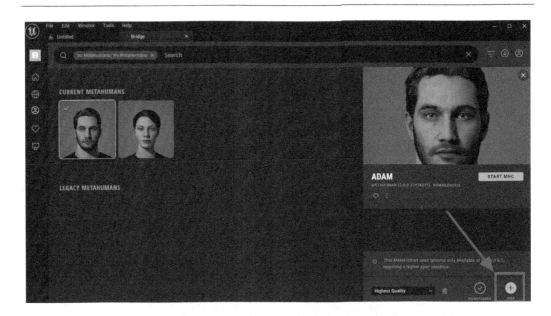

Figure 7.34: Adding the Adam character to the project

6. After a few moments, in the bottom-right corner of the interface, you will be prompted to enable a few missing plugins. These plugins will allow you to add and use MetaHumans in your project. Enable the missing plugins and restart Unreal Engine when prompted.

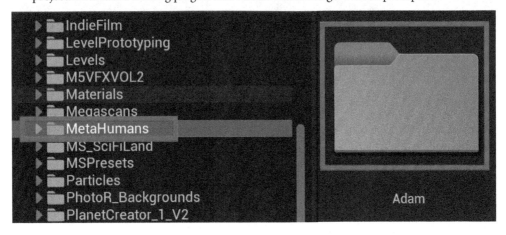

Figure 7.35: Enabling missing plugins

7. Once Unreal Engine has restarted, go to the Content folder and you should now see a MetaHumans folder, with a folder for our Adam character:

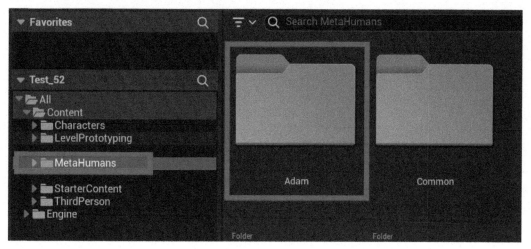

Figure 7.36: The MetaHumans folder now available in the Content Browser

8. Repeat the same process for the Eve character.

In this short section, you managed to download and import your MetaHuman characters from MetaHuman Creator into Unreal Engine. Well done!

Summary

In this chapter, our focus was on getting started with MetaHuman Creator. Here, we acquired knowledge about the various parameters available to customize our characters, including editable attributes such as body, face, eyes, hair, clothing, and the diverse range of presets.

While you successfully imported your custom character into the engine, the upcoming chapter will focus on animating your MetaHumans. There, we will dive into the concepts of rigging and retargeting, and all the necessary steps to infuse life into our characters.

8

Retargeting the MetaHumans for Unreal Engine 5

In the last chapter, we successfully created our two MetaHuman characters and imported them into Unreal Engine. In this chapter, you will learn how to prepare them to use ready-made **motion capture** (**mocap**) animation files. However, before we can do that, we will need to convert these mocap files into something that can be used by UE's MetaHumans. This process is called **retargeting**.

Mocap files exist due to traditional hand animation being a laborious process, taking weeks, if not months, to complete, and involving a large team. The development of these files is thanks to the film industry and pioneer filmmakers such as James Cameron, Tim Burton, and Peter Jackson (to name a few), with movies such as *Avatar*, *Planet of the Apes*, and *The Lord of the Rings*, where mocap was used extensively.

Since then, this technology has become affordable and can be generated using equipment such as the Rokoko suit (`https://www.rokoko.com/`), Movella's Xsens suit (`https://www.movella.com/products/motion-capture`), Sony's mocopi (`https://electronics.sony.com/more/mocopi/all-mocopi/p/qmss1-uscx`), and, more recently, online services such as Move.ai (`https://www.move.ai/`) and Wonder Dynamics (`https://wonderdynamics.com/`).

In our project, we will be utilizing ready-made mocap files, specifically from Adobe Mixamo, which has hundreds of free mocap files that we can choose from to animate our characters. We will be downloading the mocap files, importing them into UE, and retargeting them to UE Mannequins and then our two MetaHuman characters.

So, in this chapter, we will be covering the following topics:

- What is character rigging?
- What is an IK Rig?
- Downloading and importing Mixamo mocap files
- Creating an IK Rig in UE5

- Creating an IK Retargeter for UE5 Mannequins
- Creating an IK Retargeter for MetaHumans
- Testing the animation

Technical requirements

To complete this chapter, the technical requirements detailed in *Chapter 1* apply, and you need access to the MetaHumans we imported into our project in *Chapter 7*. You will also need a stable internet connection, as we will be downloading numerous animation assets from Mixamo (`https://www.mixamo.com/`).

What is character rigging?

Before we jump back into UE to start animating our characters, you must understand the concept of character rigging. **Character rigging** (sometimes referred to as **skeletal animation**) is the process of creating a digital *skeleton* or structure for a character model in animation. It is a technique used to define the range of movement for a character or object, enabling actions, gestures, and movement.

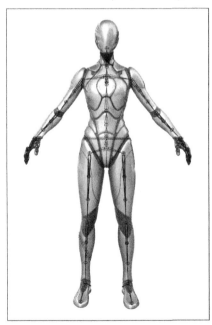

Figure 8.1: Digital skeleton in UE5

During character rigging, an artist takes a static character model and adds a series of interconnected bones to create a skeleton. These bones serve as a framework that allows animators to manipulate and control the character's movements. By assigning specific movements and constraints to the bones, animators can create lifelike movements and expressions for the character. Without rigging, characters would lack the ability to deform and move freely, making it challenging to bring them to life through animation. Ultimately, the purpose of a rig is to simplify the process of animation.

The MetaHumans in UE5 come with a built-in rig for character animation. In UE, this is referred to as an IK Rig. IK Rig? What's that?

What is an IK Rig?

IK stands for **Inverse Kinematics**, as opposed to **Forward Kinematics** (**FK**). Both techniques are used in the process of character animation. Let me explain FK first.

To animate a character using FK, animators manually manipulate the joint angles or positions over time to create a desired motion. For example, if animating a character holding a ball, an animator would adjust the positions and rotations of the shoulder and then the elbow in each frame to simulate the movement.

FK allows for intuitive control and direct manipulation of a character's movements, as animators have direct control over each joint's position and orientation. However, it can become cumbersome and time-consuming when animating complex movements or interactions between different body parts.

To address this limitation, IK is often used in combination with FK in character animation. IK enables animators to specify the position of an **end effector** (such as a character's hand or foot), and the underlying IK solver calculates the joint angles required to achieve that position. This approach simplifies the process of animating complex interactions, such as reaching for an object or maintaining balance.

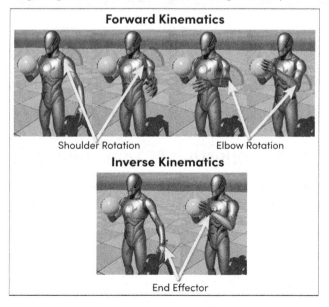

Figure 8.2: FK versus IK

So, to answer the question, in a nutshell, an IK Rig in UE is a pre-made rig (as shown in *Figure 8.3*) available to us, non-technical artists, to animate characters with ease.

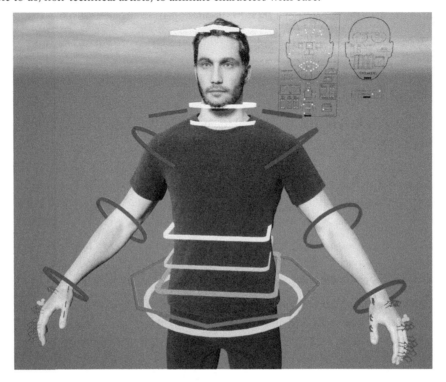

Figure 8.3: The MetaHuman IK and facial rig in UE5

UE Control Rig allows you to bypass the need to rig and animate using external DCC tools such as Maya or Blender but instead animate directly in UE. We will do exactly that later in this chapter.

Now that we have that covered, let's head over to Mixamo and download some mocap files.

Downloading and importing Mixamo mocap files

Mixamo is a large online library full of free mocap files that can be previewed in a web browser. In addition to housing this extensive library of mocap files, Mixamo also has many pre-made 3D characters.

Before we go any further, though, I need you to have a big picture of what we are trying to achieve in this chapter. Things can get a bit confusing, especially if you are doing it for the first time, so let's break it down into simple steps:

1. **Download** a character and a mocap file from Adobe Mixamo.

2. **Import** the character and the mocap file into UE.

3. **Retarget the Mixamo character** to the UE5 Mannequin character.

4. **Retarget the UE5 Mannequin character** to our MetaHumans.

5. **Test the animation** in **Sequencer**.

At the time of writing this book, the process of retargeting mocap files from Mixamo to MetaHumans involves setting up an IK Rig for the downloaded Mixamo character to match the bones of the standard UE5 Mannequin characters, which are referred to as **Manny** (the male character) and **Quinn** (the female character), then setting up an IK Retargeter from the UE5 Mannequin to the MetaHuman. But this process is made much simpler by using the ready-made IK Rig and IK Retargeter available in UE 5.2.

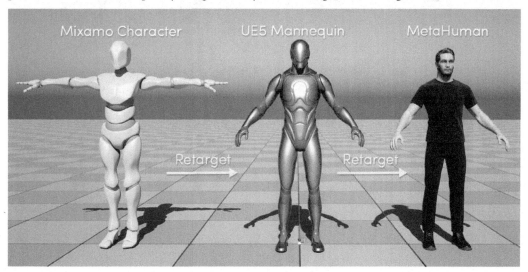

Figure 8.4: The retargeting workflow

With that, let's get into downloading and importing Mixamo mocap files.

Downloading a mocap file from Mixamo

To access the mocap files from Mixamo, you will require an Adobe ID. If you do not have one, you can learn how to create one here: `https://helpx.adobe.com/manage-account/using/create-update-adobe-id.html`.

Upon getting your Adobe ID, log in to the site and follow these instructions:

1. In the top-left section of the Mixamo interface, click the **Characters** tab. Here, you'll find a gallery of all the characters available in Mixamo.

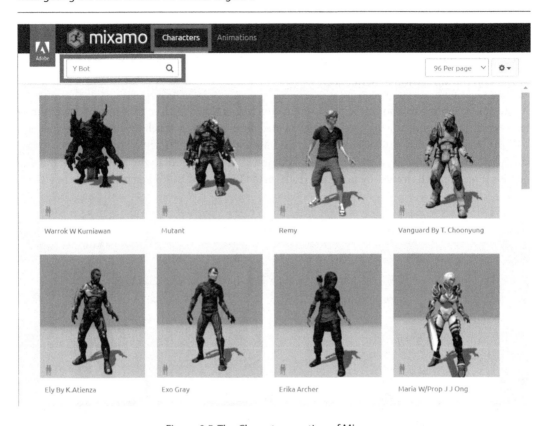

Figure 8.5: The Characters section of Mixamo

2. In the search window, type Y Bot and press *Enter*.

3. Select the **Y Bot** character and click the **DOWNLOAD** button:

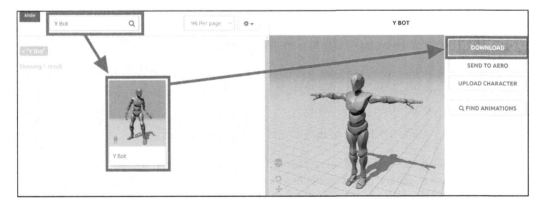

Figure 8.6: Downloading the Mixamo Y Bot character

4. In the **DOWNLOAD SETTINGS** popup, leave the settings as the defaults and click **Download**.

5. Create a folder on your desktop and name it From_Mixamo.

6. Save the Y Bot character in the new folder. You'll notice that it has an .fbx extension.

> **Note**
>
> It is very important for you to start creating meaningful naming conventions for your folders and files from now on. Things might get a bit confusing if you don't. If you are unsure, please follow the naming conventions I use in this chapter.

The next step is to download the mocap files from Mixamo.

7. Back on the Mixamo page, click the **Animations** tab. A gallery of all the mocap animations will be displayed here.

8. Click once in the search window and you'll get a drop-down list of animation genres – you can use this to filter the mocap files or just type whatever mocap you're looking for. For this exercise, let's type samba dance and press *Enter*.

9. Click on the **Samba Dancing** mocap with the Y Bot character in it and enjoy the dance routine!

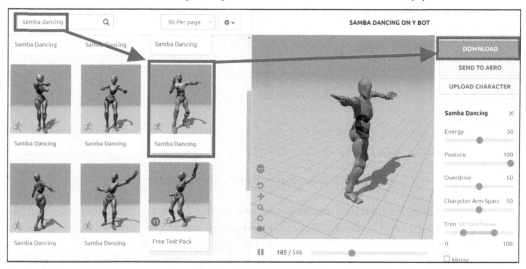

Figure 8.7: Downloading the Mixamo mocap file

10. While being entertained by the dance routine, you can use the sliders on the right of the interface to change the behavior of the mocap animation:

- **Energy**: This slider adds less or more energy to the dance routine.

- **Posture**: This slider adds the effect of a hunching or upright posture to the character.

- **Overdrive**: This slider affects the speed of the routine, from slow motion to fast motion.

- **Character Arm-Space**: This slider adds more space between the arms and the body. Use this slider if you're planning to add a larger character so the arms do not pass through the body.

- **Trim**: Use this slider to trim the routine to a specific range of frames.

11. Once you have adjusted the settings to your liking, click the **DOWNLOAD** button.

12. In the **DOWNLOAD SETTINGS** popup, change **Frames per Second** to **24** and **Skin** to **Without Skin**.

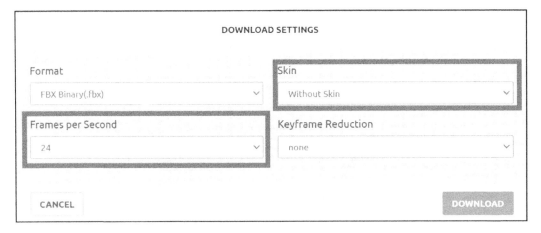

Figure 8.8: Download settings for the mocap file

In filmmaking, the preferred **frames per second** (**fps**) is 24; so, since we're making a film, we will use 24 fps for this mocap. We are choosing **Without Skin** in this instance because we already downloaded the Y Bot character earlier, which has skin attached to it.

> **Note**
> This is just a test mocap file – although it would be hilarious, we're not going to make Adam and Eve do the samba in our movie!

13. Click **DOWNLOAD** and save it in the same folder as before (**From_Mixamo**).

In this section, we successfully downloaded the Y_Bot Mixamo character and a mocap file. In the next section, we will import the character and the mocap animation file into UE5.

Importing the character file into UE

Now that we have the character and mocap animation downloaded, we need to import both files into our UE project. You will learn how to import the character file in this section and the mocap file in the next.

So, to import the character, follow these steps:

1. Open the A_New_Beginning project.

2. In Content Browser, create a new folder called From_Mixamo and open it.

3. Then, on your PC, locate the folder you downloaded the Mixamo files into, select the Y Bot. fbx file, and drag it into the **From_Mixamo** folder.

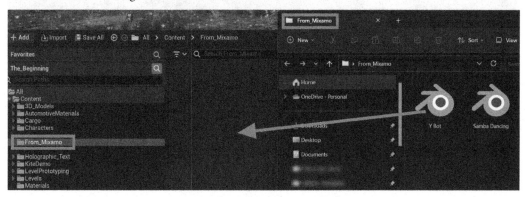

Figure 8.9: Importing the Y_Bot file via drag and drop

4. In the **FBX Import Options** dialog popup, set the following options (using *Figure 8.10* as a reference):

   - (1) Ensure **Skeletal Mesh** and **Import Mesh** are enabled (default) – these settings give the option of importing the incoming FBX file as a skeletal mesh with or without the skin. Since we are importing a character with skin and a skeleton, these need to be enabled.

   - (2) Set **Skeleton** to **None** (default) – when importing a skeletal mesh that already has a skeleton, this must be set to **None**.

   - (3) Enable **Use T0 As Ref Pose** – this setting enables the option of setting the first frame (frame 0) as the reference frame.

   - (4) Uncheck **Import Animations** – since we're not importing an animation with this import, we'll leave this unchecked.

   - (5) Set **Material Import Method** to **Create New Materials** – the materials associated with the skeletal mesh we downloaded from Mixamo will be automatically created.

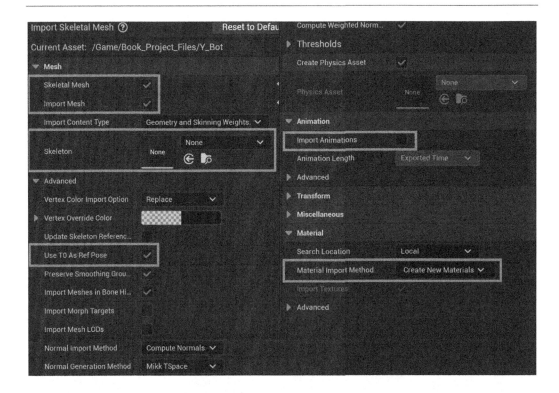

Figure 8.10: FBX Import Options dialog box

Once the import process is complete, you might get a warning dialog box – you can just ignore it by closing it.

The **From_Mixamo** folder will now have two **Materials**, a **Skeletal Mesh**, a **Physics Asset**, and a **Skeleton**.

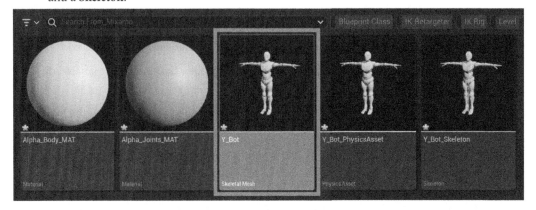

Figure 8.11: The imported Mixamo assets

Now it's time to check whether the Y_Bot character has been imported correctly. We can view it in the Level itself:

5. Create a new Level (**File | New Level**), choose the **Basic** template, and save it in the From_Mixamo folder (**File | Save Current Level As...**). You can name the Level Mixamo_To _MH_Test (Mixamo to MetaHuman Test).

6. Drag the **Y_Bot** (skeletal mesh) asset into the level, zeroize its location, and rotate it **+90** degrees to face the camera.

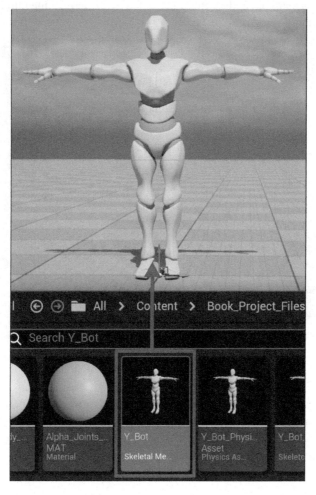

Figure 8.12: Adding Y_Bot into the Level

7. Save the project (*Ctrl + Shift + S*).

In this section, you managed to import the `Y_Bot.fbx` character into Unreal Engine using the Import dialog box. In the next section, we'll import the mocap file (`Samba Dancing.fbx`) we downloaded from Mixamo.

Importing the mocap file into Unreal Engine

To import the Mixamo mocap animation file into Unreal Engine, do the following:

1. With the project still open, drag the `Samba Dancing.fbx` file into the **From_Mixamo** folder in Content Browser.

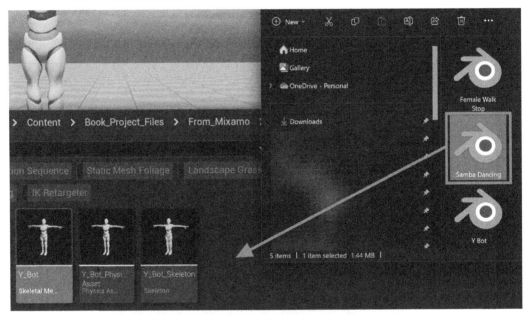

Figure 8.13: Adding the animation file into the folder

2. In the **FBX Import Options** dialog popup, in the **Advanced** section, uncheck **Use Default Sample Rate** and change **Custom Sample Rate** to 24 (this was the frame per second we chose when downloading the mocap file from Mixamo; if this value is not specified, Unreal Engine will use the default **30** frames per second):

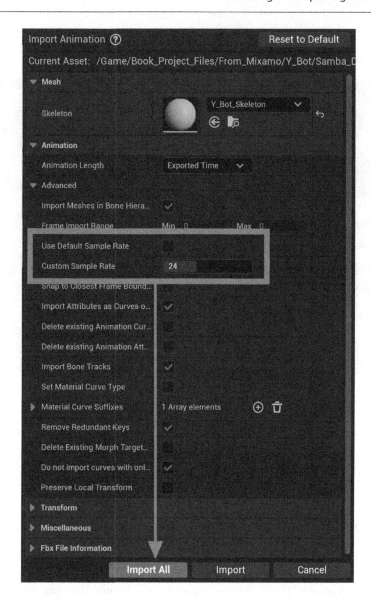

Figure 8.14: FBX Import Options dialog box

3. You'll now see the `Samba_Dancing` animation file in the folder. Double-click on the animation file to open it in the Skeletal Mesh Editor.

Figure 8.15: The Skeletal Mesh Editor

4. Close the Editor and save the project.

That's it, we imported the mocap file into Unreal Engine. In the next section, we will begin the process of creating an IK Rig for the UE5 Mannequin character.

Creating an IK Rig in Unreal Engine 5

In the last section, we imported both the Y_Bot character and the **Samba Dancing** animation into Unreal Engine. In this section, we will create an **IK Rig**, which will allow the UE5 Mannequin to inherit the bone structure of the Y_Bot and in turn use the **Samba Dancing** mocap animation on the UE5 Mannequin.

Let's begin:

1. Select **Y_Bot**, then right-click in the **From_Mixamo** folder and choose **Animation | IK Rig | IK Rig**:

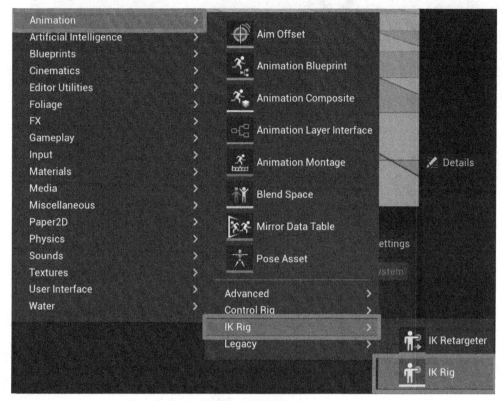

Figure 8.16: Creating an IK Rig

2. Rename the IK Rig to IKRig_Y_Bot, then double-click to open the IK Rig Editor.

3. If you do not see the Y_Bot character in the Viewport, in the **Details** panel, under **Preview Skeletal Mesh**, select **Y_Bot Skeletal Mesh**.

4. To display the skeleton structure of the Y_Bot character, in the Editor, click **Character | Bones | All Hierarchy**.

Figure 8.17: Viewing the Y_Bot bone structure

While we're here, let's quickly break down the IK Rig Editor:

- (1) **Hierarchy** tab: This tab houses the bone hierarchy of a character

- (2) **Viewport**: Here you can preview and select the bones of a character

- (3) **IK Retargeting**: This tab will be used for the retargeting process

- (4) **Preview Skeletal Mesh**: This dropdown will give an option to choose the correct skeletal mesh for the retargeting process

Figure 8.18: The Skeletal Mesh Editor

To start the retargeting (bone matching) process, we will have to create what Unreal Engine calls a **chain mapping** of the bones.

5.   In the **Hierarchy** tab, select **Spine** and *Shift* + select **Spine 2**. Then right-click and select **New Retarget Chain...**:

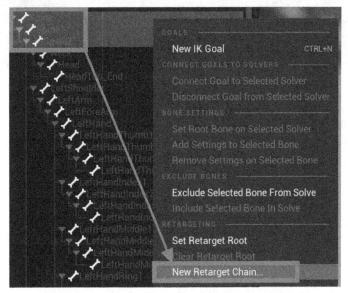

Figure 8.19: Creating the first set of Retarget Chain

6. In the **Add New Retarget Chain** popup, confirm that **Chain Name** is **Spine**, and click **Add Chain**.

7. If there is an **Add Goal to New Chain** pop-up, select **No Goal**.

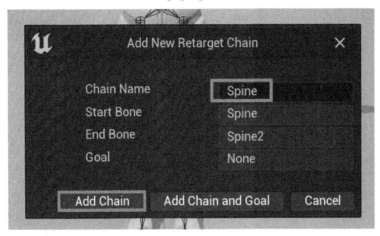

Figure 8.20: Confirming Chain Name

Once you've done this, you'll notice the first entry of the chain mapping in the **IK Retargeting** tab, as shown in *Figure 8.21*.

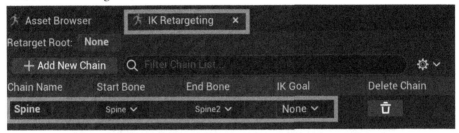

Figure 8.21: The new set of Spine chain mapping

8. Now, use the table provided to complete the rest of the bones. Ensure that you rename the chain name according to the chain names here:

Chain Name	Start Bone	End Bone	IK Goal
Head	Neck	Head	None
LeftShoulder	LeftShoulder	LeftShoulder	None
LeftArm	LeftArm	LeftHand	None
LeftThumb	LeftThumb1	LeftThumb3	None
LeftIndex	LeftIndex	LeftIndex3	None
LeftMiddle	LeftMiddle 1	LeftMiddle3	None

Chain Name	Start Bone	End Bone	IK Goal
LeftRing	LeftRing1	LeftRing4	None
LeftPinky	LeftPinky1	LeftPinky3	None
LeftLeg	LeftUpLeg	LeftToeBase	None

Figure 8.22: Chain mapping configuration

9 Once all of the bones have been completed, select all the chains in the **IK Retargeting** tab, right-click on any of the newly created chains, and select **Mirror Chain** – this will help ease the process of creating the chain mapping for the right side of the skeletal mesh.

Figure 8.23: Mirroring the right-side chain mapping

10. Now, confirm that the mapping names are correct and click **OK** for all the popups (these are the same popups you encountered before).

You should now have a complete set of chain mapping in the **IK Retargeting** tab as shown in *Figure 8.24*:

Figure 8.24: The complete set of chain mapping

11. One last thing you'll need to do before we jump into the next section is to select the **Hips** bone in the **Hierarchy** tab, right-click, and choose **Set Retarget Root**. This is done so the character's root motion can be defined and transferred to the new character proportionally.

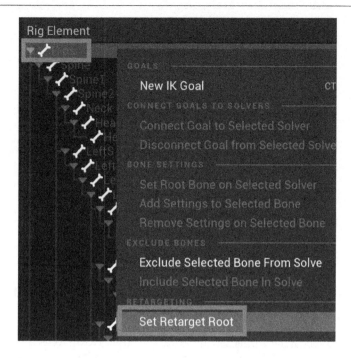

Figure 8.25: Setting Set Retarget Root for the Hips bones

12. Now save the IK Rig and your project.

In this section, you completed the process of meticulously chain-mapping the bones of the Mixamo Y_Bot character. In the next section, we will use this mapping to retarget the UE5 Mannequin character.

Creating an IK Retargeter for a UE5 Mannequin

After completing bone-mapping (chain-mapping) for the Y_Bot, we will now retarget the bones to match the bones of the UE5 Mannequin character. The UE5 Mannequin characters (Manny and Quinn) have additional bones compared to the Mixamo character; these additional bones are not needed to make the Mixamo mocap animation work. We will rectify this issue in this section.

So, let's learn how to use the **IK Retargeter**:

1. In the **From_Mixamo** folder, right-click and select **Animation | IK Rig | IK Retargeter**.
2. Rename the IK Retargeter to **RTG_Manny** and double-click to open it.
3. In the **Pick IK Rig To Copy Animation From** dialog box, choose **IKRig_Y_Bot** (as shown in *Figure 8.26*).

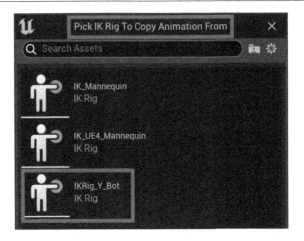

Figure 8.26: Choosing the IK Rig to copy the animation from

4.   In the **Select Target IK Rig (To Copy Animation To)** panel, choose **IK_Mannequin**.

You will now see the **IK Retargeter** Editor.

5.   In the **Details** tab, in the **Target** section, click the **Target IKRig Asset** dropdown, ensure it is **IK_Mannequin**, and in **Target Preview Mesh**, select **SKM_Manny_Simple**.

This means you have successfully selected **Source IKRig Asset** and **Target IKRig Asset**:

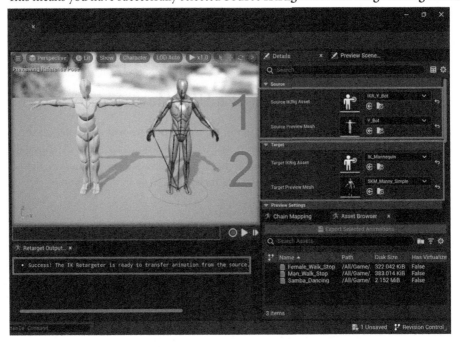

Figure 8.27: The IK Retargeter interface

6. You can see that the two characters, the Y_Bot and Mannequin, overlap each other. To set them apart so we can test the animation, under **Preview Settings**, set **Target Mesh Offset** to *200* on the X axis.

Figure 8.28: Setting the two characters apart

In the **Chain Mapping** tab (bottom right), you'll notice there are many more items listed as compared to the Y Bot IK Rig. This is because the UE5 Mannequin characters have additional bones and controls, which are not needed for Mixamo mocap to work. We will have to disable some of these mappings, but before we do that, we will need to fix the pose of the UE5 Mannequin so it mimics the T-pose (as seen in *Figure 8.28*) of the Y Bot character.

7. For the UE5 Mannequin to mimic the T-pose, in the **Hierarchy** tab, ensure the **Target** button is selected. Then, click the **Create** dropdown and select **Import from Animation Sequence**.

Figure 8.29: Importing T-pose animation sequence

8. In the popup, type MM_T_Pose in the search window, select it, then click **Import As Retarget Pose** and **Save**.

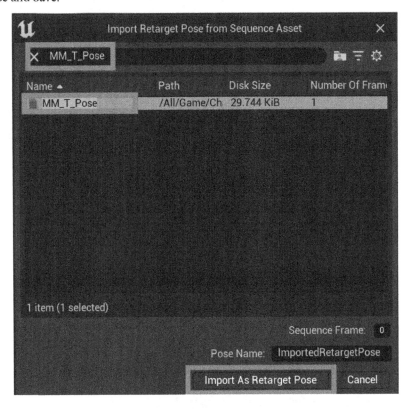

Figure 8.30: Choosing the T-pose

9. In the Viewport, you'll notice Manny is now mimicking the T-pose of the Y Bot. It is important that we match the poses to avoid unpredictable outcomes when we run the animation.

    Now we have one more task to accomplish before we are done with this section – that is, disabling the chain-mapping for the additional bones that come with the UE5 Mannequin.

10. To do this, extend the **Chain Mapping** tab as far upward as possible, as we have a long list of items in the tab. Then change the **Source Chain** dropdowns to follow *Figure 8.31* exactly. You'll have to set the bones that do not exist in the Y Bot (**Target Chain**) to **None** for the UE5 Mannequin (**Source Chain**).

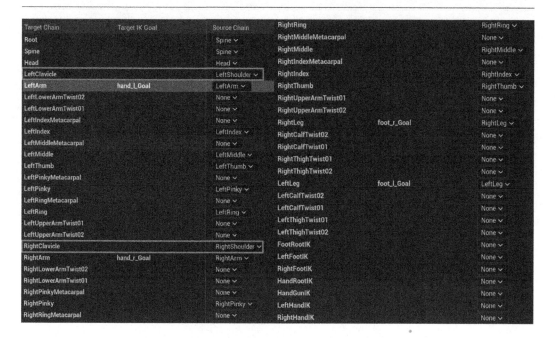

Figure 8.31: Disabling additional chain mappings

We are basically removing all the chain-mapping that does not exist in the Y Bot IK Rig; if you're unsure about this, refer back to the list of the chain-mapping we created for the **Y_Bot** IK Rig (*Figure 8.24*).

Note

The left-shoulder and right-shoulder bones of the Y Bot are referred to as **LeftClavicle** and **RightClavicle** for the UE5 Mannequin.

Once the task has been completed, you now have the Mixamo Y Bot bones matched to the UE5 Mannequin bones. The only way to find out that the bones have been matched correctly is to test the **Samba_Dancing** animation we imported in the previous section.

11. Select the **Asset Browser** tab, and double-click on the **Samba_Dancing** animation.

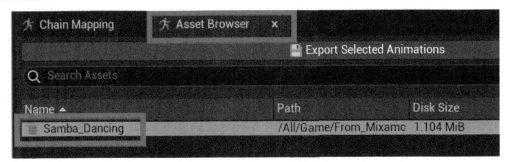

Figure 8.32: Testing the mocap animation on the UE5 Mannequin

You should see both the Y Bot and the UE5 Mannequin doing the samba in unison:

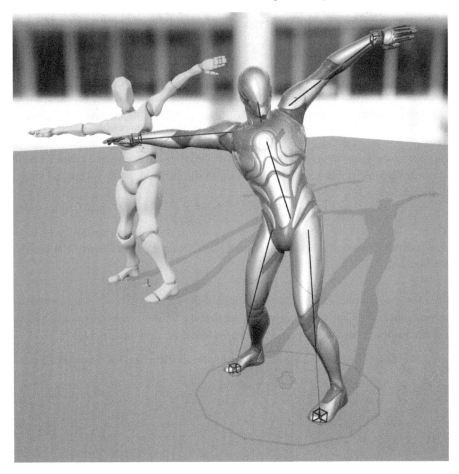

Figure 8.33: Mixamo Y Bot and UE5 Mannequin dancing in unison

Now that we have matched the mocap animation to the UE5 Mannequin, we will need to save it for later use on the UE5 Mannequin.

12. Select the **Samba_Dancing** file and click **Export Selected Animations** in the **Asset Browser** tab. In the popup, select the **From_Mixamo** folder, right-click on it, and create a new folder named `Exported_Mixamo_Animations`.

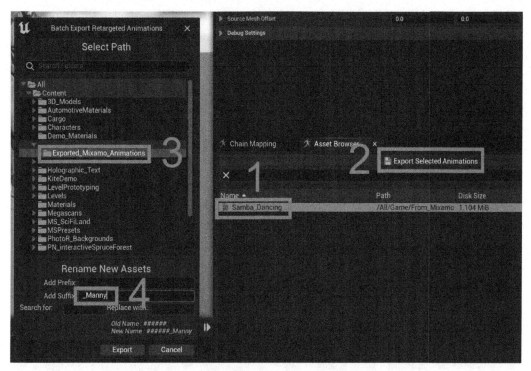

Figure 8.34: Saving the animation file for the UE5 Mannequin

13. In the **Add Suffix** window, type `_Manny` and click **Export**. This will save the **Samba_Dancing** animation as **Samba_Dancing_Manny** for easy identification later.

14. Save the IK Retargeter.

Congratulations – that was the hard part, and you did a great job! In the next section, we will retarget the UE5 Mannequin to the MetaHuman, which is a very easy task.

Creating an IK Retargeter for MetaHumans

To retarget the UE5 Mannequin to the MetaHuman, take the following steps:

1. In the **From_Mixamo** folder, duplicate the previously created **RTG_Manny** IK Retargeter and rename it to RTG_MetaHuman. Then, double-click to open it.

2. In the **Details** panel, in the **Source** section, change **Source IKRig Asset** to **IK_Mannequin**, and **Source Preview Mesh** to **SKM_Manny_Simple**.

3. In the same panel, change **Target IKRig Asset** to **IK_metahuman**, and **Target Preview Mesh** to **m_med_nrw_body**:

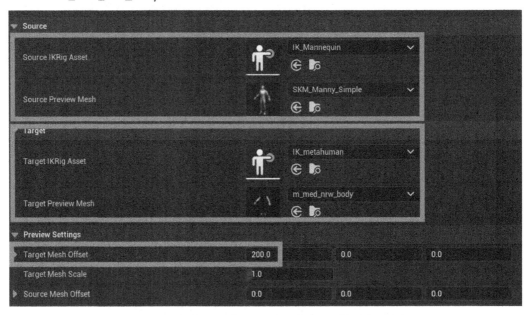

Figure 8.35: Setting the source and target IK Rig Assets

Note

The following are abbreviations of the body types of MetaHumans in UE:

- **m/f**: male/female

- **srt/med/tal**: short/medium/tall (height)

- **unw/nrw/ovw**: underweight/narrow/overweight

---

4. In the Viewport, the UE5 Mannequin (Manny) and the MetaHuman may overlap. Use **Target Mesh Offset** to separate the characters by **200** units in the Xaxis.

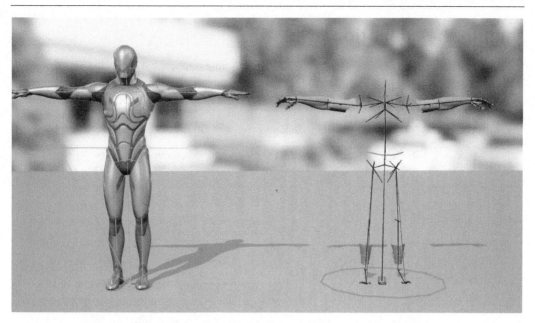

Figure 8.36: The UE5 Mannequin to Metahuman retargeting

> **Note**
>
> If your characters do not resemble what is shown in *Figure 8.36*, use the **Reset** drop-down to reset their pose.

> **Note**
>
> It is perfectly normal for the MetaHuman to be missing its head and other parts. What we are really interested in now is matching the Mixamo animation to the MetaHuman. We will learn how to add and animate facial expressions in *Chapter 9*.

5. Select the **Asset Browser** tab, double-click the **Samba_Dancing** animation, and now, both the UE5 Mannequin (Manny) and the MetaHuman are dancing in unison. Perfect!

6. As before, we will export this animation for the MetaHuman. Select the **Samba_Dancing** animation and click **Export Selected Animations** in **Asset Browser**. Then in the pop-up window, select the **MetaHumans** folder, right-click, and create a new folder named MH_Animations. In the **Suffix** window, type _MH. Now, click **Export**.

7. Save the project (*Ctrl* + *Shift* + *S*).

And we are done! In this section, we successfully retargeted the UE5 Mannequin to the MetaHuman and saved the mocap animation to be used with our MetaHuman. In the next section, we will test our animations, both for Manny and the MetaHuman, ensuring that the animations work as expected. We will be using UE Sequencer for this.

Testing the animation

We are almost at the end of the chapter. All we have to do now is to test the retargeted animations we created for the UE5 Mannequin (Manny) and our MetaHuman characters, using UE Sequencer to carry out this task. We will do a deep dive into Sequencer in *Chapter 9*, but for now, let's keep it simple:

1. In the **From_Mixamo** folder, right-click and choose **Cinematics | Level Sequence**:

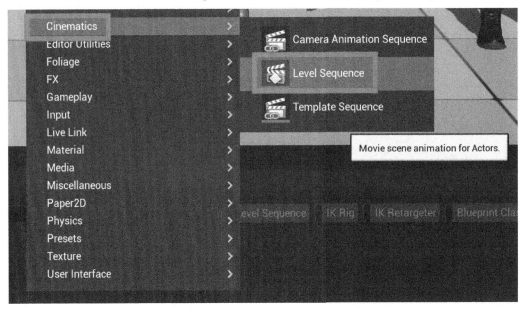

Figure 8.37: Creating the Level Sequence

2. Rename **Level Sequence** to LS_Mixamo_Test (*LS* is the naming convention we use to denote a Level Sequence).

3. Double-click to open it, then rearrange the **Sequencer** tab so it is docked with **Content Browser**.

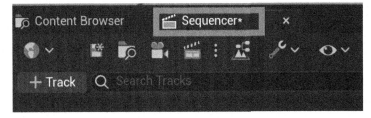

Figure 8.38: Docking Sequencer

4. Open the Level we created in the previous section – **Mixamo_To _MH_Test**.

5. Drag the following characters into the Level:

    - The **Y_Bot** character (from the **From_Mixamo** folder)

    - The **SKM_Manny_Simple** character (from the **Characters | Mannequins | Meshes** folder)

    - And our MetaHuman character, **BP_Adam** (from the **MetaHumans | Adam** folder)

6. Arrange the characters as shown in the following screenshot:

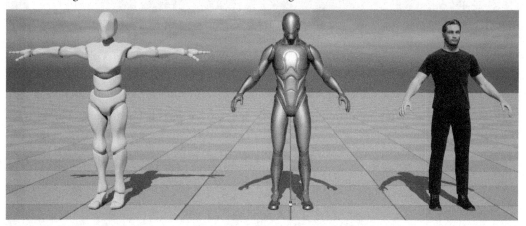

Figure 8.39: The Samba dancers line-up

7. In the Outliner, click the **Y_Bot** character and drag it into **Sequencer**.

8. The **Y_Bot** character will have two properties enabled: **Animation** and **Transform**. Click the + sign on the **Animation** property, and in the drop-down list, choose **Samba_Dancing**.

Figure 8.40: Selecting the animation for the Y Bot

The Y Bot will now have a dance pose, and in **Sequencer**, the Mixamo **Samba_Dancing** mocap **Animation** track is available, indicated by the purple-colored track:

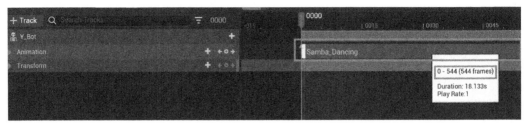

Figure 8.41: The Animation track for the Y Bot

9. To zoom in and out in the **Sequencer** timeline, press *Ctrl* and use the scroll wheel.

10. To set the end of the animation (frame 544), drag the red vertical line to the end of the track (as seen in *Figure 8.42*):

Figure 8.42: Moving the red out-marker to the end of the animation

11. To play and stop the animation, press the spacebar.

12. Use the up arrow key on your keyboard to take the play head to the beginning of the track.

13. Next, from the Outliner, drag **SKM_Manny_Simple** into **Sequencer**. You'll notice that the interface changed to the **Animation** mode.

    The UE5 Mannequin comes with a Control Rig by default, which we won't be needing in this process, so we will need to delete this from Sequencer.

14. In the **SKM_Manny_Simple** track, delete the **CR_Mannequin_Body** track:

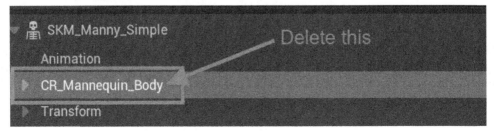

Figure 8.43: Deleting the UE5 Mannequin Control Rig

15. Change back to the **Selection** mode by pressing *Shift + 1* (or use the **Selection** mode dropdown).

16. Click the + sign on the **Animation** track of **SKM_Manny_Simple**, and in the search window, type Samba, then choose the **Samba_Dancing_Manny** animation.

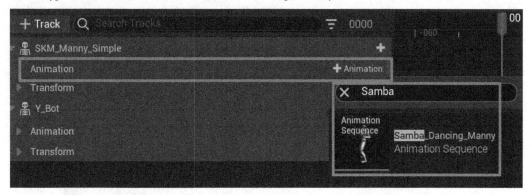

Figure 8.44: Selecting the animation for the UE5 Mannequin

17. You will now notice that the Y Bot and UE5 Mannequin have the same pose. Hit the spacebar to play the animation and use the up arrow key on your keyboard to take the play head to the beginning of the sequence.

18. Finally, let's drag our MetaHuman (**BP_Adam**) into Sequencer. Delete **MetaHuman ControlRig** and **Face_ControlBoard_CtrlRig**. Switch back to the **Selection** mode.

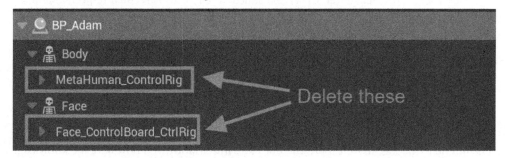

Figure 8.45: Deleting the MetaHuman Control Rig and Face rig

19. Using the same process as we have done previously, in the **BP_Adam** track, click the **Body** track + sign, choose **Animation**, and in the search window, type Samba. Select the **Samba_Dancing_MH** file we saved earlier.

Now all three characters will dance in unison! Wonderful!

Figure 8.46: All characters dancing in unison

20. Save the project.

In this section, we created Sequencer events and added the characters and their respective animations to test the IK Rig and the retargeting process.

Summary

Congratulations, you have completed the MetaHuman retargeting process! It was a rather lengthy process, but you managed to download a character and mocap animation file from Mixamo, create an IK Rig for the Y Bot, and retarget the UE5 Mannequin and the MetaHuman characters.

As I mentioned, this was just a test project, but more importantly, you now have the knowledge to take any mocap animation files from Mixamo and retarget them for use on any MetaHumans. The key thing is that you do not need to repeat the tedious chain-mapping process or create an IK Rig anymore.

In the next chapter, you will use this workflow on a walk animation we are going to use on our MetaHuman Actors.

Adding Animations and Facial Expressions to Your MetaHuman Characters

Having learned about the bone mapping (chain mapping) method through Unreal Engine's IK Retargeter in the preceding chapter, you effectively retargeted and examined a Mixamo mocap file for both the Unreal Engine Mannequin and your own MetaHuman character.

In this chapter, we will apply this acquired expertise and the established IK Rig to orchestrate the movements of the MetaHuman personas, Adam and Eve. Their actions will align with the storyboard formulated in *Chapter 3*.

Our primary objective will involve animating the MetaHumans through the utilization of pre-made mocap files. Additionally, we intend to incorporate personalized animations using Unreal Engine's **Forward Kinematics** (**FK**) Control Rig. Regarding facial animation, while our narrative doesn't require character dialogue, there's still a necessity to convey emotions through facial expressions. We will accomplish this by applying Unreal Engine's Facial Control Rig. This is going to be another packed but exciting chapter!

In this chapter, we will cover the following topics:

- Recapping the storyboard
- Adding pre-made animations in the Level Sequencer
- Using Unreal Engine's FK Control Rig
- Using Unreal Engine's Facial Control Rig

Technical requirements

To complete this chapter, you will need to meet the technical requirements detailed in *Chapter 1* and the Unreal Engine project we have been working on over the past few chapters.

Recapping the storyboard

Before we begin, let's briefly recap the storyboard we created in *Chapter 3*, just to be sure we know exactly what we're going to do:

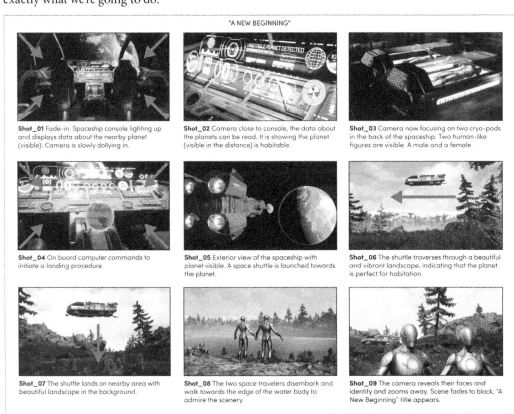

Figure 9.1: Our storyboard

Referring to our storyboard, in **Shot_08**, we have our two characters walking toward the water body after disembarking the shuttle, where they stop to admire the beautiful scenery. In the next shot, their faces and identities will be revealed, with the scene then fading to black and the *A New Beginning* title fading in.

With that said, it's not essential to depict the entire scene. Instead, we can suffice with crafting a couple of revealing shots and camera motions. My recommendations are as follows:

- **Shot_08**: Showing Adam and Eve disembarking from their shuttle and walking toward the water, with their backs to the camera.

- **Shot_09**: A close-up shot of Adam and Eve revealing their faces and identities for the first time. As the camera pulls away, Adam puts his hand on Eve's shoulder, and the scene then fades to black.

Having referred back to the storyboard to confirm our shots, we can now jump into Unreal Engine to start creating the two aforementioned shots using the Level Sequencer.

Adding pre-made animations in the Level Sequencer

We have briefly looked at the Level Sequencer before, but you never really got to understand it in detail. Starting with this chapter, the Level Sequencer is going to be your best friend. So, let's get to know it better.

Exploring Unreal Engine's Level Sequencer

Unreal Engine's **Level Sequencer** (or just **Sequencer**) is a powerful and flexible tool that allows developers and content creators to create complex, interactive, and visually appealing cinematic sequences, cutscenes, and in-game events without the need for extensive programming knowledge. It offers a timeline-based interface that simplifies the process of sequencing and blending various assets, animations, camera movements, and audio.

Let's learn about the interface's basics so that we can start using it:

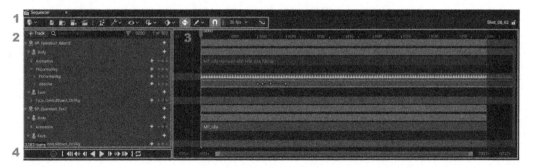

Figure 9.2: The Level Sequencer interface

Let's break down *Figure 9.2*:

- **Toolbar** (**1**): The toolbar consists of various tools, options, and settings we will be using throughout this chapter (I will be pointing them out as we create our cinematics).

- **Outliner** (**2**): The Outliner will be populated with Actors we need to animate, such as cameras, Static Meshes, Skeletal Meshes, audio, and particle effects.

- **Timeline** (**3**): The values of the properties of the Actors in the Outliner will be manipulated in the timeline using keyframes. The playback can be scrubbed back and forth using the playhead. The range of the timeline is set using the green (start) and red (end) vertical bars.

- **Playback controls** (**4**): Just like any other video editing application, these are the playback controls for toggling playing, pausing, jumping to previous and next keyframes, and looping playback.

While exploring the interface, it's worth noting that MetaHumans take up a lot of processing power – plus we have a huge landscape – so your system might get sluggish when adding them into your scene. Follow these steps to make things go a little faster:

- Temporarily disable real-time rendering by opening the **Viewport** menu and clicking on the **Realtime** checkmark (or by pressing *Ctrl + R*):

Figure 9.3: Disabling Realtime rendering

- In the top-right corner of the interface, click the **Settings** button and change **Engine Scalability Settings** to **High** or **Medium**. You will lose some slight resolution, but it will help speed things up:

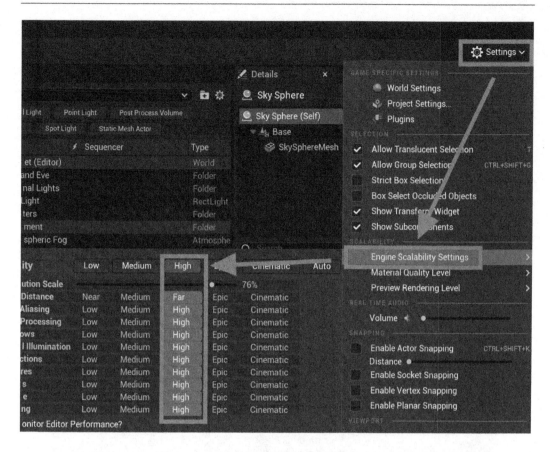

Figure 9.4: Changing Engine Scalability Settings

> **Note**
>
> Before we start using the Sequencer, I suggest having a quick look through the *Sequencer Hotkeys* documentation by Epic Games: `https://docs.unrealengine.com/5.2/en-US/Sequencer-hotkeys-in-unreal-engine/`. Using these hotkeys can be very productive. I'll also highlight some useful ones as we start animating our characters.

In the next section, you'll learn how to migrate (transfer) assets from one Unreal Engine project to another.

Migrating assets from another project

To add continuity and authenticity to our story, I wanted our characters to still be in their spacesuits when they leave their shuttle, to show their eagerness to experience the new world. Due to the complexity of setting this up, I've gone ahead and done this for you, but they are in a different Unreal Engine project. I'd like to take this opportunity to show you how you can migrate assets between projects in Unreal Engine:

1. From the downloaded project files, unzip `Book_Project_Files.zip` and double-click it to open the **Book_Project_Files** Unreal Engine project.

2. Once opened, in the Content Browser, locate the **Book_Project_Files** folder.

3. Right-click on **Book_Project_Files** and choose **Migrate...**:

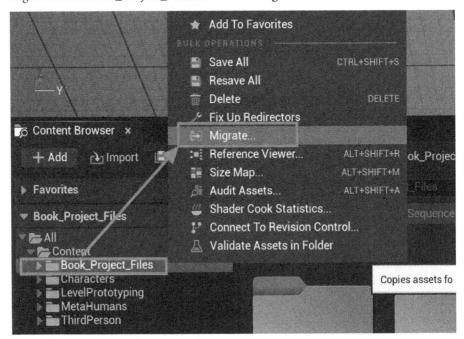

Figure 9.5: Migrating assets from another project

4.   The **Asset Report** popup will show a list of all associated files to be migrated. Click **OK**:

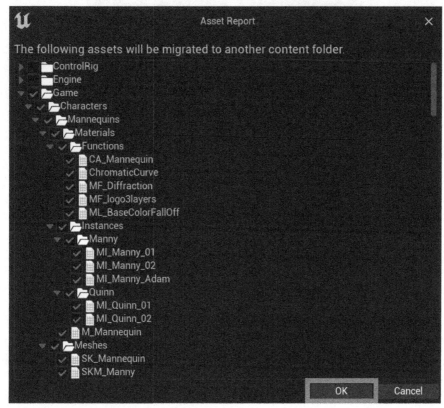

Figure 9.6: The Asset Report popup

5.   In the next popup, browse to the **A_New_Beginning** project file folder, select the **Content** folder, and then click **Select Folder**:

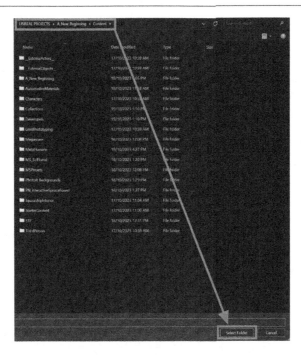

Figure 9.7: Selecting the Content folder

6. If you get a warning message, as shown in *Figure 9.8*, this is Unreal Engine's way of making sure you do not overwrite files in the destination folder. In this case, it's okay to do so. Check **Apply to All** and click **Yes**:

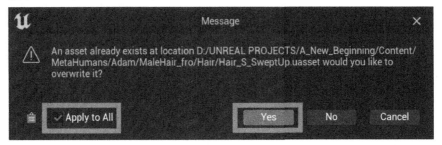

Figure 9.8: Warning message popup

7. After a few moments, the **Book_Project_Files** folder will be fully migrated to our main project. Once finished, close the **Book_Project_Files** Unreal Engine project.

You've successfully migrated a folder from one project to another. You can carry out the same steps for any assets you wish to migrate from one Unreal Engine project to another. In the next section, we will continue where we left off with our main project.

> **Note**
> The folder you just migrated consists of some assets we are going to use in the upcoming chapters, including Particle FX and Materials.

Adding MetaHumans to the Level Sequencer

In this section, we will create a new Level Sequence, add the two MetaHuman characters, and animate them. Let's proceed:

1. Open the **A_New_Beginning** project.

2. In the **Levels** folder, open the **EXT_Planet** Level. In *Chapter 5*, we added the space shuttle and two Mannequins as stand-ins. You can now delete the Mannequins from the scene.

3. From the Content Browser, in the **Book_Project_Files | MetaHumans | Adam_and_Eve_Spacesuit** folder, drag the migrated **BP_Spacesuit_Adam** and **BP_Spacesuit_Eve** into the Viewport and place them on the ground, as shown in *Figure 9.9*. Position Adam using the following values:

    -   **Location**: **X = -58411, Y = -78191, Z = -3387**

    -   **Rotation**: **X = 0, Y = 0, Z = 160**

    Then, position Eve beside Adam, like so:

Figure 9.9: Placing the MetaHuman characters on the ground

For **Shot_08**, I've positioned them here, facing toward the edge of the water body, which they will walk up to before stopping. This would be a good point to save, and then continue with the following steps.

4. Create a bookmark here using *Ctrl + 3*.

5. Before going any further, in the Outliner, duplicate **BP_Spacesuit_Adam** and **BP_Spacesuit_Eve** (Unreal Engine will add a suffix of **2** on the duplicated Actors). I will explain why we're doing this at the end of this section.

6. Hide both **BP_Spacesuit_Adam2** and **BP_Spacesuit_Eve2** by selecting them in the Outliner and pressing *H* (**Hide**). We will use them in **Shot_09** later:

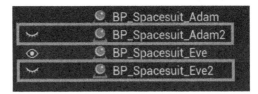

Figure 9.10: Hiding Actors in the Outliner with the H keyboard shortcut

7. In the **A_New_Beginning** folder, create a new folder, and rename it `Cinematics`.

8. Open the **Cinematic** folder, right-click inside it, then choose **Cinematics | Level Sequence**. When prompted for a name, type `Shot_08`. Then, double-click it to open the Level Sequencer.

9. From the Outliner, drag **BP_Spacesuit_Adam** into the Level Sequencer. As soon as you do that, the interface will change to **Animation** mode. In the Level Sequencer, you'll notice the **CR_Mannequin_Body** and **Face_ControlBoard_CtrlRig** tracks, as shown in *Figure 9.11*:

Figure 9.11: New tracks available in the Level Sequencer

10. In the Level Sequencer, right-click on the **CR_Mannequin_Body** track and select **Mute**. This will temporarily disable the Control Rig so that we can add the mocap animation to the Adam character (we will come back to this in the next section):

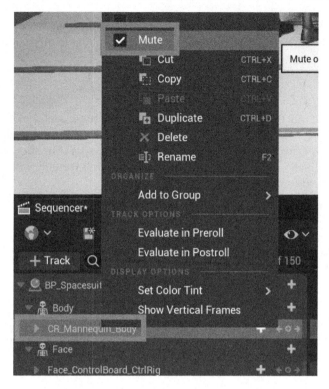

Figure 9.12: Muting/disabling the Control Rig

11. Repeat *step 10* for the **Face_ControlBoard_CtrlRig** track.

12. Now, drag and drop **BP_Spacesuit_Eve** into the Level Sequencer, and repeat the same process of muting the two tracks for the Eve MetaHuman track.

13. Switch back to **Selection** mode (*Shift + 1*) and save your project.

The Level Sequencer should now look as shown in *Figure 9.13*:

Figure: 9.13: The Level Sequencer with both characters added and tracks muted

In this section, you successfully created a Level sequence and added the two MetaHuman characters, Adam and Eve, and disabled/muted the **Body** and **Face** Control Rigs in preparation for the next step – adding the walking animation.

Note

Before we proceed with the next section, I'd like to talk about possessables and spawnables. This is an important part of the Level Sequencer workflow and the reason why we duplicated Adam and Eve in *step 5* of this section. Since both Adam and Eve appear in **Shot_08** and **Shot_09** with different animations, converting them into spawnables is the only way to get around it. Let me explain further.

A **possessable** in the Level Sequencer refers to an Actor or object in your Level that can be controlled and animated within the Level Sequencer timeline. You can think of a *possessable* as an Actor that can be *possessed* or animated by the Level Sequencer. When you add an Actor as a *possessable* in the Level Sequencer, it means you can create animation and keyframe sequences to control that Actor's properties and behavior over time. This can include things such as changing an Actor's location, rotation, scale, or visibility. When dragging or adding any Actors from the Outliner into the Level Sequencer, the Actors become possessable.

A **spawnable**, on the other hand, refers to an Actor or object that can be dynamically created and placed into the Level during a Level Sequencer animation. It allows you to instantiate Actors at specific points in time within your cinematic sequence. A spawnable Actor is useful when you have multiple Actors or shots taking place in the same scene.

Posseable Actors will always be listed in the Outliner, whereas spawnable Actors are removed or destroyed when the sequence ends.

More details about this feature can be found here: `https://docs.unrealengine.com/5.2/en-US/spawn-temporary-actors-in-unreal-engine-cinematics/`. We will also use the spawnable workflow after adding the walk animations.

Adding the walk animations

Now that we have both characters in the Level Sequencer, we can start adding the walk animations:

1. From the downloaded **Chapter_08** folder, drag both `Man Walk Stop.fbx` and `Female Walk Stop.fbx` into the **From_Mixamo** folder. In the **FBX Import Options** popup, click **Import All**. Both animations will be imported simultaneously.

2. Then, in the **From_Mixamo** folder, open the `RTG_Manny` IK Retargeter file. In the **Asset Browser** area, you'll now have the `Female_Walk_Stop` and `Man_Walk_Stop` animation files. Select both files and click the **Export Selected Animations** button. Save the animation in the **Exported_Mixamo_Animations** folder:

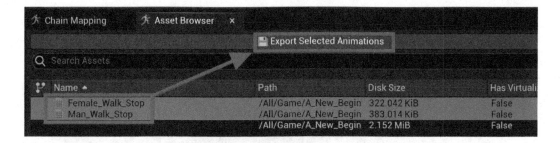

Figure: 9.14: Adding the walk animations

3. In the Level Sequencer, ensure that the playhead is at the beginning of the sequence (use the up arrow shortcut key). Then, select the **Body** track of the Adam character and click **+ Track | Animation**. From the search bar, choose the **Man_Walk_Stop** animation sequence:

Figure 9.15: Adding the walk sequence to the Adam character

4. The Level Sequencer will now have the walk **Animation** track (in purple). Scrub the playhead to see the walk animation – you'll see Adam walking forward and stopping.

> **Note**
>
> If you don't see the **Animation** track (purple line), just close the Sequencer and re-open it.

5.   We will need to make this sequence five seconds long. Drag the playhead to frame 150 and press the right bracket key (*]*). This will mark the end of the sequence indicated by a red vertical bar.

6.   When playing back the animation, you'll notice Adam resetting to his original position. To remedy this, right-click on the **Man_Walk_Stop** purple track and click **Properties**. From there, change the **When Finished** dropdown to **Keep State**. This will keep the current state of Adam at the end of the animation:

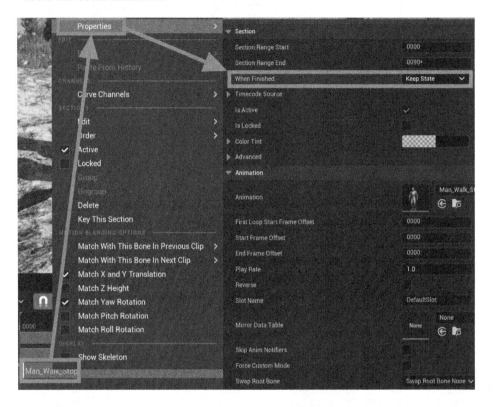

Figure 9.16: Changing Adam's animation state

7.   Now, repeat *steps 1* to *4* for Eve's character, but for Eve's animation, choose, **Female_Walk_Stop**.

In our situation, both Adam and Eve are used in the same location in **Shot_08** and **Shot_09**. For them not to appear in both shots, we will need to convert them into spawnables. This will give control to the Level Sequencer to remove them from their location before loading the next shot. It's easier if I were to show you. Let's go!

8.   While still in the **Shot_08** Level sequence, right-click on **BP_Spacesuit_Adam** and choose **Convert to Spawnable**:

Figure 9.17: Converting BP_Spacesuit_Adam into a spawnable

A lightning bolt icon will appear to indicate that **BP_Spacesuit_Adam** is now a spawnable Actor:

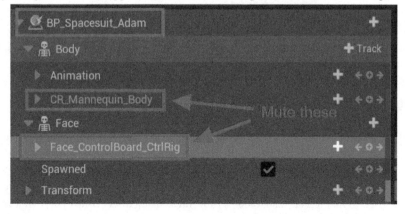

Figure 9.18: Lightning bolt indicating a spawnable Actor

9. At this point, you may have to mute the **CR_Mannequin_Body** and **Face_ControlBoard_CtrlRig** tracks again.

10. Then, repeat the spawnable conversion for **BP_Spacesuit_Eve** and save your project.

    Now that both characters have been converted into spawnables, you will not see them listed in the Outliner. Here is the result of the instructions:

Figure 9.19: Adam and Eve at the end of Shot_08

In this section, you created a new Level sequence and added the two MetaHuman characters in their spacesuit. Then, we added the walk animation to both characters, made them walk toward the water body, and converted them into spawnable Actors. In the next section, we will create the next shot, **Shot_09**, of Adam and Eve in their final position, and we will utilize the **FK Control Rig** to animate Adam placing his hand on Eve's shoulder.

Using Unreal Engine's FK Control Rig

In the previous section, you successfully added the walk animation to both MetaHuman characters using the Level Sequencer. In this section, for the final shot, we will have both Adam and Eve on a ledge, looking at the distance and admiring the new planet, and animate Adam placing his hand on Eve's shoulder. To do this, we will use the FK Control Rig – as mentioned in *Chapter 8*, the FK Control Rig is used to manipulate a character's movement using direct control of each joint's position and orientation.

Creating the final shot

Referring to the storyboard again, in this final shot, all we need to do is animate Adam placing his left hand on Eve's left shoulder. Let's start:

1. Move the view to frame Adam and Eve from the front, as shown in *Figure 9.20*, and create bookmark 4 using *Ctrl + 4*. Rotate the Directional Light and lower the **Intensity** to **10 LUX** to mimic *Figure 9.20*:

Figure 9.20: Placement of Adam and Eve for Shot_09

2. In the **Content Browser | Cinematics** folder, create a new Level sequence by right-clicking and selecting **Cinematics | Level Sequence**. Name it **Shot_09** and double-click to open it.

3. In the Outliner, select both **BP_Spacesuit_Adam2** and **BP_Spacessuit_Eve2** and press *Shift + H* to unhide both Actors.

Since we've created a new sequence, Adam and Eve will reset to their A-pose. This is fine. Now, we will add an idle animation to both characters so that they don't look stiff in the next section.

> **Note**
>
> You must save the project often. As I mentioned earlier, dealing with MetaHumans takes a toll on your system resources, so to avoid disappointments, save often!

Adding an idle animation

In this section, we will add both MetaHumans into the new sequence and add an idle animation to both our characters. Here's how to do it:

1. Drag **BP_Spacesuit_Adam2** from the Outliner into the Level Sequencer.

2. As in the previous section, you will need to mute/disable the **CR_Mannequin_Body** and **Face_Control_Board_CtrlRig** tracks.

3. Next, using the same technique as shown in *Figure 9.15*, add the **MM_Idle** animation to Adam. This is an idle animation that will make Adam strike a pose and have a slight body movement – click the **Play** button or tap the spacebar to view the animation.

4. Add **BP_Spacesuit_Eve2** into the Level Sequencer and repeat the same steps, but instead of searching for MM_Idle, search for MF_Idle.

5. As you may have noticed, Adam is facing away from Eve (not good body language!). We will have to mirror his pose so he's facing Eve. In the **Characters | Mannequins | Animations | Manny** folder, right-click and select **Animation | Mirror Data Table**. Then, in the **Select Skeleton** popup, choose the **SK_Mannequin** skeleton, click **Accept**, and name it MM_Idle_Mirror – this will create a **Mirror Data Table** function that will mirror Adam's pose:

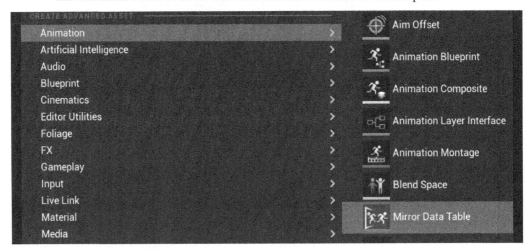

Figure 9.21: Creating the Mirror Data Table property

> **Note**
>
> A **Mirror Data Table** function simply allows for animations to be mirrored from one side to another. You can find out more about this process here: https://docs.unrealengine.com/5.1/en-US/mirroring-animation-in-unreal-engine/.

6. Back in the Level Sequencer, right-click on Adam's **Animation** track (the purple one), select **Properties | Mirror Data Table**, and choose **MM_Idle_Mirror**:

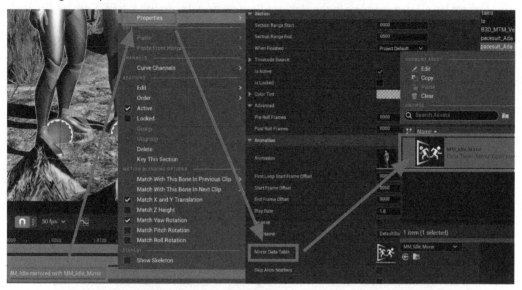

Figure 9.22: Mirroring Adam's pose using the newly created Mirror Data Table

7. Scrub the playhead – Adam's pose will now be inverted and he'll be facing Eve.

8. Drag Eve's animation using the white vertical bar to the end of the track so that it repeats for the duration of the sequence:

Figure 9.23: Extending Eve's Animation track

9. Play the sequence to check the animation and save your project.

In this section, we introduced an idle animation for both Adam and Eve, imbuing them with motion to alleviate rigidity. Subsequently, Adam's animation was mirrored using the **Mirror Data Table** function. In the next section, we will use the **FK Control Rig** to animate Adam's hand.

Adding the FK Control Rig and an Additive layer

Now that we have Adam and Eve in the right position, we're going to use the **FK Control Rig** to do some manual keyframe animation. We're going to do this by exposing some control points on Adam's left hand and rotating them so that his left arm moves up and rests on Eve's left shoulder. To do this, follow these steps:

1. Right-click on the **Body** track for **BP_Spacesuit_Adam2** and choose **Edit With Control Rig**:

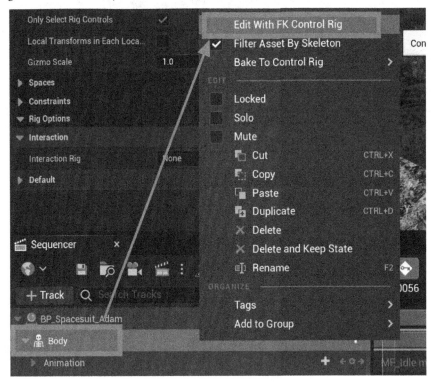

Figure 9.24: Adding an FK Control Rig to Adam

2. In the **Options For Baking** popup, change **Tolerance** to **1.0** and click **Create**.

    After a few seconds, an **FKControlRig** track will be created. The track will have triangle-shaped keyframes for every frame of the idle animation. This process is also known as **baking** the animation.

3. To reveal all the baked animation keyframes of the entire rig, click the triangle on the left of the **FKControlRig** track. Click it again to collapse the track. You can also use the *V* keyboard shortcut to both expand and collapse tracks:

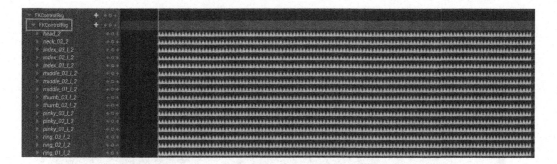

Figure 9.25: FKControlRig's baked data

To craft Adam's hand animation, our approach involves generating an **Additive** layer as opposed to modifying the existing baked data. This approach preserves the integrity of the baked data while allowing us to establish keyframes for hand animation on a distinct layer. Should errors occur, prompting a desire to recommence the process, simply removing the **Additive** layer allows for a fresh start.

4. Ensure that the playhead is at the beginning of the sequence and **FKControlRig** is unmuted. Then, on the **FKControlRig** track, click the **+ Section** button and choose **Additive**:

Figure 9:26: Adding the Additive track

5. A new track will be created – press *F2* and rename it `Additive`. This is for our reference only. The sequence tracks should now look like what's shown in *Figure 9.27*:

Figure 9:27: The Additive layer added to the Sequencer

Save your project before continuing.

6. Next, switch to **Animation** mode (if you're not already in it, hit *Shift + 8*). You should be able to see Adam's control points; if not, ensure the **Hide Control Shapes** checkmark is unticked:

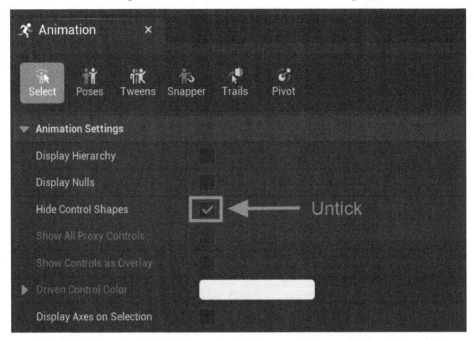

Figure 9.28: Disabling Hide Control Shapes

7. Select the **Additive** layer and press the *V* key to expose all the control points.

8. Scroll down until you come across the **lowerarm_twist_02_l_2** control point.

9. Position the playhead at frame **60**, select all the tracks from **lowerarm_twist_02_l-2** to **upperarm_l_2**, and press the *Enter* key. This will create keyframes for all the selected tracks at frame **60**:

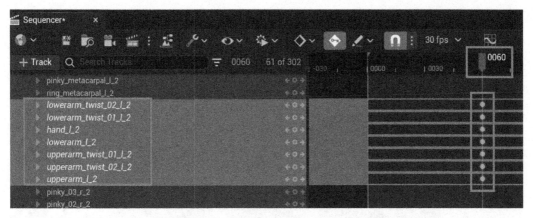

Figure 9.29: Creating new keyframes at frame 60

10. The selected tracks are the only control points we will be rotating to move Adam's arm. Open each track and use the following information to create the next keyframes:

Track	Rotation.Roll	Rotation.Pitch	Rotation.Yaw
At frame 64			
lowerarm_l_2	-23	9.5	-11
At frame 73			
lowerarm_twist_01_l_2	7.5	-1.2	2
hand_l_2	-33	-1.6	17
lowerarm_l_2	6.7	8.5	10
upperarm_twist_01_l_2	-6.5	-2	-1
upperarm_twist_02_l_2	2.5	0.7	0.5
upperarm_l_2	-21	24	8.8
At frame 89			
lowerarm_twist_01_l_2	-15	12	-5
hand_l_2	-84	-40	35
lowerarm_l_2	45	5	29
upperarm_twist_01_l_2	-7	-8	-8
upperarm_twist_02_l_2	33	10	0.7
upperarm_l_2	-23	58	40

Figure 9.30: Track information

The figures in the table work for the animation I created; your milage may differ but feel free to change the keyframes and move Eve into Adam's arms if necessary. You can see the before and after results in *Figure 9.31*:

Figure 9.31: The before and after results of Adam's hand animation

11. Also, **BP_Spacesuit_Adam2** and **BP_Spacesuit_Eve2** will need to be converted into spawnable objects, as we did in the previous section. Otherwise, they will appear in **Shot_08** too.

12. Now, press play to test the animation and then save the project.

In this section, you created the final shot, used the Level Sequencer to add an idle animation to Adam and Eve, and used the **FK Control Rig** to create a keyframe animation on Adam's left hand. In the next section, we will be looking at using Unreal Engine's Facial Control Rig to add facial expressions for both Adam and Eve.

Using Unreal Engine's Facial Control Rig

In the previous section, you learned how to use a pre-made animation and **FK Control Rig** to add a custom keyframe animation. By default, the MetaHumans come expressionless, so in this section, we will add facial expressions to Adam and Eve using the **Face_ControlBoard_CtrlRig** track.

Just like the Body Control Rig, the **Facial Control Rig** provides a system of controls, parameters, and connections that allow animators and creators to modify the facial features and expressions of a MetaHuman character. This includes controlling various aspects of the face, such as eyebrow movement, eye blinking, lip curling, and more. The rig simplifies the process of creating intricate facial animations by providing a user-friendly interface and a set of pre-built controls that are intuitive to use:

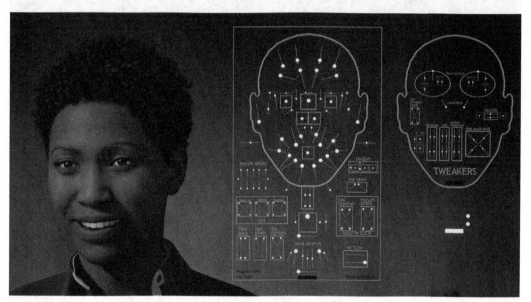

Figure 9.32: The MetaHuman facial controllers

To add facial expressions to the MetaHumans, follow these steps:

1. Check that you're still in **Animation** mode (*Shift + 8*).

2. In the Level Sequencer, select either Adam or Eve's track, then click the **Face** track triangle to reveal **Face_ControlBoard_CtrlRig**. In the previous section, we deliberately muted (disabled) this track; if it still is muted, unmute (enable) it by right-clicking on the track and unchecking the **Mute** checkbox.

3. In the **Animation** tab, click the **Poses** button. Then, in the pop-up window, browse to **Content | MetaHumans | Common | Common | PoseLibrary | Face | Expressions** and select the **Joy-02_Amusement** pose:

Figure 9.33: Accessing the MetaHuman facial pose library

4.   After selecting the pose, in the lower half of the **Control Rig Pose** pop-up panel, click **Select Controls | Paste Pose**:

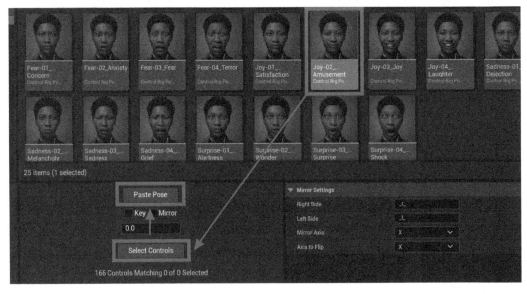

Figure 9.34: Using the MetaHuman pose library

Now, both Adam and Eve will have pleasant smiles. Instead of tweaking the facial controllers, to ease the process, we used one of the pre-existing face poses in the pose library in the **MetaHuman** folder that met our purpose. Now, for the last time in this chapter, save your project:

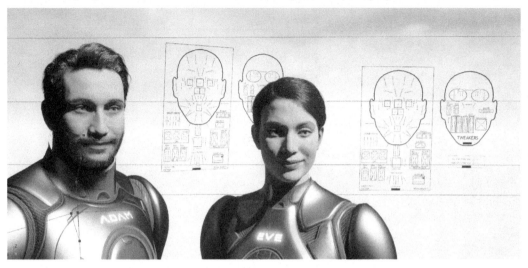

Figure 9.35: Adam and Eve with their respective facial rigs

However, if you wish, you can use the facial controllers on the screen to tweak the expressions yourself. I suggest experimenting with them and coming up with some interesting expressions of your own.

> **Note**
>
> Explaining every controller that exists on the Facial Control Rig is beyond the scope of this book, but there is a detailed video by Adam Walton on the Unreal Engine YouTube channel that I suggest watching if you want to understand every slider and what it does: `https://youtu.be/GEpH3o44_58`.

Summary

Our work for this chapter is now complete. If you've reached this point and successfully kept pace, kudos to you!

In this chapter, we extensively explored the utilization of pre-existing animations, integrated supplementary animations onto Adam using the FK Control Rig, and employed the Facial Control Rig to introduce various facial expressions. By achieving this, you've acquired the proficiency to forge custom character animations within Unreal Engine.

Moving forward to the next chapter, we'll continue utilizing the Level Sequencer, add virtual cameras, manage multiple levels, and assemble the Master Sequence.

Part 4:
Production:
Shooting the Scene

In this part, you will learn pivotal techniques for refining the cinematic aspects of your Unreal Engine project. *Chapter 10* introduces the art of adding and animating virtual cameras using the Sequencer, enabling you to craft dynamic and visually compelling scenes. You'll then progress to *Chapter 11*, where you'll elevate your storytelling by enhancing set dressing, retiming shots, and incorporating Niagara particles for added visual impact. Finally, in *Chapter 12*, you'll discover the art of setting a mood with lighting and post-processing effects, bringing a nuanced atmosphere to your virtual world.

This part includes the following chapters:

- *Chapter 10, Adding and Animating Virtual Cameras Using the Level Sequencer*
- *Chapter 11, Enhancing Set Dressing, Retiming Shots, and Adding Niagara Particles*
- *Chapter 12, Setting the Mood with Lighting and Adding Post-Processing Effects*

10

Adding and Animating Virtual Cameras Using the Level Sequencer

In *Chapter 4*, we delved into Unreal Engine's Film framework, exploring the creation of individual shots that are subsequently organized into sequences. These sequences are then amalgamated to form a comprehensive Master Sequence, constituting an entire film. This structural approach closely mirrors the conventional filmmaking process and is accomplished within Unreal Engine through the utilization of the Level Sequencer.

In this chapter, we shall finalize the individual shots, integrate them into sequences, and ultimately assemble the Master Sequence. Additionally, you will gain insight into the inherent intuitiveness and ease of management offered by this framework.

So, we will be covering the following topics:

- Creating individual shots using the Level Sequencer
- Creating the sequences
- Managing multiple Levels
- Assembling the Master Sequence
- Animating the virtual cameras

Technical requirements

To complete this chapter, you will need to meet the technical requirements detailed in *Chapter 1* and the Unreal Engine project we have been working on for the past few chapters.

Creating individual shots using the Level Sequencer

In *Chapter 4*, we created the first sequence (the spaceship interior) with four camera shots and the second sequence (the space scene) with a single camera shot. Then, in *Chapter 5*, we created the third sequence (the planet), which consists of four camera shots.

In this section, we will revisit these individual shots to add a virtual camera for each of them, and in the following sections, combine all these shots into a Master Sequence. The plan is to use the *Master Sequence > Sequence > Shot* method covered in *Chapter 4*. Let's start:

1. Open the **A_New_Beginning** project.
2. Then, in the **Level** folder, double-click to open the **INT_Spaceship** Level. Press *1* to go to **Bookmark 1** (the spaceship flight deck view).
3. In the **Cinematics** folder, create a new Level Sequence by right-clicking, and then selecting **Cinematics | Level Sequence**. Rename it Shot_01 and double-click the Level Sequence to open it.
4. To create a camera from this point of view, in the **Viewport** menu, click **Create Camera Here | Cine Camera Actor**:

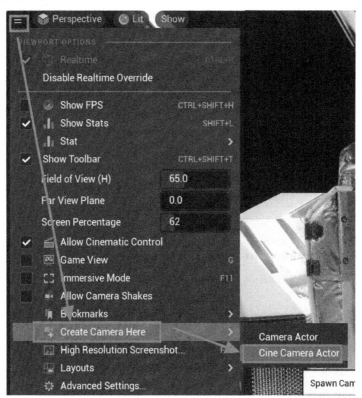

Figure 10.1: Creating a camera for Shot_01

5. Next, in the Outliner, rename the camera `Cam_01` and drag it into the Level Sequencer:

Figure 10.2: Dragging Cam_01 into the Level Sequencer

The Level Sequencer now has the **Cam_01** track, which includes **Camera Aperture**, **Current Focal Length**, **Manual Focal Distance (Focus Settings)**, and a **Transform** track (we'll go through these more in the next chapter). This operation also created a **Camera Cuts** track, also known as the **Camera Shots** track:

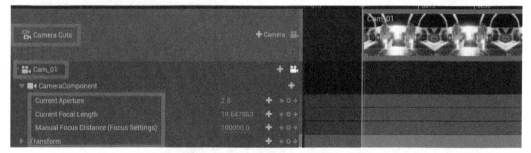

Figure 10.3: Cam_01 properties and the Camera Cuts track

Whenever a camera is added to the Level Sequencer, it will automatically be set to **Pilot** mode (indicated in the top-left corner of the **Viewport** interface). This will lock the camera, allowing you to position the camera for the shot you're trying to capture.

6. We won't need to pilot the camera just yet, so click the **Eject** button to *un-pilot* the camera:

Figure 10.4: The camera's pilot mode and the Eject button

7. Save the project (*Ctrl + Shift + S*) and close the Level Sequencer.

    We will repeat the same process for the rest of the shots. We will revisit these shots in the upcoming section to create the camera animations.

8. Jump to **Bookmark 2** – this is a close-up view of the spaceship flight deck console where a holographic screen will be displayed:

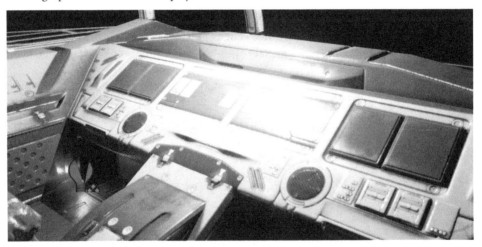

Figure 10.5: View of Shot_02

9. In the **Cinematics** folder, create another Level Sequence, rename it Shot_02, and open it. Then, create a **Cine Camera Actor** property, rename it Cam_02, and drag it into the Level Sequencer. Eject the camera and close the sequence.

10. Jump to **Bookmark 3** – the cryo-pods view. Create another Level Sequence, rename it Shot_03, and open it. Then, create another camera here, rename it Cam_03, and drag it into the Level Sequencer. Eject the camera and close the sequence:

Figure 10.6: View of Shot_03

11. For the final spaceship internal shot, jump back to **Bookmark 1** and move the view close to the console. We will use this view to show a holographic screen indicating the landing clearance given by the onboard computer:

Figure 10.7: View of Shot_04

12. Create another Level Sequence, rename it Shot_04, and open it. Then, create a camera here, rename it Cam_04, and drag it into the Level Sequencer. Eject the camera and close the sequence. Finally, save the project.

We're done creating shots for the **INT_Spaceship** sequence, so let's create shots for the **Space** sequence.

13. In the **Levels** folder, open the **EXT_Space** Level. Then, in the **Cinematics** folder, create a new Level Sequence, rename it Shot_05, and open it. As before, create a camera, rename it Cam_05, drag it into the Level Sequencer, eject it, close the Level Sequencer, and save the project:

Figure 10.8: View of Shot_05

14. Next, open the **EXT_Planet** Level and jump to **Bookmark 1** – this is the shot where the space shuttle traverses the landscape. Create the Level Sequence and name it Shot_06. Then, open it, add a camera, and rename it Cam_06.

15. Jump to **Bookmark 2** and move closer to the space shuttle. Here, create a new Level Sequence and rename it Shot_07. Then, create **Cam_07**:

Figure 10.9: View of Shot_07

16. Lastly, add the cameras to **Shot_08** and **Shot_09** in the same way.

17. Close and save the project.

In the next section, we will add these shots to their respective sequences before adding them to a Master Sequence.

Creating the sequences

In the previous section, we completed all the individual shots for our film. In this section, we will create the three sequences of our film. The creation of these three sequences is crucial in controlling the visibility of tracks in the Master Sequence, which will be achieved through the **Level Visibility** track available in the Level Sequencer (Level management will be covered in the next section).

So, let's get started:

1. Open the **INT_Spaceship** Level.

2. In the **Cinematics** folder, create a new Level Sequence, rename it Seq_01, and open it. This is the first sequence that will contain the first four shots (**Shot_01** to **Shot_04**).

3. Click the + **Track** button and select **Shot Track**:

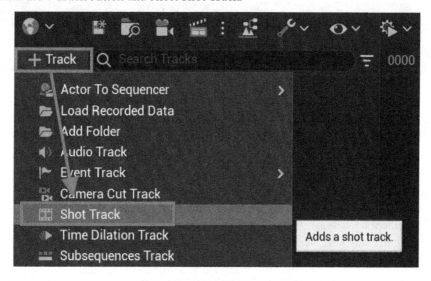

Figure 10.10: Adding Shot Track

4. Click the + **Shot** button on the **Shots** track and, from the popup, choose **Shot_01**. This is our first shot from the **INT_Spaceship** sequence:

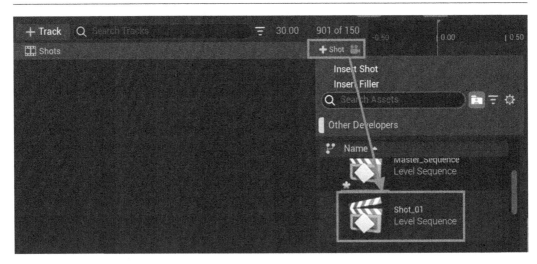

Figure 10.11: Adding Shot_01 to Seq_01

5. To be able to view the **Shot_01** camera, click the camera icon in the **Shots** track. This will lock the view to the **Shots** track:

Figure 10.12: Clicking on the Shots track's camera icon

> **Note**
>
> You won't be able to move the camera in lock mode. To unlock it, click the camera icon again or use *Shift + C*.

Since we have a total of four shots in this sequence, let's make each shot 5 seconds long (this is just a temporary setting). Typically, a film is shot in 24 **frames per second** (**FPS**), which gives films a cinematic look, as opposed to games, which are usually set to 60 FPS to give them a smooth look. So, to give our virtual film a cinematic look, we will *shoot* in 24 FPS too.

6. In the **Sequencer** toolbar, click the button next to **30 fps** and change it to **24 fps**:

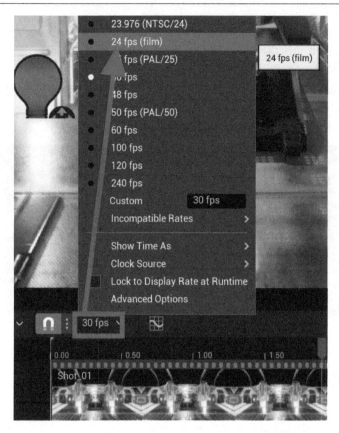

Figure 10.13: Changing the Level Sequencer's FPS to 24

7. In a **24 fps** sequence, a 5-second shot is 120 frames. If we multiply 120 by 4 (shots) we get 480 frames. So, click once in the Level Sequencer, press *Ctrl + T*, and type 480. The playhead will jump to frame 480. Now, press the right bracket key (*J*) to mark the end of the sequence with a red vertical bar.

8. Click the **Save the Sequence** button to save the sequence. Any time you see the asterisk on this icon, as depicted in *Figure 10.4*, save your work – just to be on the safe side:

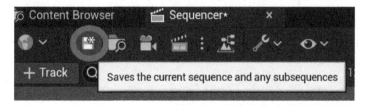

Figure 10.14: The button to save the sequence/project

9. Let's add the next shot. Ensure the playhead is at frame **120** (use the *Ctrl* + *T* shortcut and type 120), then click the + icon on the **Shots** track and choose **Shot_02**. You'll now see the **Shot_02** view.

10. Add **Shot_03** and **Shot_04** in the same way. You can use the comma (,) and period (.) keys to jump from one shot to another.

11. Once done, drag **Shot_02** and **Shot_04** downward to arrange the timeline, as shown in *Figure 10.15*:

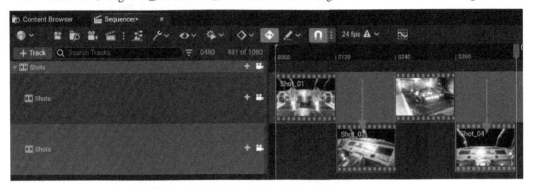

Figure 10.15: Separating the shots for clarity

12. Lock the **Shots** camera and scrub the playhead to view all four shots.

13. Use the previous steps to create the next two sequences:

- **Seq_02**, which consists of **Shot_05**

- **Seq_03**, which consists of **Shot_06**, **Shot_07**, **Shot_08**, and **Shot_09** – for **Shot_09**, extend the duration of the shot to 10 seconds (240 frames)

Our three sequences are now complete, but before we can add them into a Master Sequence, we'll need to figure out how to manage their visibility when moving from one sequence to another during playback. We'll tackle that next.

Managing multiple Levels

In this project, we had to create multiple Levels since our story comprises different locations (Levels). To be able to load these different Levels in the Level Sequencer, we will require the use of the **Levels** panel. Let me show you how to do it:

1. Create a new Level, choose the **Empty Level** template, and save it as Main_Level in the **Levels** folder. Your screen should now be black.

2. Next, from the **Window** menu, choose **Levels**:

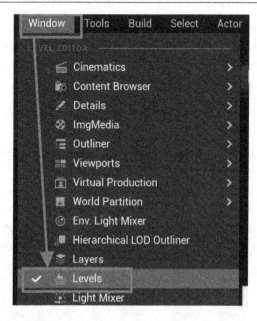

Figure 10.16: Opening the Levels panel

3. The **Levels** panel will pop up in the middle of the screen. Dock it somewhere so that it is easily accessible, as shown in *Figure 10.17*:

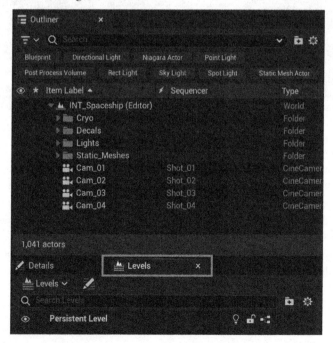

Figure 10.17: Docking the Levels panel

4. You'll notice that the **Levels** panel already consists of a cyan-colored **Persistent Level** (which is another word for the current Level). From the **Levels** folder in the **Content Browser** area, drag the **INT_Spaceship**, **EXT_Space**, and **EXT_Planet** Levels into the empty area in this panel.

5. Then, in the **Levels** panel, do the following:

    I.   Double-click on the **INT_Spaceship** Level to make it **Persistent Level**. It will turn to cyan-colored text.

    II. Right-click on **INT_Spaceship**, choose **Change Streaming Method**, and select **Always Loaded**. Do the same for the **EXT_Space** and **EXT_Planet** Levels.

    III. Click on the eyeball icons for the **EXT_Planet** and **EXT_Space** Levels to hide them in the Level:

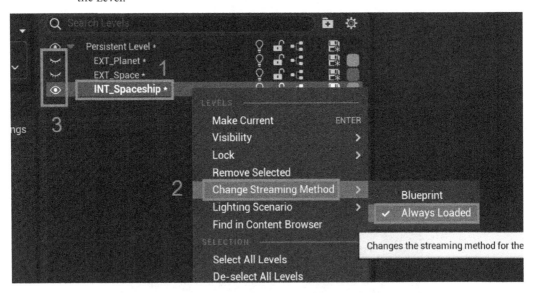

Figure 10.18: Configuring the Levels in the Levels panel

Let's review what you just did. You added the three Levels by dragging them into the **Levels** panel, which will now allow you to control their visibility in the Level Sequencer. You then right-clicked on each of the Levels and changed the streaming method to **Always Loaded**, ensuring the Levels are always loaded during playback and not controlled via blueprint scripting (visual programming language in Unreal Engine). Lastly, you disabled the visibility of the **EXT_Space** and **EXT_Planet** Levels using the **Toggle Visibility** switch (eye icon) – their visibility can now be toggled on or off using **Level Visibility Track** in the Level Sequencer.

With that, in the next section, we will create the Master Sequence and use the **Level** panel to set the visibility of each Level during playback.

Assembling the Master Sequence

In the previous section, you created the three sequences and added the three existing Levels to the **Levels** panel. In this section, we will add all the sequences to a Master Sequence and control their visibility during playback. Here's how to do it:

1. In the **Cinematics** folder, create a new Level Sequence, rename it Master_Sequence, and open it.

2. Change the **FPS** settings to **24** (all the Level sequences must be set to 24 FPS).

3. Ensure the playhead is at the beginning of the sequence and add a **Shot** track (as shown in *Figure 10.10*). In the **Shot** track, click the **+ Shot** button and add **Seq_01**.

4. Press *Ctrl + T* and type 1080 – this will set the duration of the Master Sequence to 45 seconds, with each shot being 5 seconds long (for now).

5. Press the right square bracket (*]*) to set the end marker.

6. Using the period (.) key, jump to the end of the first sequence, then add the second and third sequences, as shown in *Figure 10.19*:

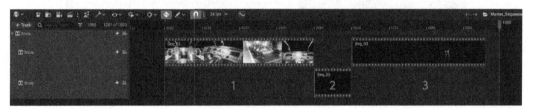

Figure 10.19: Master sequence with all three sequences

7. Click the green **+ Track** button on the Level Sequencer and select **Level Visibility Track**:

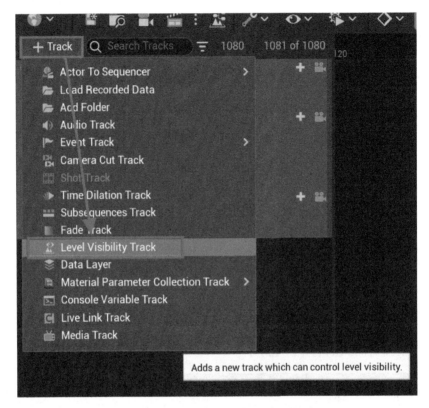

Figure 10.20: Adding Level Visibility Track

8.   Since we have three sequences, using **Visibility Trigger**, add three **Visible** tracks and three **Hidden** tracks. Each sequence will be visible and hidden at any given time:

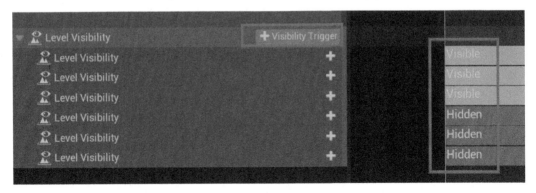

Figure 10.21: Adding three Visible and three Hidden tracks

9. Right-click the first visible **Level Visibility** track (green) and choose **Properties**. Then, under **Level Names**, click the + icon, type INT_Spaceship, and press *Enter*. To avoid re-typing, I'd suggest selecting the text and pressing *Ctrl + C* to copy the text to your system's memory:

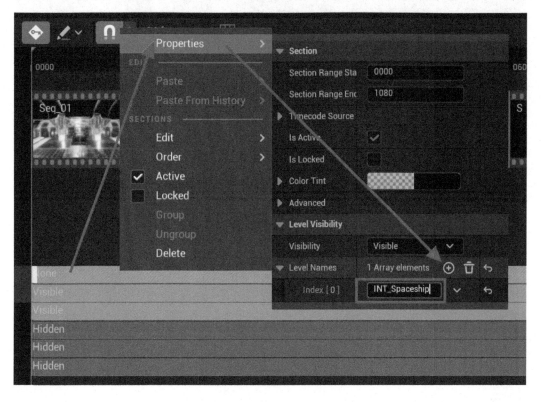

Figure 10.22: Configuring each track to the right Level

10. Now, right-click on the first **Hidden** track (red), go to **Properties**, click the + icon, and press *Ctrl + V* to paste the same text. Then, press *Enter* to confirm the text. The names must be entered accurately as per the names of the Levels displayed in the **Levels** panel.

11. Since we used the first visible and first hidden track for the **INT_Spacehip** Level, let's use the second visible and second hidden track for **EXT_Space**, and the third visible and third hidden track for **EXT_Planet**, as shown in *Figure 10.23*:

Figure 10.23: Adding Visible and Hidden tracks

12. Trim the tracks by dragging the edges of the tracks and aligning them, as shown in *Figure 10.24*:

Figure 10.24: The assigned and neatly arranged Level Visibility tracks

> **Note**
>
> Logically, the **Visible** tracks will make the assigned Level visible, and the **Hidden** track will hide the assigned Level during playback and rendering.
>
> I've trimmed the tracks by selecting and dragging the edge of each track so that they take up minimal space in the Level Sequencer. You can scrub the playhead to check whether the Levels are indeed loading. The **EXT_Planet** track will take a few extra seconds to load due to its sheer complexity.

13. The Master Sequence is now complete, so you can save the project.

To do a bit of a recap, what you have just created is a *Master Sequence > Sequence > Shot* nested system. If you double-click on any of the sequences, you'll drill down into the sequence shots, and if you double-click on the individual shots, you have access to the shot itself, as shown in *Figure 10.25*:

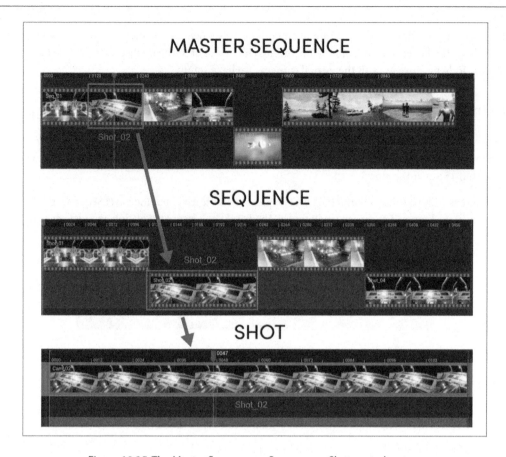

Figure 10.25: The Master Sequence > Sequence > Shot nested system

To move back up in the hierarchy, at the top right of the Level Sequencer interface, use the left arrow to navigate one Level up or click the **Master Sequence** button to return to the Master Sequence:

Figure 10.26: The breadcrumb navigation

This is a great workflow as we can jump in and out of the sequences and shots with ease. We will learn more about the Level Sequencer in the upcoming chapters, but in the final section of this chapter, we will conclude by animating all the virtual cameras we have set up.

Animating the virtual cameras

In this section, you will finally get to animate all the virtual cameras we've added to all the shots in the previous section. More specifically, in **Shot_05**, **Shot_06**, and **Shot_07**, you will also animate the space shuttle as per the storyboard.

But before we jump back again into the Level Sequencer, let's learn about the Level Sequencer's playback controls. In the bottom-left corner, you'll find all the Level Sequencer's navigation and playback controls:

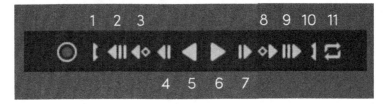

Figure 10.27: The sequencer playback controls

Here are what the controls are and their equivalent shortcuts:

- **1**: This sets the start maker indicated with a green vertical line ([)
- **2**: This jumps to the start of the timeline (up arrow key)
- **3**: This jumps to the previous keyframe (,)
- **4**: This jumps to the previous frame (left arrow key)
- **5**: Play in reverse
- **6**: Play forward (spacebar)
- **7**: This jumps to the next frame (right arrow key)
- **8**: This jumps to the next keyframe (.)
- **9**: This jumps to the end of the timeline (*Ctrl* + up arrow key)
- **10**: This sets the end maker indicated with a red vertical line (])
- **11**: This toggles between looping and non-looping playback

With that, let's animate the first sequence.

Animating the first sequence

Let's start with **Shot_01**, our opening shot:

1. From the Master Sequence, double-click on **Seq_01**, then **Shot_01**.

2. Click on the **Cam_01** track, then the camera icon, to activate the camera:

Figure 10.28: Activating the Shot_01 camera

3. Ensure the playhead is at the beginning of the timeline (use the up arrow key). If you need to, press the G key to go into **Game View** mode to hide all the overlay icons.

4. We're going to create a 5-second camera dolly (moving the virtual camera physically as opposed to zooming in) from this point, toward the flight deck. So, select the **Cam_01** track and press S to set the first keyframe – you'll notice a pink circle on the **Transform** track at frame **0**.

5. Now, drag the playhead to frame **119** and move **Cam_01** close to the console, as seen in *Figure 10.29*. Press S to set the end keyframe:

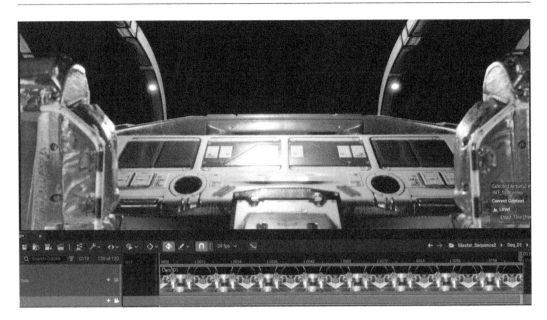

Figure 10.29: The Shot_01 end frame

6. Select the two keyframes, right-click on one of them, and in the popup, choose **Linear**. Let me quickly explain the options here:

    •   **Cubic (Auto)**: The default mode. This mode attempts to smooth out the curve between the keyframes and eases in and out both the start and end keyframes.

    •   **Cubic (User)**: This mode is similar to **Cubic (Auto)**, but the tangents will be locked for any further automatic edits when adding or moving keyframes.

> Note
> **Tangents** are handles that stick out of a keyframe, allowing animation curves to be smoothed out. They are also known as Bezier handles in other 3D applications.

    •   **Cubic Break**: This mode is like **Cubic (Auto)**, but the tangents are broken to allow you to customize the angles in the **Curve Editor** area.

    •   **Linear**: Linear tangents have no smoothing nor easing applied, causing abrupt starts and stops when reaching any keyframes.

    •   **Constant**: The current value of the keyframe will be maintained until reaching the next keyframe:

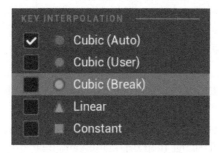

Figure 10.30: Sequencer interpolation modes

As we want the camera to have a constant linear movement, we will set these keyframes to **Linear**.

7.   Scrub the playhead or press the spacebar to play the animation.

Congratulations! You've just created your first virtual camera animation. I find the animation a tad fast as an opening shot, but we will fine-tune the timings in the next chapter.

> **Note**
>
> If you're finding it a challenge to create the keyframes, ensure that the **Camera** track is selected; it'll be indicated by a blue highlight. You could also click directly on the **Transform** keyframe button.

Now, let's work on **Shot_02**. In the next chapter, we will need to place a holographic image in this shot, so here, we'll create a subtle five-second push-in camera movement toward the console (just enough time for the audience to read the text).

Simply click the left arrow key to jump back to **Sequence 1** and double-click **Shot_02**. Then, follow the previous steps to create a linear animation. The end frame will look like what's shown in *Figure 10.31*:

Figure 10.31: The Shot_02 end frame

Now, let's work on **Shot_03**:

1. Click the left arrow key to jump back to **Sequence 1** and double-click on **Shot_03**.

2. This is the cryo-pod scene. Since we're here, we might as well add our two space travelers to the cryo-pods. In the **Content Browser** area, in the **3D_Models** folder, create a new folder and rename it Characters.

3. In the **Book_Project_Files | 3D Models | Characters** folder, drag **Manny_Sleep** and **Quinn_ Sleep** into the pods and change their orientation and their scale to **1.8** to fit the cryo-pods.

4. Then, create a linear camera animation, moving from screen right to screen left in five seconds (120 frames), as shown in *Figure 10.32*:

Figure 10.32: The beginning and end frames for Shot_03

5. For **Shot_04**, which is similar to **Shot_02**, the holographic display will indicate that the shuttle launch sequence has started. Animate a subtle movement of the camera from its default position closer to the console in five seconds, as shown in *Figure 10.33*:

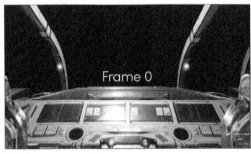

Figure 10.33: The beginning and end frames for Shot_04

We're done with the first sequence, so save the project. We will now continue with the second sequence, which contains only one shot, but in this shot, we will also animate the space shuttle leaving the spaceship and moving toward the planet.

Animating the second sequence

In this section, we will continue to use the Level Sequencer to animate the camera and space shuttle leaving the spaceship:

1. Open **Seq_02**, then **Shot_05**.

2. Next, add the camera animation. At frame **0**, drop a keyframe at the current position. Then, move the camera to screen right and add the end keyframe, as shown in *Figure 10.34*:

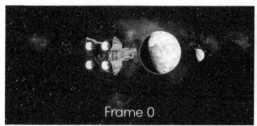 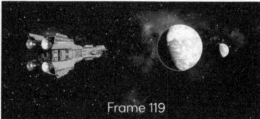

Figure 10.34: The beginning and end frames for Shot_05

3. Change the keyframe interpolation to **Linear**.

4. To ensure the shuttle is added to the right Level, double-click on the **EXT_Space** Level in the **Levels** panel so it becomes the current Level.

5. From the **Book_Project_Files | 3D _Models | Shuttle_Flight_Mode** folder, drag **Shuttle_FlightMode** into the Level. Scale the shuttle up to **2.0** and position it, as shown in *Figure 10.35*:

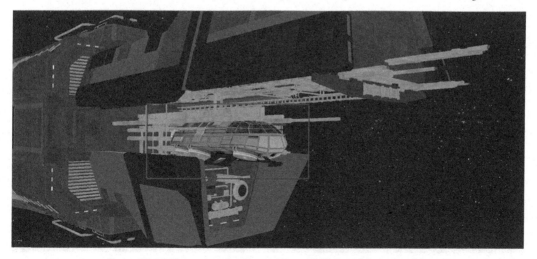

Figure 10.35: The space shuttle positioned in front of the spaceship

Now, let's animate it launching from the spaceship.

6. Drag **Shuttle_FlightMode** from the Outliner into the Level Sequencer and press *S* to create a transform keyframe at frame **0**.

7. Jump to frame **119**. Select **Shuttle_FlightMode** in the Outliner. Then, using the *X axis* (red axis), drag the shuttle toward the planet.

8. Create a keyframe at frame **119**, then convert the keyframes into **Linear** frames and preview the animation.

> **Note**
>
> The steps in this chapter are here as a guideline – feel free to exercise your creativity to tell your story. Right now, we're just interested in creating the initial animations; we will refine and enhance the scenes in the next chapter.

Once you have completed the instructions and are happy with the animation, save the project and move on to the last sequence.

Animating the last sequence

In this final sequence, **Seq_03**, we have the last four shots, **Shot_06**, **Shot_07**, **Shot_08**, and **Shot_09**. Let's get going:

1. Jump into **Sequence 3**, then **Shot_06**. In this shot, we'll place the space shuttle at the top right of the screen, behind the trees, and animate it flying from screen right to screen left. We will not animate the camera in this shot.

2. Double-click the **EXT_Planet** Level in the **Levels** panel to make it the current Level. This is to ensure that if we add any Actors to the Level, they will belong to this Level:

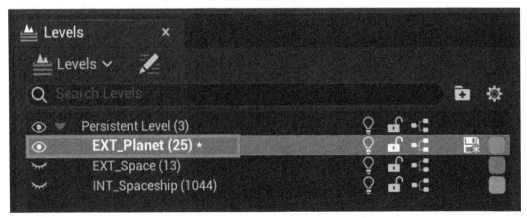

Figure 10.36: Making EXT_Planet the current Level

3. From the **3D Models** folder, drag **Shuttle_FlightMode** into the scene and place it using the following values:

    • **Location**: X = -58700, Y = -107800, Z = 1800

    • **Rotation**: X = 0, Y = 0, Z = -90

    • **Scale**: X = 3.0, Y = 3.0, Z = 3.0

4. Drag **Shuttle** into the Level Sequencer and drop a **Transform** keyframe at frame **0**.

5. Jump to frame **119** and drag the shuttle to the left of the screen using the *X* axis (red-axis). Then, press *S* to create a keyframe and convert the keyframe into a **Linear** frame.

6. Now, go back to frame **0**, drag the shuttle off the camera view to the right, and press *S*. Then, drag the shuttle off the camera view to the left for the end keyframe as well, and press *S* again. This will look as if the space shuttle enters the view from screen right and leaves on screen left:

Figure 10.37: The beginning and ending frames for Shot_06

Now, let's work on **Shot_07**. In this shot, we will animate the space shuttle landing. The space shuttle comes withthe landing gears deploying and doors opening animations. We can use this to our advantage to make the shot look believable, but it is going to need some extra effort. Let's begin:

1. Open **Shot_07**. By default, the space shuttle will be on the ground, as shown in *Figure 10.9*. Click on it in the **Viewport** area to ensure it's the right static mesh, and drag it from the Outliner into the Level Sequencer.

2. Using the *Z* axis (blue axis), drag it upward, almost to the top of the shot, as shown in *Figure 10.41*. Use the following values for precise placement:

    • **Location**: X = - 57180, Y = -69823, Z = -950

    • **Rotation**: X = 0, Y = 0, Z = 170

    • **Scale**: X = 2.0, Y = 2.0, Z = 2.0

3. Create a keyframe at frame **0**. This is the starting position of the landing sequence.

4. Jump to frame **70** and use the following values to position the shuttle:

   - **Location**: X = -57240, Y = -69823, Z = -2410

   - **Rotation**: X = 3, Y = 4, Z = 140

   - **Scale**: X = 2.0, Y = 2.0, Z = 2.0

5. Create a keyframe at frame **70**. This is the end position of the landing sequence. Now, let's add the animation for lowering the landing gear and opening the doors.

6. With the playhead at 0, select **Shuttle**. Then, in the **Animation** track, click the **+ Animation** button, and choose the **Shuttle_Anim** animation. You'll now have the familiar purple **Animation** track:

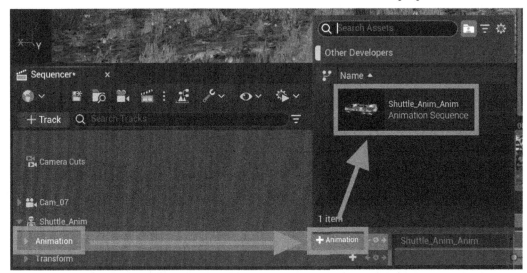

Figure 10.38: Adding the Animation track to the space shuttle

7. Since the shuttle animation comes with a take-off sequence instead of a landing sequence, we will need to reverse it. So, right-click on the **Animation** track, select **Properties**, and enable **Reverse**:

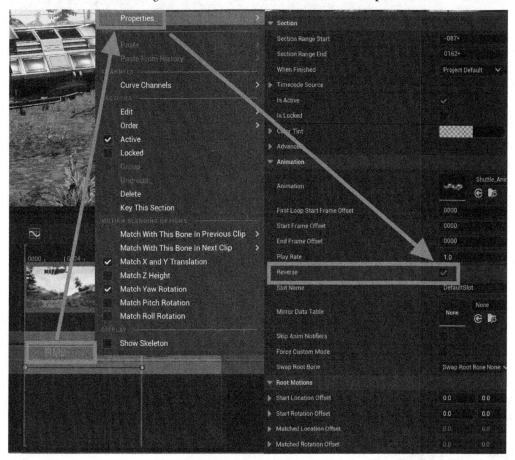

Figure 10.39: Reversing the animation

8. Now, right-click the **Animation** track again and select **Properties**, but this time, set **Section Range Start** to **-086** and **Section Range End** to **0162**. This will set the exact timing when the landing gear gets deployed and the doors open:

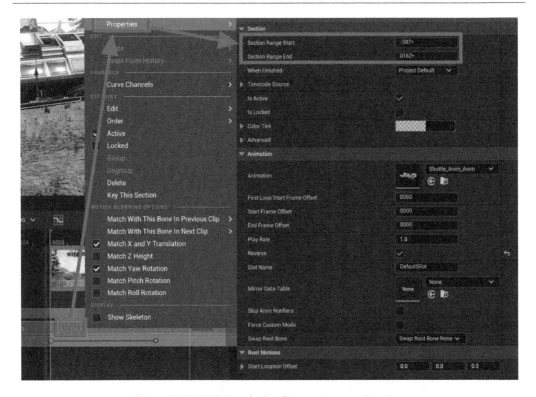

Figure 10.40: Retiming the landing sequence animation

If done correctly, when you play the animation, you'll have a five-second landing sequence with the landing gear deploying and doors opening. I feel that this shot needs to be prolonged, but we'll take care of that in the next chapter:

Figure 10.41: The beginning and end frames for Shot_07

> **Note**
>
> **Shot_08** and **Shot_09** are GPU processor intensive. Unreal Engine crashing is not unusual, so save often. I'd also suggest changing the **Engine Scalability** settings to **High** or **Medium** – this will lower the resolution while you set up the camera animation.

Next is **Shot_08**. This is a rather simple shot. In this shot, Adam and Eve arrive at the edge of the body of water and stop walking. We will create a subtle dolly shot moving the camera in sync with their movement. Select **Cam_08** and create a keyframe at frame **0**. Dolly the camera forward, then create an end keyframe at frame **119**, as seen in *Figure 10.42*. Remember to change both keyframes to **Linear** by right-clicking on one of them and choosing **Linear** from the popup:

Figure 10.42: The beginning and end frames for Shot_08

Shot_09 is the revealing shot, where we will finally reveal the identity of the two characters, Adam and Eve, and we will leave it to the audience to interpret the story. We will do a close-up of Adam and Eve, enough for the audience to read their names, and pull the camera way back for the ending shot, then fade to black. We will add the fading effect in the Master Sequence. Let's get to it:

1. Jump into **Shot_09**. In the Level Sequencer, select **Cam_09**. Set its location using these values:

   - **Location**: X = **-58380**, Y = **-78309**, Z = **-3233**

   - **Rotation**: X = **0**, Y = **0**, Z = **93**

2. Set a keyframe at frame **0**. Copy the keyframe by selecting it and pressing *Ctrl + C*, jump to frame **48**, and paste the keyframe. This should give the audience two seconds to realize who they are:

Figure 10.43: The beginning frame of Shot_09

3. To give the camera a slow pull-out, jump to frame **160** and set the camera using the following location and rotation:

    - **Location**: **X = -58304, Y = -79678, Z = -3246**
    - **Rotation**: **X = 0, Y = 0, Z = 100**

4. Then, at frame **239**, set the camera with the following location and rotation:

    - **Location**: **X = -58297, Y = -93647, Z = -1794**
    - **Rotation**: **X = 0, Y = 0, Z = 100**

    Between frame **160** and frame **239**, the camera will move much faster to give it a dramatic fade-out.

The final timeline is shown in *Figure 10.44*:

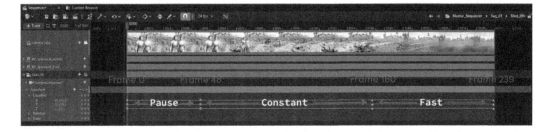

Figure 10.44: The final timeline for Shot_09

Take note of the keyframe interpolation settings on the keyframes. Frames **0** and **48** are **Cubic (Auto)** and frames **160** and **239** are **Linear**. From frame **0** to frame **48**, the camera will have a two-second pause, then start to pull away slowly but with a constant speed until frame **160**. From frame **160** to **239**, the camera speeds up.

I feel that this camera animation will give a dramatic look, which at the end shows the vast landscape where we leave our two space travelers to start a new beginning as the film fades to black.

Summary

In this chapter, you've accomplished 80% of the necessary tasks for completing the film. You've successfully crafted individual shots, assembled the three sequences along with the Master Sequence, and brought the cameras to life, which is undeniably the most crucial aspect of the entire film.

Nonetheless, there's still a bit more to be done. In the upcoming chapter, we will meticulously examine each shot, ensuring that we incorporate all the missing elements, a process commonly referred to as *set dressing* in the film industry. We will also fine-tune the timing of camera animations and make lighting adjustments to perfectly match the mood of our film.

It promises to be an exciting journey, so I look forward to meeting you in the next chapter!

11

Enhancing Set Dressing, Retiming Shots, and Adding Niagara Particles

Set dressing in film refers to the process of arranging and decorating the physical elements of a film set to create a realistic and visually appealing environment for a scene. This includes everything from the placement of furniture and props to the selection of colors and textures for walls, floors, and other surfaces. Set dressing is a crucial aspect of production design and helps to establish the setting, mood, and atmosphere of a scene or film.

Within our virtual film project, we will identify the absence of some critical elements essential to our storytelling, including the absence of a **heads-up display** (**HUD**) inside the shuttle and smoke effects when the shuttle lands. These omissions will be systematically addressed on a shot-by-shot basis, ensuring the completeness and coherence of our narrative. Moreover, you'll gain insights into the process of reshaping shot timing within the Sequencer and basic skills in creating dynamic particle effects using Unreal Engine's robust Niagara system.

In this chapter, we will be covering the following topics:

- Identifying missing set dressing elements
- Adding set dressing elements to each shot
- Creating Niagara particles

Technical requirements

To complete this chapter, you will need the technical requirements detailed in *Chapter 1* and the Unreal project we have been working on over the past few chapters.

Identifying missing set dressing elements

Throughout the course of this book, we have leveraged projects available on the Unreal Engine Marketplace and objects acquired from platforms such as Sketchfab. This strategic approach has significantly streamlined our workflow, saving us valuable time. However, it's important to note that there are still certain components that are conspicuously absent and hold immense importance in advancing our narrative.

In the subsequent sections, I will be adding the following elements on a shot-by-shot basis:

- **Shot_01**: Adding a HUD that turns on to indicate a habitable planet has been found
- **Shot_02**: Animating the camera focus settings for a **depth-of-field** (**DOF**) effect
- **Shot_03**: Adding cryo-pod smoke effects to mimic a cold environment
- **Shot_04**: Adding a holographic HUD indicating the space shuttle is launching
- **Shot_05**: Adding a jet trail to the launching space shuttle
- **Shot_06**: Adding animals in the foreground and a flock of birds flying in the distance
- **Shot_07**: Slowing down the shot and adding smoke and debris particle effects to the landing space shuttle
- **Shot_08** and **Shot_09**: Adding animals in the background of the scene

I believe that these elements will not only enhance the aesthetics but also infuse greater realism into our film. So, let's start adding them.

Adding set dressing elements to each shot

Using the previous list of set dressing elements, let's start enhancing each of our shots.

Shot_01 – Adding a HUD that turns on to indicate a habitable planet has been found

In this very first shot, we will add a HUD on the flight deck console area. As the camera moves closer to the console area, the HUD will turn on and the text will read that a habitable planet has been found.

We will do this by adding a simple plane and dragging and dropping a pre-made material I made using some simple **Material** nodes, then, using the Sequencer, the HUD will be turned on using keyframe animation. Let's start:

1. Open the **A_New_Beginning** project, then, in the **Cinematics** folder, open **Master_Sequence**.

2. Jump into **Shot_01** and press the *G* key to hide the overlay icons. Then, drag the playhead to frame **119** (the last keyframe).

3. Using the green + icon, add a plane to the scene. Then, set its location, rotation, and size using the following values:

   - **Location: X = 205, Y = 3300, X = 303**

   - **Rotation: X = 70, Y = 0, Z = 180**

   - **Scale: X = 3.5, Y = 3.5, Z = 3.5**

   This will place a plane static mesh in the console area, as seen in *Figure 11.1*:

Figure 11.1: Plane static mesh for HUD_01

4. After setting the previous values, in the Outliner, rename the plane HUD_01.

5. In the **Content Browser | Materials | Hud** folder, drag the **MI_HUD_01** material onto the **HUD_01** plane (ensure it is the material instance and not the master material!):

Figure 11.2: The completed HUD_01 plane

Et voilà – you have just created the first HUD for **Shot_01**!

Note

To create the HUD, I used Adobe Illustrator to create the UI, which was converted into a `.png` file with transparency. The `.png` file was then imported into Unreal Engine as a texture file. In the **Materials** folder, you can open the **M_HUD_01** master material to study how the HUD was constructed.

Now, let's animate the HUD as if it is being switched on by the onboard computer in the opening scene:

1. The current camera setting is slightly out of focus at frame **119**, so to ensure the HUD is in focus, change the **Manual Focus Distance (Focus Settings)** value of **CAM_01** to **400.0** units, as seen in *Figure 11.3*. This will increase the camera's focus range:

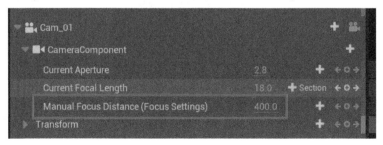

Figure 11.3: Setting Shot_01 Manual Focus distance

2. Now, jump back to frame **0** and drag the **HUD_01** static mesh into the Sequencer.

3. Select the **HUD_01** track. Then, in the **Details** panel, search for the **Actor Hidden In Game** property and click the **Create keyframe** button (diamond icon). This will enable the **Visibility** track in the Sequencer:

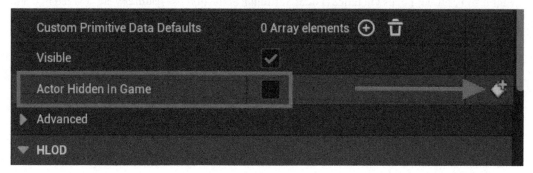

Figure 11.4: Creating a Visibility track using the Actor Hidden In Game keyframe icon

4. Next, in the Sequencer, drop a keyframe at frame **0** on the **Visibility** track. Then, uncheck the **Visible** check mark. The track should turn red, indicating the visibility of **HUD_01** is off.

5. Drag the playhead to frame **60** and click the **Visibility** checkbox, as seen in *Figure 11.5*. The track after frame **60** will turn green, indicating that after frame **60**, **HUD_01** will be visible in the scene:

Figure 11.5: Switching on the Visibility track at frame 60

6. Finally, tap the spacebar to test the animation and save the project.

In this section, you added a HUD to **Shot_01** and created a simple animation of turning it on using the **Visibility** track. In the next section, we will continue with **Shot_02**, with a close-up view of the HUD and creating a rack focus.

Shot_02 – Animating the camera focus settings for a DOF effect

In the previous chapter, you noticed that, whenever you drag a camera into the Sequencer, several tracks will automatically be created: **Camera Cuts Track**, **Camera Current Aperture**, **Current Focal Length**, and **Manual Focus Distance (Focus Settings)**. Some of these features were covered in detail in *Chapter 2* of this book, but before we proceed, let's have a quick refresher on what these properties do, in the context of Unreal Engine:

- **Camera Cuts Track**: This dictates the currently active **Cine Camera** actor during playback in the Sequencer. You can have multiple cameras in your scene, and using this track, you can cut between them.

- **Camera Current Aperture**: This refers to the size of the diaphragm in the camera lens (also known as an f-stop). The wider the aperture, the shallower the DOF, and vice versa; that is, if you would like to achieve a shallow DOF, the aperture of the camera should be set to a smaller f-stop such as *F/1.4*.

- **Current Focal Length**: The focal length of the camera is calculated by measuring the center of the lens and the sensor. Shorter lenses will give a wider **field of view** (**FOV**), and longer lenses will provide a narrower FOV. To get a shallow DOF, longer lenses are preferred – anything between 55 mm and 200 mm.

- **Manual Focus Distance (Focus Settings)**: This controls the focus distance of an actor relative to the camera's current position. The eye dropper (marked in *Figure 11.6*) is a very useful tool for selecting an actor to be focused directly on in the Viewport:

Figure 11.6: Camera Manual focus setting

In **Shot_02**, since the HUD is already in place from our previous shot, let's use the **CAM_02 Manual** focus setting to animate the DOF and draw attention to the text on the HUD:

1. Jump into **Shot_02**. Then, if it is not already open, select the **CAM_02** track, press the *V* key to reveal the **Camera** component tracks, and adjust the following properties:

   - **Camera Current Aperture: 2.1**

   - **Current Focal Length: 18.0**

   - **Manual Focus Distance (Focus Settings): 100**

2. Next, at frame **0**, drop a keyframe for all three properties. This will make the HUD slightly out of focus.

3. Then, jump to frame **60**, change **Manual Focus Distance** to **200**, and add a keyframe.

4. Scrub the playhead, and you'll now see the DOF effect, as seen in *Figure 11.7*:

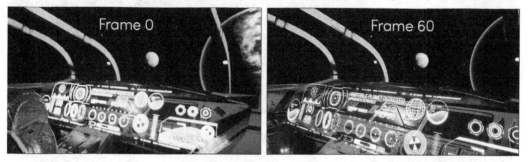

Figure 11.7: Shot_02 DOF effect

Now you have successfully added a DOF effect to the shot, the viewers' eyes are drawn to the text on the HUD.

Shot_03 – Adding cryo-pod smoke effects to mimic a cold environment

For **Shot_03**, which features a **cryo-pod** scene, we can introduce a touch of authenticity by incorporating smoke emerging both from the bottom of the pod and the ceiling. This will create the impression that the space travelers were undergoing a freezing process during their journey. So, jump to **Shot_03**, and then we'll start:

1. In the last chapter, you added a 5-second animation to this shot. If it's not already locked, lock the **Shots** camera using *Shift + C* to play the animation. By locking the camera in the **Camera Cuts** track, you'll be able to view the shot(s) through all the active camera(s). Unlock the camera by using the same keyboard shortcut to move freely in the scene:

Figure 11.8: Locking and unlocking the Shots camera using Shift + C

2. From the **Particles | Cryo_Smoke** folder, drag **P_Cryo_Smoke** into the scene using the following **Location** values: **X = 340, Y = -590**, and **Z = 380**.

Now, you'll have smoke dropping from the ceiling and from under the pod:

Figure 11.9: Shot_03 with the added smoke

This particle originates from the **Starter Content** folder that we installed earlier in the book, and I tweaked it a little to suit our scene. Later in this chapter, I'll introduce you to Unreal Engine's powerful Niagara particle system, but for now, let's move on to the next scene.

Shot_04 – Adding a holographic HUD indicating the space shuttle is launching

In **Shot_04**, we are going to add a second HUD that indicates that the space shuttle is ready to launch. But, in this case, it is not a straightforward replacement – if we replace **HUD_01** in this shot, it will replace the HUD for **Shot_01** and **Shot_02** as well. That sounds tricky. Well, not really. We'll use the same techniques we used for **Shot_01**, deactivating the **HUD_01 Visibility** track and activating **HUD_02**. So, jump into **Shot_04**, and let's go:

1. In the Outliner, duplicate **HUD_01** (using *Ctrl + D*) and rename it HUD_02.

2. With **HUD_02** selected, from the **Material | HUD** folder, drag the **MI_HUD_02** material into the **Element 0** material slot in the Outliner. This will replace the **MI_HUD_01** material with the **MI_HUD_02** material:

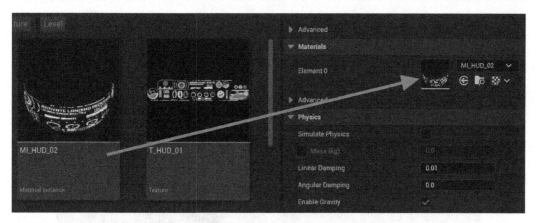

Figure 11.10: Replacing the HUD material

3. Then, drag both **HUD_01** and **HUD_02** into the Sequencer.

4. While both tracks are being selected, in the **Details** panel, click the keyframe button of the **Actor Hidden In Game** property. This will add a keyframe automatically at frame **0** for both tracks in the Sequencer.

5. Next, disable the visibility of **HUD_01** by unchecking the **Visibility** checkbox (as we did back in *Figure 11.5*).

So, in this section, we replaced **HUD_01** with **HUD_02** to show a different message on the HUD by simply activating one track and disabling the other using the **Visibility** track.

Shot_05 – Adding a jet trail to the launching space shuttle

Within the **Outer Space** scene, we will incorporate a jet trail for the departing space shuttle, enhancing its authenticity and realism. In **Shot_05**, let's proceed with this adjustment:

1. In the **Particles | Jet_Trail** folder, drag **P_JetTrail** into the Viewport (this is a particle I made with Unreal Engine's Niagara particle system; I will be covering how to create a Niagara particle later in the chapter).

2. In the last chapter, we added a 5-second animation of the space shuttle launching. Since we will be attaching jet trails to the back of the shuttle, drag the playhead to somewhere between frames **30** and **40**. This will allow the shuttle to be visible for us to add the particle effect to.

3. Unlock the camera by pressing *Shift + C*. Then, select the **Shuttle_FlightMode** static mesh in the Viewport or the Outliner and press *F*. This will bring us closer to the shuttle.

4. With the static mesh still selected, right-click the **Location** property of the shuttle and select **Copy**. Then, in the Outliner, select **P_JetTrail**, right-click its **Location** value, and press *Ctrl + V* to paste the **Location** value of the shuttle. The jet trail will now be positioned at the pivot point of the space shuttle, as seen in *Figure 11.11*:

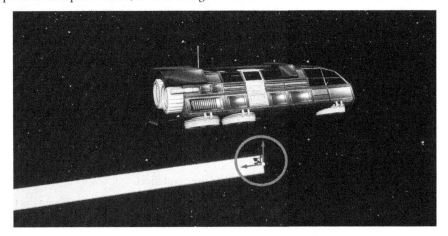

Figure 11.11: Positioning the jet trail to the space shuttle

5. Using the XYZ axis, relocate and rotate the jet trail to the rear end of the space shuttle, closer to one of the exhausts. Then, duplicate the jet trail with *Ctrl + D* and relocate it next to the other exhaust. You can see the result in *Figure 11.12*:

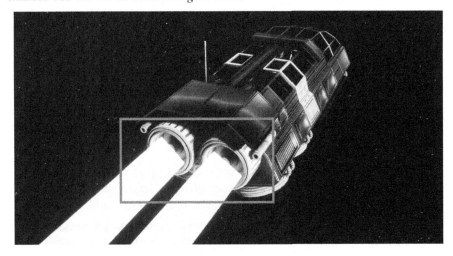

Figure 11.12: Relocated and duplicated jet trails

6. Next, you will need to parent the two jet trails to the space shuttle, to allow the two trails to travel together with the shuttle. So, in the Outliner, drag **P_JetTrail** onto **Shuttle_FlightMode**; if done correctly, you'll see a green check mark:

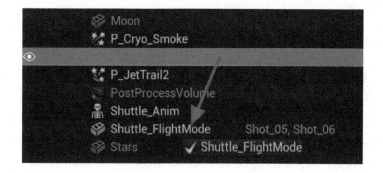

Figure 11.13: Parenting the jet trail to the shuttle

7. Next, repeat *step 6* for **Jet_Trail2**. Both **P_JetTrail** and **P_JetTrail2** will now be the child of **Shuttle_FlightMode**, as seen in *Figure 11.14*:

Figure 11.14: Parent/child relationship

8. Lock the shot camera and play the animation. You'll see the shuttle launching and the jet trail clearly visible!

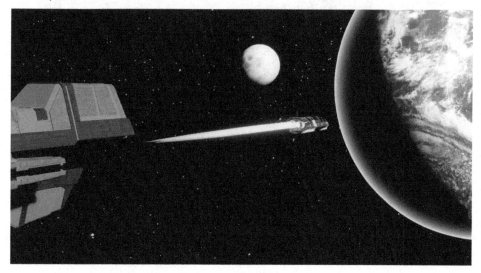

Figure 11.15: A closer view of the space shuttle jet trails

In this section, we added a jet trail to the space shuttle by attaching two instances of a slightly modified Niagara particle system. In the next section, we'll jump into the next sequence to add more enhancements.

Shot_06 – Adding animals in the foreground and a flock of birds flying in the distance

In this shot, we will make the **Planet** scene come to life by adding some animals and maybe a flock of birds. We will need to find these, though. As always, we will browse the Unreal Engine Marketplace, and we're lucky enough to get some realistic-looking animals. Let's begin:

1. Before jumping into **Shot_06**, open the Epic Games Launcher and click the **Marketplace** tab. From here, in the search window, type `animals`, and under **Max Price**, click **Free**.

2. There are two packs available: **African Animals Pack** and **Animal Variety Pack**. Go ahead and add these packs to your project, as we did back in *Chapter 4* with the spaceship interior project:

Figure 11.16: Free animal packs

3. Back in our project, check that we have both packs available in the Content Browser.

4. Navigate to the **AnimalVarietyPack | DeerStagAndDoe | Animations** folder, and double-click on any of the animations to open the Animation Editor. Then, in the **Asset Browser** tab, double-click the list of animations to find a suitable animation for our scene. I've chosen the **ANIM_DeerStag_IdleLookAround** animation:

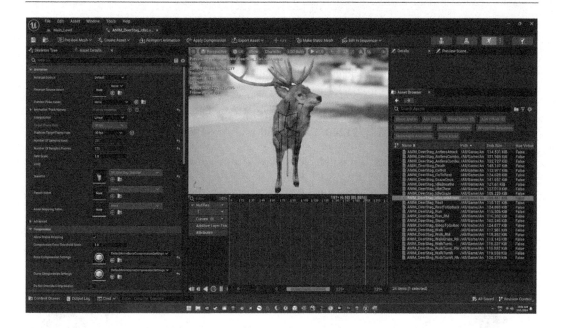

Figure 11.17: Animation Editor and Asset Browser

5. Now, jump into **Shot_06** – this is the space shuttle traversing the landscape scene, a perfect place to place some animals in the foreground and a flock of birds in the background.

6. Double-click on **EXT_Planet** level in the **Levels** panel. Then, from the Content Browser, drag the chosen animation file into the Viewport. Then, drag it into the Sequencer.

7. Next, in the Sequencer, click the **+ Track** button; then, in the search window, type `idle`. From here, scroll down to look for the animation we selected:

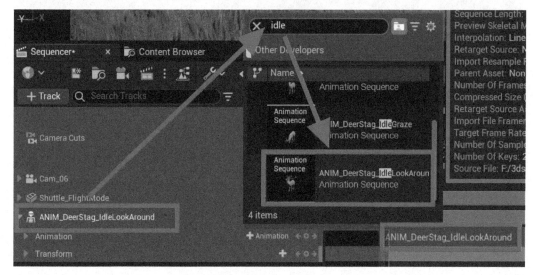

Figure 11.18: Adding the stag animation

8. Go ahead and add a few more deer in the foreground, giving them different animations.

    Now, let's add some birds, which I have placed in the **Particles** folder. These birds were taken from the **Rural Australia** package, which is available on the Marketplace for free too; however, you can use a different bird package if you wish.

9. In the **Particles | Birds** folder, drag **NS_Birds** into the viewport. Then, set **Location** to the following coordinates: **X = -51240**, **Y = -95980**, and **Z = -1900**.

By following these instructions, this will have the birds fly at a low altitude while the space shuttle flies overhead. Super!

Figure 11.19: The completed Shot_06 element

In this section, you added some animated animals in the foreground and birds flying in the distance to add more realism to the scene. In the next section, we will tackle **Shot_07**, the exciting space shuttle landing sequence.

Shot_07 – Slowing down the shot and adding smoke and debris particle effects to the landing space shuttle

In this section, we will add some particle effects to the landing sequence to make it more realistic. But before we do that, we'll have to lengthen **Shot_07** by 2 seconds to slow down the landing sequence and replicate how a shuttle actually touches down.

Slowing down the shot

In the last chapter, I mentioned that 5 seconds for this shot is a tad fast, so let's increase it to a 7-second shot. In this case, we will need to shift **Shot_08** and **Shot_09** by 2 seconds:

1. Jump one level up, to **Seq_03**, where **Shot_07** to **Shot_09** are displayed. Drag the playhead to frame **408**, then nudge **Shot_09** until it snaps to the playhead:

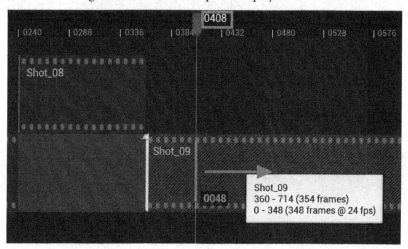

Figure 11.20: Nudging Shot_09 to the right

2. Do the same for **Shot_08**, dragging it so that it snaps with the beginning of **Shot_09**.

3. Now, you'll have room to extend **Shot_07** by dragging the end of **Shot_07** to the beginning of **Shot_08**, as shown in *Figure 11:21*:

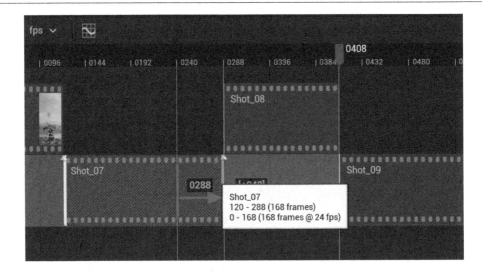

Figure 11.21: Extending Shot_07

You now have an extra 2 seconds in **Shot_07** to play with.

4. Next, make sure to jump back into **Shot_07**, place the playhead at frame **124**, and then drag the last keyframe to the playhead. We have extended the animation to slow down the landing phase of the space shuttle:

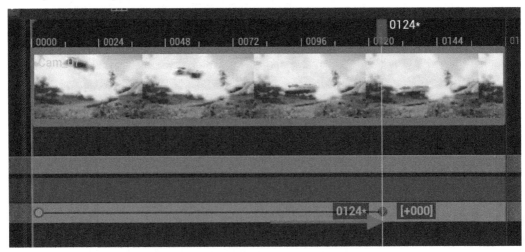

Figure 11.22: Slowing down the landing animation by extending the keyframe

5. Next, to slow down the shot a tad more, let's adjust the play rate of the animation. Right-click on the **Animation** track, select **Properties**, and change the **Play Rate** value to **0.8**. This will slow the animation by 20%:

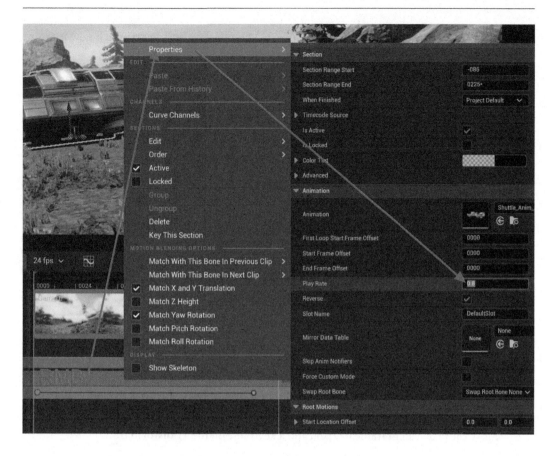

Figure 11.23: Adjusting the play rate of the animation

Hit the spacebar to play the animation – you'll find the timing makes much more sense, with the shuttle slowing down toward the end. In the next section, we will continue working on the landing sequence by adding some particle effects.

Adding particle effects

In this section, we will finally add some particle effects as the shuttle is about to touch down. We will use the particle effects available in the **Particles** folder, but we will need to time it so that the particles become denser as the shuttle comes closer to the ground and dissipate as it touches down. So, let's get started:

1. From the **Particles | Landing_FX** folder, drag the **P_Smoke_C** particle into the viewport.
2. Use the following **Location** coordinates so that it is placed near the landing shuttle: **X** = **-57538**, **Y** = **-70600**, and **Z** = **-4397**.

3. In the **Details** panel, change its **Scale** value to **20** on the *x*, *y*, and *z* axes. You'll now see some smoke in the scene.

4. Next, drag the **P_Smoke_C** actor into the Sequencer, then add a **Transform** track by clicking the **+ Track** button and choosing **Transform**:

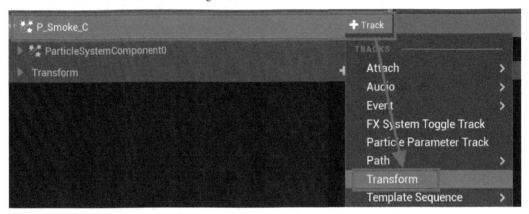

Figure 11.24: Adding a Transform track

For an easy fade-in and fade-out of the smoke that emerges when the shuttle is about to land, we will add the particle close to the ground, underneath the shuttle, and just as it is about to touch down. Using keyframes, we will raise it up above the ground so that it looks as if the smoke is much denser, then, as the shuttle touches down, we will lower the particle back to the ground.

5. Move the playhead to frame **017** and add a keyframe on the **Transform** track.

6. Drag the playhead to frame **063**. Using the *z* axis (blue axis), raise the particle up until the smoke becomes very dense – I used a value of **-3705** on the *z* axis.

7. For the fade-out, jump to frame **143**, copy the keyframe from frame **063**, and paste it at frame **143**. This will copy the same value from frame **143** to **063**.

8. To see what we have achieved so far, click **Play** to test the effect:

Figure 11.25: The three stages of the smoke particles for Shot_07

9. We're not done just yet. Let's add some debris. From the **Particles | Blowing_Particles** folder, drag **NS_Blowing_Particles** into the scene and place it using the following coordinates: **X = -58632, Y = -73064**, and **Z = -2511**.

10. We do not need to animate these particles, so save the project, and we are done with this shot!

Figure 11.26: The final shot of Shot_07

For the next two shots, **Shot_08** and **Shot_09**, I'll leave it to you to add more animals into the scene from the animal packs downloaded earlier in this chapter, to make the planet come alive with a vibrant and diverse ecosystem of creatures, each contributing to the rich tapestry of life.

Before we end this chapter, I'd like to show you how I made the blowing particles we used in **Shot_07**, using Unreal Engine's powerful Niagara particle system.

Creating Niagara particles

Unreal Engine's Niagara particle system is a vital tool for developers and artists, empowering you to create dynamic particle effects with unprecedented customization. Not only does it enhance the visual quality of your scenes by allowing you to craft realistic weather systems or magical spells, but it also optimizes performance, making it essential for creating immersive interactive experiences in various fields, from gaming and visual effects to architectural visualization.

The Niagara particle system consists of three main components:

- **Niagara system**: The Niagara system is a container of one or more Niagara emitters, which in turn consist of modules.

- **Niagara emitters**: Emitters are where the particles are generated, controlling how and when particles are generated, how they look, how they behave, and what happens to them over time. You will have a better understanding as we proceed in this section.

- **Niagara modules**: Modules are individual components within an emitter that control various aspects of particle behavior, such as movement, rendering, collision, and sound:

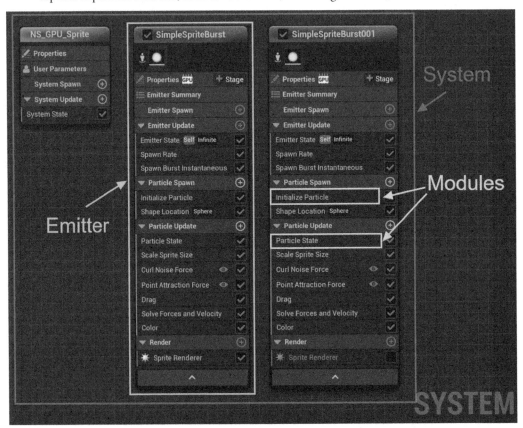

Figure 11.27: The Niagara system

Without jumping into something too complex, let's create a simple particle effect, similar to the one we used in **Shot_07** to mimic the debris as the space shuttle was touching down:

1. In the Content Browser, navigate to the **Particles | Blowing Particles** folder.

2. We already have the **NS_Blowing_Particles** Niagara system that was pre-created for **Shot_07**; however, let's create another from scratch. Right-click in the empty area of the Content Browser, choose **FX**, and click on **Niagara System**:

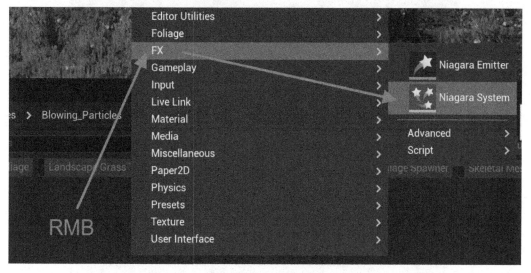

Figure 11.28: Creating a Niagara particle system

3. You'll be presented with a popup and a list of starting points for your particle system. Choose the **New system from selected emitter(s)** option and click **Next**:

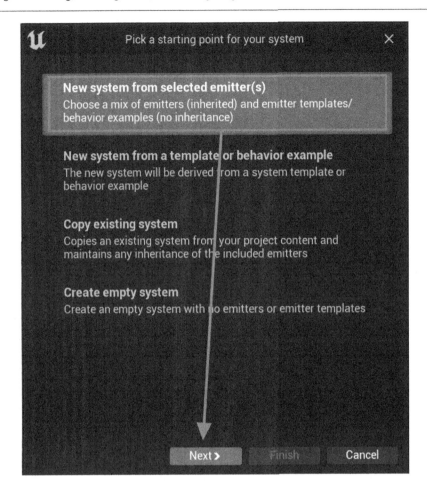

Figure 11.29: Choosing from the list of options

4.   In the next panel, you'll be presented with a choice of pre-made templates; scroll through to check out the various types of particles you can use in your future projects. You will also notice **Dynamic Beam**, which was used as jet trails in **Shot_05** earlier in the chapter. For now, select **Blowing Particles** and click the green + button, then **Finish**:

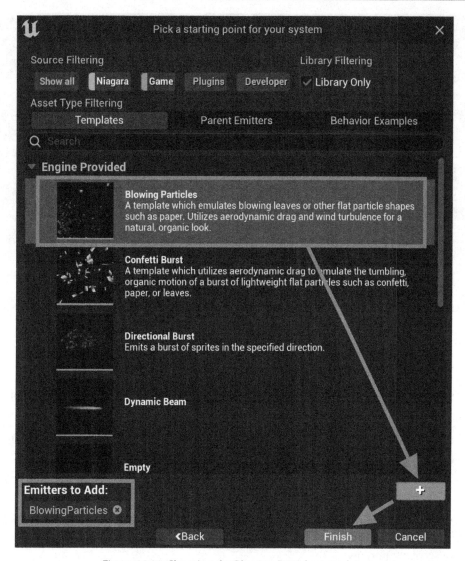

Figure 11.30: Choosing the Blowing Particles template

5. You'll be prompted for a name – let's name it **NS_Blowing_Particles_2**.

6. Double-click on the Niagara system you just created. You'll now be presented with the **Niagara Editor**:

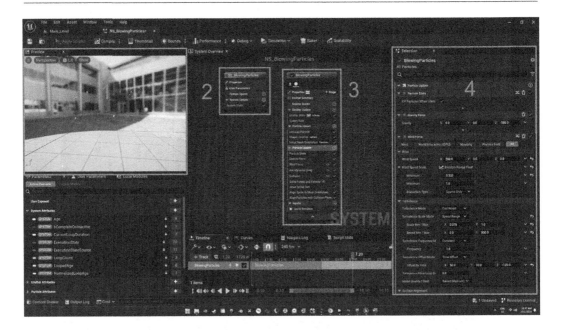

Figure 11.31: The Niagara Editor

This editor may look intimidating, but let's focus on the basic stuff for now:

- The **Preview** window (**1**): In this panel, you'll see a preview of the particles as you work on them.

- Niagara system container (**2**): This manages all the emitters that exist in this system.

- The emitter/s (**3**): This emitter generates and controls the particles. Notice the name associated with this emitter – yes, it was from the list of templates we chose earlier, as shown in *Figure 11.30*.

- The **Selection** panel (**4**): The properties of each of the emitter's modules are listed here. Yes – this looks complicated, but fret not; we are only going to make some slight tweaks to serve our purpose.

- The **Compile** and **Save** buttons (**5**): To save changes, click on **Compile**, then **Save**, before you close the editor.

7. Since we used a template that was close to the kind of debris particles we are after, let's make some minor changes and add it to our scene. In the editor, in the **Blowing Particles** emitter, select the **Spawn Rate** module, and change the **SpawnRate** value from **15** to **50.0**:

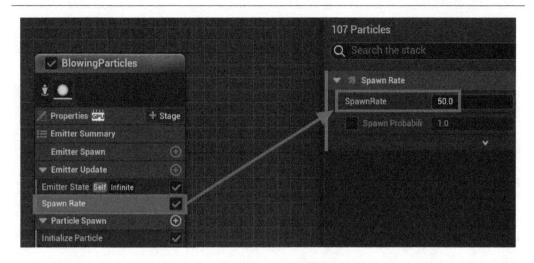

Figure 11.32: Increasing the spawn rate

This will make the debris move a lot faster than before, which is more suitable for our scene.

8. Next, in the **Initialize Particle** module, change the **Color Mode** from **Direct Set** to R**andom Hue/Saturation/Value**. Then change the color of the particles to brownish, as seen in *Figure 11.33*:

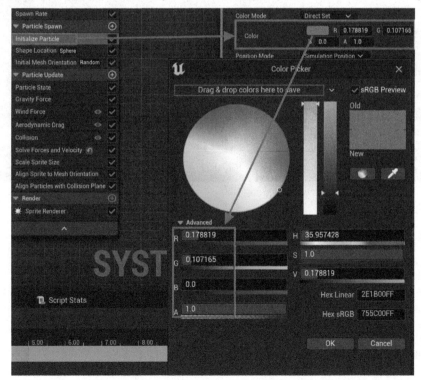

Figure 11.33: Changing the particles' color

9. One last thing – let's increase the wind force so that the particles are scattered in every direction as the shuttle lands. Click the **Wind Force** module and change the **Wind Speed** value on **X**, **Y**, and **Z** to **500**:

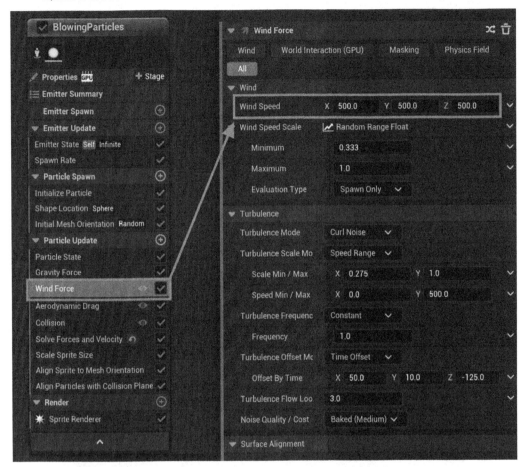

Figure 11.34: Increasing the wind force

10. Compile and save the editor. You can now drag **NS_Blowing_Particles_2** into the scene in **Shot_07** as additional particles if you wish.

We aren't going to go much deeper than this but feel free to reopen the particle system, tweak the settings, and come up with your own unique look or create another with a different template. The more you practice, the more you will learn.

Here is a good resource to start learning Niagara in more detail: `https://docs.unrealengine.com/5.2/en-US/overview-of-niagara-effects-for-unreal-engine/`

Summary

In this chapter, we explored the art of enhancing the visual composition of our shots through set dressing. We introduced essential storytelling elements that were previously absent, delved into a straightforward shot retiming process within the Sequencer, and had the opportunity to create a Niagara particle system while gaining insight into its workflow.

In the upcoming chapter, we will put the finishing touches to our film by establishing the desired ambiance through lighting, incorporating postprocessing elements, and exploring the various rendering choices offered within Unreal Engine.

12
Setting the Mood with Lighting and Adding Post-Processing Effects

Lighting is the most crucial aspect of any film, akin to a painter's brushstrokes on a canvas. Stories have been vividly brought to life throughout the film era using the enchanting palette of colors, masterfully achieved through a dance of natural and artificial lighting. It's the alchemy of light and shadow that imbues each frame with emotion, depth, and a touch of cinematic magic, making it an art form that transcends mere technicality.

Post-processing, on the other hand, refers to the application of various visual effects and adjustments to a scene prior to being rendered. These effects are applied during the final stage of rendering, enhancing the overall look and feel of the film.

So, in this chapter, you're going to learn the fundamentals of lighting in Unreal Engine 5, including lighting terminology, types of lights, and how to set the mood for each of the shots. Then we will further enhance the shots using Post Process effects such as Bloom, Color Grading, and Lens Flare.

In this chapter, we will be covering the following topics:

- Looking for lighting references
- Understanding lighting in Unreal Engine 5
- Setting the mood with lighting
- Adding Post Process effects

Technical requirements

To complete this chapter, you will need the technical requirements detailed in *Chapter 1* and the Unreal project we have been working on throughout the book.

Looking for lighting references

Getting references for lighting a virtual film is paramount for achieving realism and visual coherence in the digital world. References provide a solid foundation for understanding how real-world lighting behaves, helping CG artists replicate those effects convincingly. They guide decisions on color, intensity, direction, and shadows, ensuring that the virtual elements seamlessly blend with the live-action or digital environment.

References can be found on sites such as FILMGRAB (`https://film-grab.com/`), Pinterest (`https://www.pinterest.com/`), ArtStation (`https://www.artstation.com/`), and ShotDeck (`https://shotdeck.com/`).

> **Note**
>
> ShotDeck is a subscription-based service that provides extensive information on each movie shot, including color scheme, aspect ratio, film format, frame size, shot type, lens size, type of composition, lighting type, and so on, which is very useful for filmmakers. There is a 2-week trial with no up-front payment information, which I strongly encourage you to try out.

The genre of our virtual film can be defined as science fiction, adventure, and mystery, so I collected references from some of my favorite movies, such as Jurassic World, Aliens, and Prometheus, and googled beautiful landscapes and placed some of the results in PureRef (`https://www.pureref.com/`), as seen in *Figure 12.1*.

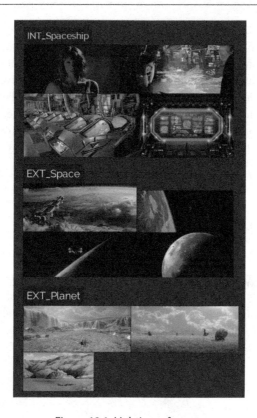

Figure 12.1: Lighting reference

We will refer to these images as a guide once we start lighting our scenes and using the Post Process effects. Feel free to add and use as many reference images as you need.

Now, before we jump back to our project and start adding lights or adjusting lights in our shots, let's understand some of the lighting features available in Unreal Engine 5.

Understanding lighting in Unreal Engine 5

Two of the most exciting features that came with Unreal Engine 5 when it was first launched were Nanite and Lumen. We covered the significance of the Nanite features back in *Chapter 5* when you were learning about Quixel Megascans and Quixel Bridge, but we have not really touched on Lumen.

Lumen is a global illumination system that was introduced in Unreal Engine 5. It is designed to provide dynamic and realistic lighting in real time, making it easier for developers to create visually stunning and immersive environments. Lumen in Unreal Engine represents a significant advancement in real-time global illumination, offering dynamic and realistic lighting without the need for pre-baked data. This enhances the overall visual quality and allows developers to create more immersive and visually appealing virtual environments.

In the realm of film production, particularly in the context of a fully computer-generated movie like ours, the process that demands the most computational power is undoubtedly lighting. 3D artists need to exercise great caution when incorporating lights into their scenes because each additional light contributes to a heightened computational "expense." This cumulative cost becomes significant when it's time to convert the movie into a final output file, a step referred to as **rendering**. Thanks to Lumen, the anxiety surrounding the idea of saturating a scene with numerous lights and enduring a time-consuming iterative process is now a thing of the past. When lights are in dynamic mode (which is the default setting), you have the freedom to adjust their properties to your heart's content.

In the coming sections, you'll learn lighting terminology and the types of lights and properties available in Unreal Engine.

Lighting terminology

Using *Figure 12.2*, let's first understand the terminology around lighting:

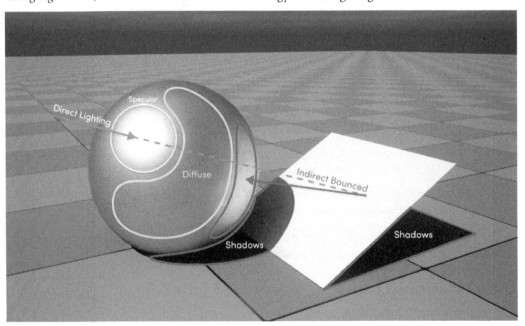

Figure 12.2: Lighting terminology

Here are the terms:

- **Direct lighting**: Light that falls onto a surface without any interference. The light travels directly to the surface and that surface receives the full color spectrum of light, usually producing hard-edge shadows.

- **Specular**: A specular highlight is the bright spot of light that appears on shiny objects when illuminated.

- **Diffused lighting** (or **Diffused reflection**): The direct illumination of an object by an even amount of light interacting with a light-scattering surface. Diffused light is not directly emitted from a primary source of light.

- **Indirect (bounced) lighting**: Unlike direct lighting, which shines light directly on an object or area, indirect lighting is designed to bounce or diffuse light off surfaces, such as walls, ceilings, or floors, to create a more subtle and uniform illumination. Indirect light will also be affected by the color of the surfaces the light is bouncing off and that color will scatter onto surrounding surfaces.

- **Shadows**: The absence of light when light is blocked by an object. In Unreal Engine, shadows are created using light's perspective and a snapshot of a mesh actor's position. The light information is projected onto another mesh actor/surface on the opposite side of the obstruction.

Rendering and shading terms

Now, let's look at some key terms needed when creating realistic and visually appealing images and animations:

- **Global Illumination** (**GI**): A rendering technique that simulates the way light interacts with surfaces and objects in a 3D scene, accounting for the complex interplay of direct and indirect lighting to create more realistic and natural-looking images. This is also known as indirect illumination.

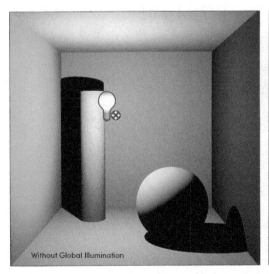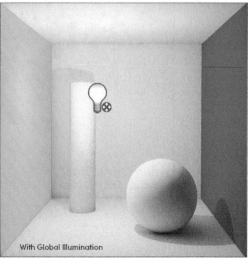

Figure 12.3: With and without global illumination (Lumen)

- **Ambient occlusion**: A shading and rendering technique that simulates the soft, subtle shadows that occur in areas where objects or surfaces are close together, obstructing some of the ambient (indirect) light. It adds depth and realism to 3D scenes by darkening crevices and corners, enhancing the perception of depth and contact between objects.

- **Albedo**: An expression of the ability of surfaces to reflect light from the sun. Light-colored surfaces return a large part of sunrays back to the atmosphere (high albedo), whereas dark surfaces absorb the rays from the sun (low albedo). The albedo/base color of a material on an object will directly affect how much light, and what color, gets reflected back onto surfaces.

Different light types

Unreal Engine 5 offers various light types. Each serves a certain purpose. Let's find out what they are and what they do:

- **Directional Light (Sun)**: Simulates light from a distant source, like the Sun, with parallel rays. *Directional Light casts light based on its rotation, angle, and direction only. The light's not affected by its translation or position.*

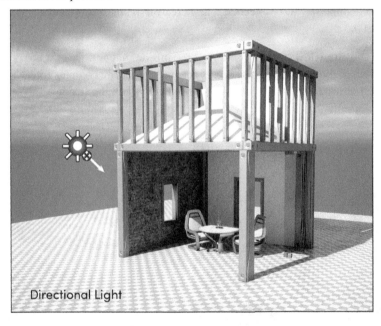

Figure 12.4: Directional Light

- **Point Light (Omni)**: Working much like a real-world lightbulb, this is omnidirectional lighting that emits light from a single source in all directions. *Its translation or position will affect the light, but the angle or rotation will not affect the light.*

Figure 12.5: Point Light

- **Spot Light**: This emits light in a specified cone shape and can be used to focus light on specific areas, creating dramatic effects or simulating sources such as flashlights or stage lights. *Its translation, rotation, and position will affect the light.*

Figure 12.6: Spot Light

- **Rect (Rectangular) Light**: This is a square-ish-looking region/shape of light that emits light from a rectangular plane with a defined width and height. It is useful for simulating rectangular areas such as televisions or monitor screens, overhead light fixtures, or a studio softbox. *Its translation, rotation, and position will affect the light.*

Figure 12.7: Rect Light

- **Sky Light**: This captures the current scene's lighting illumination and uses it to light the scene, creating ambient lighting and global illumination effects. You can think of it more as a "collector" of the environment illumination, which is reflected onto the objects in the scene.

Figure 12.8: Sky Light

- **HDRI** (standing for **High Dynamic Range Imagery**) **Backdrop**: Essentially a 360-degree panoramic image, captured using specialized equipment able to capture a wide range of exposure levels and color. The image is then wrapped onto a spherical object and used as a light source in a 3D scene. Applying the HDRI Backdrop to the scene makes it look more lifelike and convincing. The HDRI Backdrop is enabled through the **HDRI Backdrop** plugin in the **Plugins** editor.

Figure 12.9: The scene lit with HDRI Backdrop only

- **Sky Atmosphere**: This component employs a physics-based approach to render skies and atmospheres. Its versatility extends to crafting Earth-like atmospheres, complete with dynamic time-of-day transitions, including picturesque sunrises and sunsets. Equally, it allows for the creation of unconventional, otherworldly atmospheres.

Figure 12.10: Sky Atmosphere

- **Exponential Height Fog**: A versatile tool used for simulating realistic atmospheric effects in your virtual environments. It allows developers and artists to create the illusion of fog, haze, or other volumetric effects that add depth and atmosphere to a scene.

Figure 12.11: Exponential Height Fog

- **Volumetric Cloud**: A feature that allows developers to create realistic, three-dimensional cloudscapes within their virtual environments. These volumetric clouds are not just flat, 2D textures but actual 3D cloud volumes that interact with lighting and the environment, adding depth and authenticity to the sky in Unreal Engine.

Figure 12.12: Volumetric Cloud

Lighting tools

Unreal Engine also offers lighting tools, such as the **Env. (Environment) Light Mixer** and the **Light Mixer** for the fast and easy setup and manipulation of lights in any given scene. Let's have a closer look at both of them:

- **Env. Light Mixer** is a dockable editor window, accessible through the **Window | Env. Light Mixer** menu. This panel allows for the rapid addition of environment lights such as **Directional Light**, **Sky Light**, **Sky Atmosphere**, **Exponential Height Fog**, and **Volumetric Sky**, speeding up your workflow, as all of the properties can be found in one location.

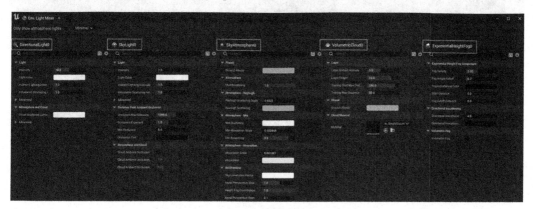

Figure 12.13: The Env. Light Mixer interface

More detailed information on **Env. Light Mixer** can be found here: `https://docs.unrealengine.com/5.2/en-US/environment-light-mixer-in-unreal-engine/`.

- **Light Mixer**, accessible through the **Window | Light Mixer** menu, offers a specialized interface designed to cater to the artistic needs of lighting. This interface empowers artists to individually manage lights, adjust their visibility, and easily access essential settings to achieve their desired visual results. Lights can also be organized into collections, making it more convenient to work with groups of lights.

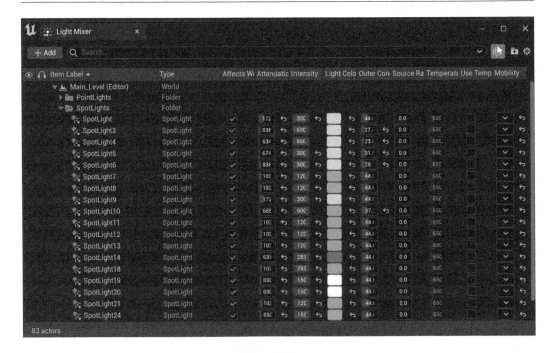

Figure 12.14: The Light Mixer interface

More detailed information on **Light Mixer** can be found here: `https://docs.unrealengine.com/5.2/en-US/using-the-light-mixer-in-unreal-engine/`.

To summarize, the Light Mixer primarily concentrates on overseeing standard light types and functions in conjunction with the Environment Light Mixer. The Environment Light Mixer focuses on environmental lighting elements such as the sky, clouds, atmospheric lights, and skylights.

Common lighting properties

Now that you have been introduced to the types of lights and the tools you can use to augment their properties, let us look at the common lighting properties that you will be augmenting:

- **Intensity**: This property determines how bright a light source is. You can adjust the intensity to make lights appear dim or extremely bright.

- **Light Color**: Here, you can set the color of the light, which plays a crucial role in establishing the mood and atmosphere of the scene.

- **Attenuation Radius**: This property controls how a light's brightness diminishes with distance from the source and affects how far the light can reach.

- **Source Radius**: For area lights, such as rectangular lights, the **Source Radius** property controls the size of the light source, which impacts the softness or hardness of shadows it produces.

- **Source Length**: This refers to the shape of the light. By changing its shape (making it longer), a point light can be turned into a tube light.

- **Temperature**: Adjusting the color temperature can simulate various types of light, from warm incandescent to cool fluorescent.

- **Affects World**: This switch disables the light and it will not appear during rendering.

- **Shadows**: You can enable or disable shadows for a light source and adjust shadow quality, softness, and bias.

- **Indirect Light Intensity**: This controls the strength or brightness of indirect lighting in a scene.

- **Volumetric Light Scattering Intensity**: This controls the amount of light scattered through volumes such as fog and clouds.

- **IES Profiles**: These are used to accurately simulate real-world lighting conditions. They can be applied to light sources such as point lights or spotlights, allowing for the precise recreation of the actual lighting behavior of specific real-world light fixtures. By utilizing **Illuminating Engineering Society** (**IES**) profiles, you can achieve highly realistic and authentic lighting effects in your virtual scenes.

In this section, you delved into lighting terminology and gained a deeper comprehension of the available light types in Unreal Engine and their respective functions. You also explored two essential lighting tools, namely, the Environment Light Mixer and Light Mixer, which facilitate the swift addition or removal of lights and fine-tuning of their attributes. Furthermore, you saw a comprehensive breakdown of the typical light properties you'll encounter when making adjustments in Unreal Engine.

In the next section, we will return to our project and begin establishing the desired ambiance through lighting.

Setting the mood with lighting

Now that you have a better understanding of lighting terminology, features, and types, let's jump back into our virtual film and set the lighting using the reference images we collected in the previous section as a guide. As most of the lighting is already set up from the project files we downloaded from the Unreal Engine Marketplace, we will add and adjust the properties of a few lights in our existing shots.

Illuminating the spaceship console area

For the spaceship console area, we will add a Rect Light. As the HUD turns on at frame 60, the console area should be lit up as if the HUD is illuminating it, adding a bit more subtle realism to the scene. Let's get started:

1. Open the A_New_Beginning project, load the Master Sequence, and jump into **Shot_01**.

2. Delete **PointLight56** (it's the light in the middle of the flight deck).

3. Using the **+ Place Actor** button, click **Lights | Add Rect Light**. Then position the light using the following coordinates:

   - **Location**: X = 210, Y = 3270, Z = 400

   - **Rotation**: X = 180, Y = -90, Z = 180

4. Next, change the **Light** properties to the following:

   - **Mobility**: **Moveable**

   - **Intensity**: **5.0**

   - **Attenuation Radius**: **500**

   - **Source Height**: **150**

   - **Light color**: **R = 0, G = 0.3, B = 0.3**

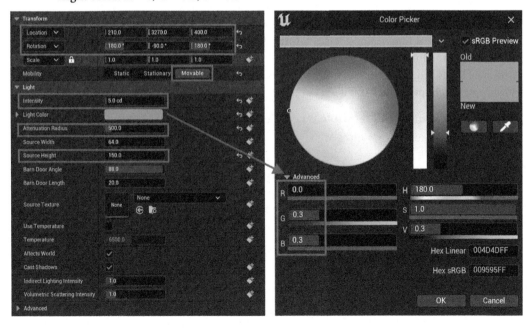

Figure 12.15: Adding the Rect Light to Shot_01

This will place a Rect Light in the console area, but we only need it to illuminate after frame 60. Let's work on that now.

5. Drag **Rect Light** into **Sequencer**. You'll be presented with two **Rect Light** properties, **Intensity** and **Light Color**. We are going to add keyframes to **Intensity**. So, at frame 59, add a keyframe by pressing *S*, and set **Intensity** to **0**. Then, at frame 60, add another keyframe and change **Intensity** to **5**, as shown in *Figure 12.16*:

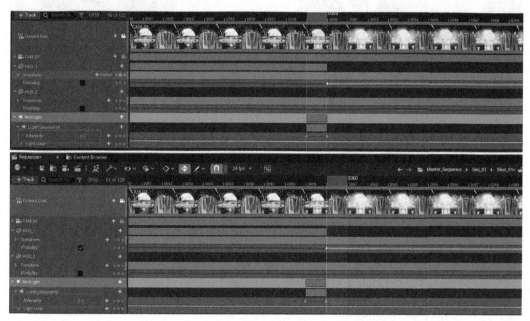

Figure 12.16: Keyframing Rect Light Intensity

6. Hit **Play** to test the sequence. At this point, you may want to adjust the intensity to suit the scene. Once you're happy, save the project.

Figure 12.17: The completed Shot_01 with Rect Light

Since we added a keyframe at frame 59 with **Intensity** of **0** and, in the next frame, frame 60, changed **Intensity** to **5**, it looks as if the HUD is casting a teal-colored light in the console area when it switches on. Why did I choose a Rect Light instead of any other lights? The Rect Light provides even illumination for large areas, and adjusting **Source Height** to **150** units makes it into a rectangle-shaped light that covers almost the whole dashboard.

In the next section, we will skip **Shot_02** and jump to **Shot_03**, where we will change the Point Lights color to indicate that the Cryo-Pods have been activated.

Changing the Cryo-Pod area light color

In **Shot_03**, there are several Point Lights in the scene, which are currently emitting a red color. To indicate that the Cryo-Pods have been activated, we will use **Sequencer** to turn their color from red to green. Let's begin:

1. Jump into **Shot_03**. Here, we have a 5-second shot with the camera being animated. Also, if you remember back in *Chapter 11*, we added smoke effects to the scene.

2. From the **Lights** folder in the Outliner, select and drag the following lights into **Sequencer**: **PointLight9**, **PointLight15**, **PointLight28**, **PointLight29**, **PointLight30**, **PointLight33**, **PointLight38**, and **PointLight40**.

Once done, you'll have a long list of all the Point Lights with **Intensity** and **Light Color** exposed in **Sequencer**.

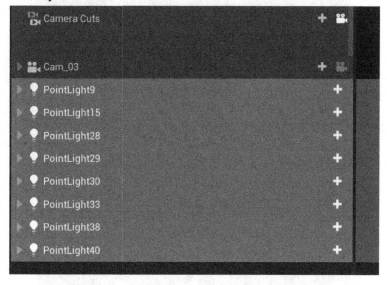

Figure 12.18: All Point Lights added to Sequencer

3. Drag the playhead to frame 60. In the **Details** panel, click the create keyframe icon for the **Light Color** property.

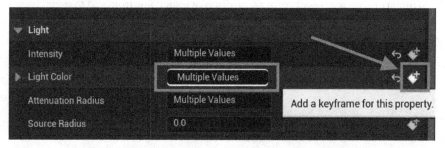

Figure 12.19: Creating a Light Color keyframe for all the Point Lights

Since all the Point Lights are selected, this action will add a keyframe to *all* Point Lights in **Sequencer**. **Light Color** will indicate **Multiple Values** due to more than one light being selected in **Sequencer**.

4. Now drag the playhead to frame 61. Then click once in the **Light Color** swatch, change the color to green (**R = 0.0, G = 1.0, B = 0.2**), and press **OK**. This will both change the color of all the Point Lights to green and create keyframes for all selected lights at the same time.

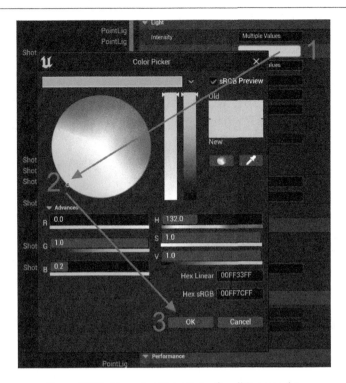

Figure 12.20: Changing Light Color for all Point Lights

In **Sequencer**, you will now notice a transition of light color from red to green from frame 60 to frame 61, as shown in *Figure 12.21*:

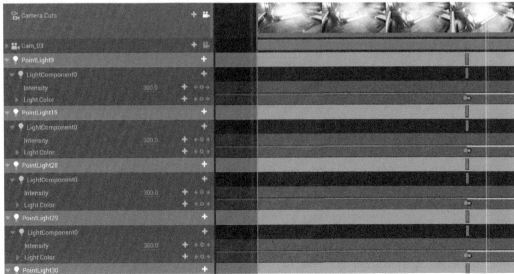

Figure 12.21: Color transition from red to green for selected Point Lights

5.   Use **Collapse All Nodes** from the **View Option** menu to collapse all the tracks at once, so our **Sequencer** view goes back to normal.

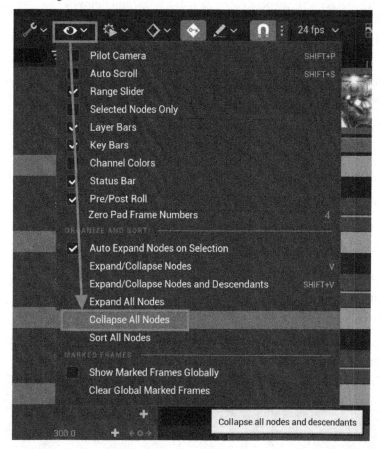

Figure 12.22: Using the Collapse All Nodes function

6.   Now play the sequence to view the Point Lights changing color halfway through the shot, and then save your project again.

In this section, you successfully animated the change of light color on multiple Point Lights in the scene by selecting all the Point Lights in **Sequencer** and adding keyframes using a single click! In the next section, we will adjust the atmospherics on the planet so that all the shots are evenly lit.

Adjusting the planet atmospherics

According to the reference screenshot in *Figure 12.1*, it's a bright and sunny day and the planet has green foliage with blue skies and fluffy clouds in the distance. As we already have most of these elements in the shots, we will adjust Directional Light so that each shot casts the right amount of light intensity and the shadows do not obscure the elements in the shots.

We will do this by adjusting the direction, rotation, and angle of the light. And since there is only one Directional Light, we are going to need to keyframe the Directional Light for each of the shots:

1. First, double-click on **Seq_03** and jump into **Shot_06**.

2. Ensure that we are working in the correct level by double-clicking **EXT_Planet** in the **Levels** panel.

3. In the **Details** panel, adjust **DirectionalLight** with the following properties:

    - **Location**: X = 0, Y = 0, Z = 0
    - **Rotation**: X = 60, Y = -40, Z = -160
    - **Mobility**: **Moveable**
    - **Intensity**: **4.0 lux**

    This will cast a nice early morning sunlight in our environment, so we can clearly see the animals in the foreground, the space shuttle flying overhead, and the birds flying in the distance.

4. Now drag **DirectionalLight** into **Sequencer**. Then click the **+ Track** button on the **DirectionalLight** track and choose **LightComponent0**.

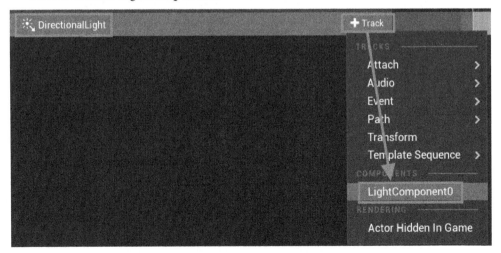

Figure 12.23: Adding the LightComponent0 property

5. Next, click the **+ Track** button on the **LightComponent0** track and choose **Transform**.

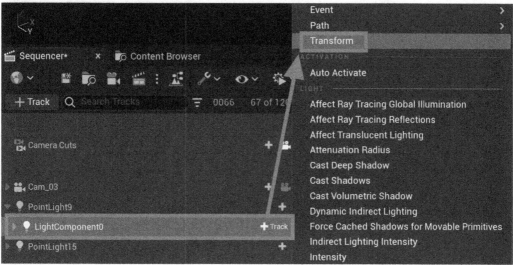

Figure 12.24: Adding the Transform property for DirectionalLight

This will add the **Transform** property to **DirectionalLight**.

6. Finally, we will add a keyframe to the rotation value, so the **DirectionalLight** rotation values are permanently fixed for this shot. So, ensure the playhead is at the beginning of the sequence and click the keyframe button on the **Transform** track to complete the process.

Figure 12.25: Adding the Transform keyframe at the beginning of the sequence

Here is what our environment looks like now:

Figure 12.26: DirectionalLight setup for Shot_06

7. You are going to continue the same process for the rest of the shots. We will keep the Directional Light's **Location**, **Mobility**, and **Intensity** values the same, but change its **Rotational** value like so:

    • For **Shot_07**, set these **Rotational** values: **X = 60**, **Y = -60**, **Z = -10**

    • For **Shot_08**, set these **Rotational** values: **X = 60**, **Y = -35**, **Z = -170**

    • For **Shot_09**, set these **Rotational** values: **X = -83**, **Y = -35**, **Z = 45**

And with that, our lighting setup for all nine shots are complete!

In the next section, we will add post-processing effects to enhance the look of our film. What are Post Process effects? Let's find out.

Adding Post Process effects

Post Process effects in Unreal Engine refer to a set of techniques and visual enhancements applied after the 3D scene has been generated. These effects are used to improve the overall visual quality and create specific artistic or realistic looks for the final output. Post Process effects are a key element of the graphics pipeline in Unreal Engine and play a significant role in shaping the visual style and mood of a project.

Figure 12.27: The opening scene with Post Process effects applied

In *Chapter 4*, we used the **Exposure** feature in the **Post Process Volume** (**PPV**) to lock the exposure of the scene. Now, in this section, we will explore the rest of the features in detail. As a quick overview, here are some common Post Process effects in Unreal Engine:

- **Bloom**: Creates a soft, glowing effect around bright objects, simulating the way light spreads and flares in the real world.

- **Exposure**: Typically refers to the controls and parameters that allow you to adjust the exposure and overall brightness of your scene.

- **Chromatic Aberration**: Simulates the dispersion of light, which results in color fringing at the edges of objects.

- **Dirt Mask**: A texture-based feature that enhances the **Bloom** effect in designated screen areas. It's handy for crafting a distinct camera lens appearance, complete with its flaws, or simulating the presence of dirt and dust on the lens.

- **Lens Flare**: Simulates the scattering of light when viewing bright objects due to imperfections in the camera lens.

- **Image Effects / Vignette**: Darkens the edges of the screen to draw focus toward the center and create a more cinematic effect.

- **Depth of Field**: Blurs objects in the foreground or background to simulate the focus of a camera, enhancing the cinematic quality of the scene.

- **Color Grading**: Adjusts the colors and tones of the image to achieve a particular mood or style. This can involve changes in contrast, saturation, brightness, and more.

- **Film**: This includes properties such as **Slope**, **Toe**, **Shoulder Black Clip**, and **White Clip** that meet the **Academy Color Encoding System** (**ACES**) for television and film. These properties ensure that consistent color is preserved across multiple formats and displays while also future-proofing the source material to not have to adjust it for each new medium that comes along.

> **Note**
>
> ACES is a professional color management and image interchange system developed by the Academy of Motion Picture Arts and Sciences. It was created to standardize and improve the way digital and film content is created, distributed, and archived in the motion picture and television industry. ACES is designed to ensure consistent and high-quality color reproduction across different devices and workflows.

- **Global Illumination**: The PPV settings for **Global Illumination** enable you to select the type of dynamic global illumination to use and include **Lumen**, **Screen Space (Beta)**, and **Stand Alone Screenspace (Deprecated)**. For our project, we will stick to **Lumen**.

- **Reflections**: This enables you to select from types of dynamic reflections such as **Lumen**, **Screen Space**, or **Stand Alone Screenspace (Deprecated)**. Again, we will stick to **Lumen**.

- **Film Grain**: Adds a grainy texture to the image to achieve a film-like or vintage look.

- **Screen Space Reflections**: Simulates reflections on surfaces based on what is visible on the screen.

- **Anti-Aliasing**: Reduces jagged edges (or *jaggies*) to create smoother, more visually pleasing edges on objects.

- **HDR Tonemapping**: Adjusts the dynamic range of the image to display a wide range of lighting conditions more accurately.

- **Motion Blur**: Blurs moving objects to capture the sense of motion, such as fast camera pans or moving characters.

These post-processing effects, among others, are essential tools in Unreal Engine, allowing you to fine-tune the visual quality and aesthetics of your projects, whether you want to achieve a realistic, cinematic, or stylized look.

We are not going to use every Post Process effect as some of them won't give us the look we're going for. We are going to be experimenting mainly with **Bloom**, **Chromatic Aberration**, **Dirt Mask**, **Lens Flare**, **Vignette**, **Color Grading**, **Film**, and **Film Grain**. Effects such as **Depth of Field** are better off being controlled in the **Camera** settings, and **Anti-Aliasing** will be covered in *Chapter 13*.

> **Note**
>
> Before we proceed though, a word of caution, if not done correctly, adding these effects could be disastrous to the look of your production. I suggest we use them sparingly, enough to add the right amount of aesthetics to tell our story.

Now that we have an idea of the effects that are available at our disposal, let's jump back into our project and start adding some of them to the shots. To add the previously described effects to our shot, we will use the PPV. The PPV is a special type of volume that can be added to a level. Multiple PPVs can be added to define the look of a specific area, but in our case, we will use a single PPV to achieve the results needed.

The **INT_Spaceship** and **EXT_Space** sequences share the same PPV while the **EXT_Planet** sequence has one of its own, located in the `Environment` folder. Be sure to select the appropriate level in the **Levels** panel to have access to the respective PPV.

Here's how to access the effects:

1. Open the `A_New_Begnning` project and load the Master Sequence. Then, in the **Levels** panel, double-click on the **EXT_Space** level to access the PPV for both levels.

2. In the Outliner's search window, type `Post`. This will single out the PPV that is currently in the level. Select the PPV to reveal the extensive list of categories in the **Details** panel, as shown in *Figure 12.28*:

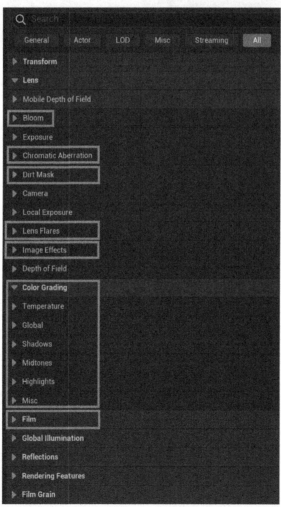

Figure 12.28: The categories of the Post Process effects

Use **Collapse All Categories** to have a compressed view of all the categories so they can be accessed swiftly.

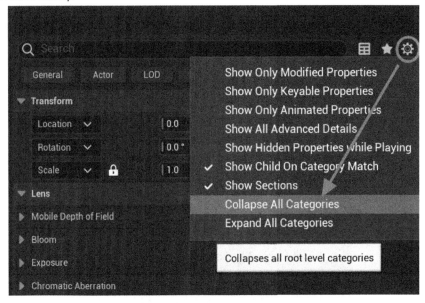

Figure 12.29: Collapsing the categories

Now that we have the PPV setup, let's start adding the effects.

Adding the Bloom effect

Bloom enhances the lighting in your scene by creating a soft, glowing effect around bright objects, simulating the way light can bleed into the camera lens. It creates haloing, which produces glow effects from bright objects such as light and shiny materials, which is perfect for our sci-fi adventure mystery film. Let's add this to our scene:

1. Jump into **Shot_01**, access the Post Process effects (as shown in *Figure 12.28*), and locate **Bloom** in the **Lens** category.

2. From here, enable the **Method** check mark and choose **Standard** from the drop-down menu. Then enable **Intensity** and set it to **2.0**.

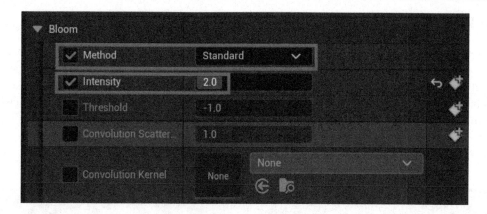

Figure 12.30: Setting the Bloom effect

Here is a before and after of the results:

Figure 12.31: The Bloom effect before and after

3. Scrub the playhead to check **Bloom Intensity** for the other **INT_Spaceship** shots (**Shot_02**, **Shot_03**, and **Shot_04**). If you find their **Bloom** settings overwhelming, you can jump into individual shots and keyframe the properties in **Sequencer**, as you did for the Directional Light in the previous section.

> **Note**
>
> As a quick reminder, all the properties in the PPV that have a diamond shape with a + icon are keyframeable. Use this feature to quickly add animation to the properties in **Sequencer**.

Adding the Chromatic Aberration effect

Chromatic aberration (also known as color fringing or chromatic distortion) is an optical phenomenon that occurs when a lens or other optical system fails to focus all colors of light on the same point. It results in a distortion of colors and can be seen as fringes of color along the edges and boundaries of objects in an image. Although filmmakers try to avoid this at all costs, it has become somewhat artistic in recent years. Let's add the effect:

1. In **Shot_01**, locate the **Chromatic Aberration** effect in the list of Post Process effects.

2. Enable **Intensity** and set it to **1.0**, then enable **Start Offset** and set it to **0.2**.

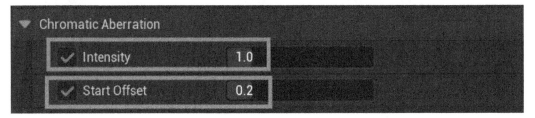

Figure 12.32: Setting the Chromatic Aberration effect

Intensity is the amount of aberration to simulate an artifact of a real-world lens. **Start Offset** sets the effectiveness range of the effect. Here is the result:

Figure 12.33: The Chromatic Aberration effect before and after

Adding the Dirt Mask effect

Dirt Mask is a texture-driven effect that can be useful to create a specific look for camera lens imperfections, something such as scratches and dust on the lens. Here's how to view the **Dirt Mask** effect:

1. In **Shot_03**, drag the playhead to frame 50.

2. Enable the **Dirt Mask Texture** check mark.

3. In the dropdown, search for `T_ScreenDirt02_w`.

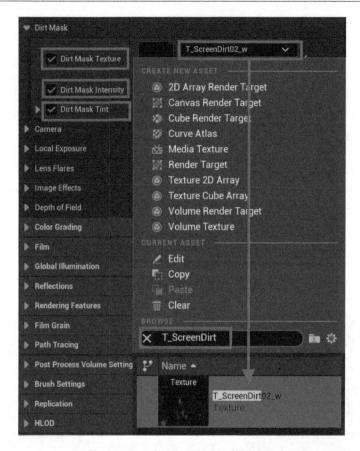

Figure 12.34: Setting Dirt Mask Texture

4. Enable **Dirt Mask Intensity** and set it to **200** (this is just to showcase the effect; in reality, you may want to tone it down a little) and use **Dirt Mask Tint** to adjust the color of the effect you are going for.

    Here is the result:

Figure 12.35: The Dirt Mask effect before and after

Adding the Lens Flares effect

Lens flare is an optical phenomenon that occurs in photography and cinematography, as well as in the human eye. It appears as streaks, circles, or polygons of light that can appear in an image or video when bright light sources, such as the sun or artificial lights, are in or near the camera's field of view. Lens flare is caused by the scattering, reflection, and refraction of light within the lens system or camera.

Here's how to add the **Lens Flares** effect:

1. Drag the playhead to frame 517 and then locate the **Lens Flares** options.

2. Enable **Intensity** and set it to **30**. Then enable and set **BokehSize** to **10** or as needed. The larger **BokehSize**, the larger the bokeh on the screen.

    Bokeh is a term used in photography and cinematography to describe the aesthetic quality of the out-of-focus areas in an image, typically in the background or foreground. It refers to the way the lens renders the points of light that are not in focus, creating a soft, blurry, and often pleasing background or foreground. Bokeh is characterized by smooth, circular, or polygonal shapes formed by blurred highlights and points of light.

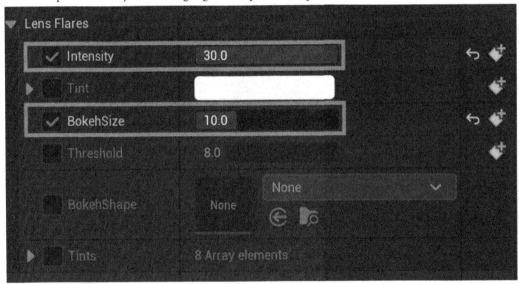

Figure 12.36: Setting the Lens Flares effect

The **Lens Flares** effect will be obvious if the camera is looking right at a light source. That is not the case in any of our shots, so it would not make much sense to have it switched on. However, we explored this option just so you could see it.

Figure 12.37: The Lens Flares effect before and after

Adding the Vignette effect

A **Vignette** effect is a photographic or artistic technique that involves darkening or fading the edges of an image, drawing the viewer's attention toward the central subject or focal point and creating a sense of depth. This effect is characterized by a gradual transition from the center of the image, which remains relatively well-lit or unaltered, to the outer edges, which become progressively darker or blurred.

To access this Post Process effect, in the **Image Effects** category, enable the **Vignette** effect and adjust the **Vignette Intensity** value as needed.

Figure 12.38: Setting the Vignette effect

Here is the result of using **Intensity** of **0.8** – the higher the number, the darker the edges of the screen (and vice versa):

Figure 12.39: The Vignette effect before and after

Adding the Color Grading effect

Color grading is the post-production process of adjusting and enhancing the colors and tones of a film to achieve a specific visual style, mood, or atmosphere. It plays a crucial role in shaping the final look and feel of a movie, contributing to the storytelling and emotional impact of the film.

Color grading is a process of creative choices, as it can be used to enhance visual storytelling. It also involves psychology, as certain colors can evoke certain emotions, as shown in *Figure 12.40*.

Figure 12.40: Establishing the look and feel of a film

> **Note**
>
> For an interesting look at how color is used in film, read this article: `https://www.studiobinder.com/blog/how-to-use-color-in-film-50-examples-of-movie-color-palettes/`.

In Unreal Engine, the **Color Grading** effect is made up of several main categories, including **Temperature**, **Global**, **Shadows**, **Midtones**, **Highlights**, and **Misc**:

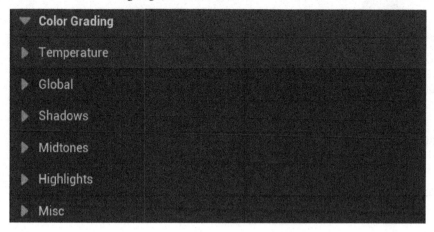

Figure 12.41: The Color Grading categories

I'll break down the main categories so you can understand their functions.

Temperature

The **Temperature** effects consist of the following:

- **Temperature Type**: The two types here are as follows:

  - **White Balance**: This ensures that white objects appear white and that other colors are rendered correctly, without any unwanted color cast.

  - **Color Temperature**: This sets the warmth or coolness of color values and is calculated in degrees Kelvin.

- **Temp:** Enable this to set the color temperature. Color temperature is a characteristic of visible light that describes the color appearance of a light source, typically measured in units called **Kelvin** (**K**). It is a way to quantify the color of light, particularly in relation to how *warm* or *cool* it appears to the human eye. Color temperature is a key concept in lighting and photography, as it helps define the color quality of a light source and how it can affect the appearance of objects and scenes. Typically, daylight is equivalent to 6,500 Kelvin, as shown in *Figure 12.42*:

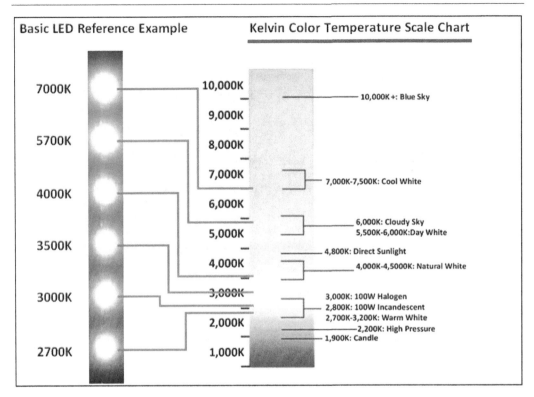

Figure 12.42: Color temperature chart

- **Tint**: Depending on the previous **Temp** settings, **Tint** will adjust the temperature value further by adjusting the cyan and magenta color ranges.

Figure 12.43: The Temperature effects

Global, Shadows, Midtones, Highlights, and Misc

The next categories in the Color Grading effects are as follows:

- **Global**: The properties in this section are a global set of color corrections. These settings will adjust the color grading of the scene globally.

- **Shadows**: The properties in this section control the dark/shadow area only.

- **Midtones**: The properties in this section control the gamma/midtones only.

- **Highlights**: The properties in this section control the bright/highlights area only.

- **Misc**: This includes settings for further color correction, but we'll focus on the Color Grading LUT in the upcoming section.

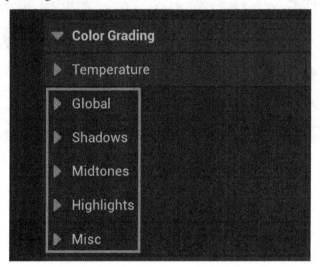

Figure 12.44: The Global, Shadows, Midtones, Highlights, and Misc categories

Now let's break down what each of the first four categories' properties do:

- **Saturation**: This refers to the intensity or vividness of colors in an image. It determines how *colorful* or *color-rich* an image appears. When you increase the saturation, colors become more vibrant and pronounced, while decreasing saturation desaturates the colors, making them appear more muted or grayscale.

- **Contrast**: This will adjust the tonal range of light and dark color values in your scene. Lowering the intensity will remove highlights and lighten the image, resulting in a washed-out appearance, whereas a higher intensity will tighten the highlights and darken the overall image.

- **Gamma**: This will adjust the luminance intensity of the image to accurately reproduce colors. Raising or lowering this value will result in the image's midtones being washed out or too dark.

- **Gain**: This will adjust the luminance intensity of the image's whites (highlights) to accurately reproduce colors. Raising or lowering this value will result in the image's highlights being washed out or too dark.

- **Offset**: This will adjust the luminance intensity of the image's blacks (shadows) to accurately reproduce colors. Raising or lowering this value will result in the image's shadows being washed out or too dark.

Each of these properties is controlled using their respective panel, as shown in *Figure 12.45*.

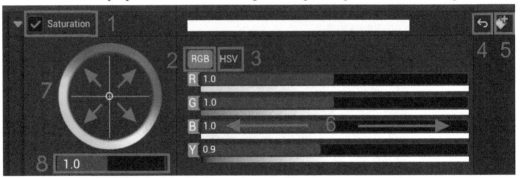

Figure 12.45: The Color Grading controls

Let's quickly understand the controls:

- (**1**) This checkmark enables/disables the effect (I find this useful when checking the before and after results of the settings)

- (**2**) Click this if you prefer to use the **RGB** (standing for **Red**, **Green**, **Blue**) values

- (**3**) Click the **HSV** button to use the **HSV** (standing for **Hue**, **Saturation**, **Value**) values

- (**4**) This button will reset the saturation values to the default settings

- (**5**) Use this button to be able to keyframe the values in the Level Sequencer

- (**6**) Use the sliders to control the RGB/HSV values

- (**7**) Use the color wheel to control the color values instead of the sliders.

- (**8**) This is the main slider for controlling the saturation (or the selected category) value

Go ahead and adjust the **Global**, **Shadows**, **Midtones**, and **Highlights** category properties as you see fit. Color grading involves an iterative process of adjusting settings as you work toward achieving the desired visual style, so keep going until you're happy with the results.

Misc (Miscellaneous)

In this category, we'll be looking at the **Color Grading LUT** properties. **LUT**, which stands for **Lookup Table**, is a mathematical table or set of data used in image processing and color grading. In the context of image and color manipulation, a LUT is a predefined array of values that serves as a reference for transforming input colors to specific output colors. It essentially acts as a color filter, allowing you to apply consistent and controlled color adjustments to images, film, or 3D graphics.

In the **Misc** category, enable **Color Grading LUT**, from the drop-down search for LUT. You'll find that there are four default choices of LUTs: **LUT_Afternoon**, **LUT_Daytime**, **LUT_Morning**, and **LUT_Night**. Cycle through them to see the effect of each in your scene.

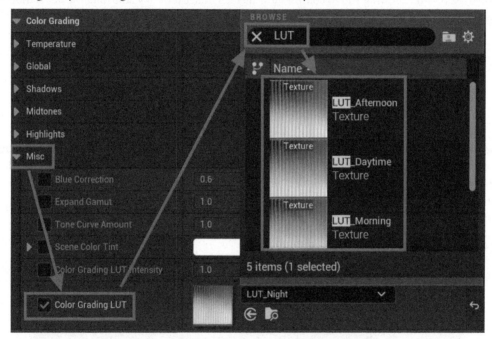

Figure 12.46: Setting the LUT

LUTs are a fast way to achieve about 90% of your desired color grading. You can easily change color styles with LUTs. After you're satisfied with the style, you can fine-tune the final appearance using the adjustments explained in this section.

> **Note**
>
> You can even create a LUT of your own, using image editing software such as Photoshop. I created the various looks in *Figure 12.40* using a LUT. Here are step-by-step instructions on how you can create your very own LUT: https://docs.unrealengine.com/5.2/en-US/using-look-up-tables-for-color-grading-in-unreal-engine/.

In the next section, we will continue with the next category, which focuses on properties that meet the ACES standards.

Film (tone mapper)

In Unreal Engine, a **tone mapper** is a tool or component that adjusts the overall tone and color balance of a rendered image to achieve a desired look. It's often used to simulate the way cameras and the human eye perceive light and color in the real world.

In simpler terms, the tone mapper in Unreal Engine helps you fine-tune the visual presentation of your game or film, allowing you to control how the final image looks by adjusting various settings to achieve a specific aesthetic or mood. These controls are accessible through the **Film** category.

> **Note**
>
> More technical information on the tone mapper can be found here: `https://docs.unrealengine.com/5.2/en-US/color-grading-and-the-filmic-tonemapper-in-unreal-engine/`.

The **Film** category includes properties such as **Slope**, **Toe**, **Shoulder**, **Black Clip**, and **White Clip**. These properties meet the **Academy Color Encoding System** (**ACES**), which is the industry standard for ensuring that consistent color is preserved across multiple formats and displays (we will dive into details about ACES and color management in the next chapter).

The properties in the **Film** category work much like curve adjustment in applications such as Photoshop or After Effects. Let's get into the details:

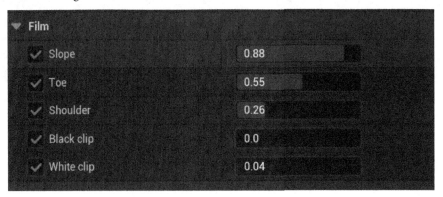

Figure 12.47: Tone mapping chart

Let's go through the properties:

- **Slope**: This slider adjusts the steepness of the S-curve (as shown in *Figure 12.48*). The larger the value, the steeper the curve, and hence the darker the image; the smaller the number, the shallower the slope, and hence the lighter the image.

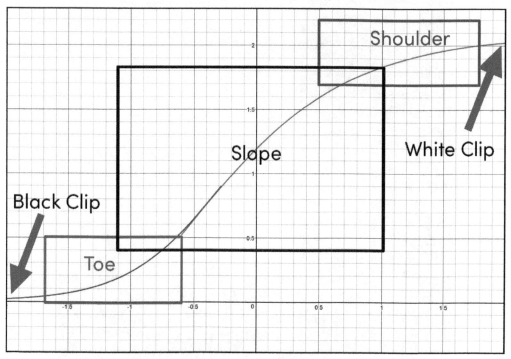

Figure 12.48: Tone mapping chart

- **Toe**: This slider will darken or lighten the dark values or shadow area of the image.
- **Shoulder**: This slider will darken or lighten the bright values or highlight area of the image.
- **Black Clip**: This will clip the black values so the image does not get underexposed. In general, this value should not be adjusted as it will give undesirable results.
- **White Clip**: This will clip the white values so the image does not get overexposed. Again, in general, this value should not be adjusted as it will give undesirable results.

To enable a preview of the S-curve in Unreal Engine, click **Show | Visualize | HDR (Eye Adaptation)**.

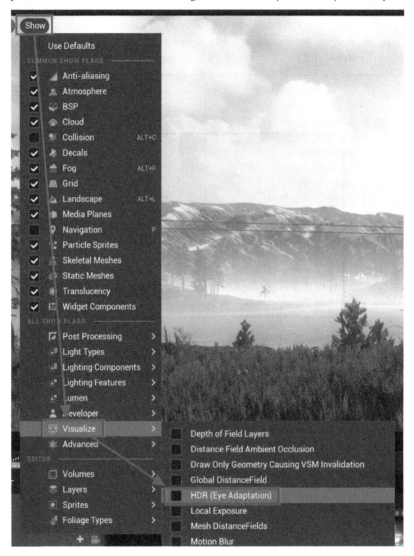

Figure 12.49: Enabling the S-curve

The **HDR (Eye Adaptation)** overlay will show a representation of *Figure 12.48*, which you can use to adjust the properties visually. *Figure 12.50* clearly shows how the S-curve is adjusted to give a desired look. Once you have reached the desired results using the **Film** settings, you can disable the visualizer by unchecking **HDR (Eye Adaptation)**:

Figure 12.50: The (tone mapper) S-curve with shallow, normal, and steep settings

This concludes the color grading section. In the next section, we will jump to the next category, which is **Film Grain**.

Adding the Film Grain effect

Film grain is a visual texture or pattern that resembles the small, random particles or grains that are characteristic of traditional photographic film. It is often intentionally added to films and photographs to create a specific aesthetic, simulate the look of analog film, or achieve artistic effects.

Here's how to use these settings:

1. In the **Film Grain** category, enable **Film Grain Intensity**, and drag the slider to achieve the intensity of grain as needed.

2. If needed, use **Film Grain Intensity Shadows**, **Film Grain Intensity Midtones**, and **Film Grain Intensity Highlights** to emphasize the grain in these areas.

3. Another way of adding film grain is by using film grain textures via the **Film Grain Texture** dropdown, as shown in *Figure 12.51*. Enable **Film Grain Texture**, then, in the dropdown, search for film. Now choose either one of the two textures.

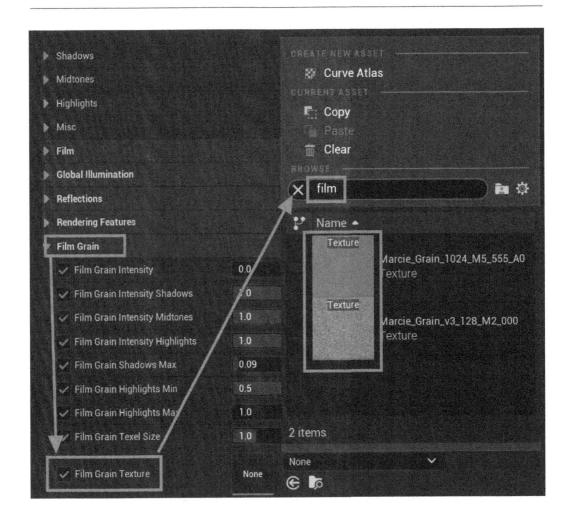

Figure 12.51: Adding Film Grain

These grain textures are sometimes captured from actual celluloid film stock. You can search for such textures online, and here is a good example: https://www.behance.net/gallery/59398743/Film-Grain-Textures-8K-FREE-PACK.

If you find the **Film Grain** effect not to your liking, you can always disable it.

With that, we've wrapped up our discussion on Post Process effects – we delved into most of the crucial effects that will assist us in defining the visual aesthetic we aim to achieve. More technical details of the Post Process effects can be found here: `https://docs.unrealengine.com/5.2/en-US/post-process-effects-in-unreal-engine/`.

Summary

In this chapter, you've acquired the foundational knowledge of lighting within Unreal Engine 5, understanding lighting terminology, various light types, and how to create specific moods for your scenes. We also looked at how to enhance your visuals through Post Process effects such as **Bloom**, **Color Grading**, **Lens Flares**, and others.

In the next chapter, we will delve into color management, rendering and preparing our shots for editing in an external application, and incorporating sound effects, music, and titles to complete our virtual film. See you there.

Part 5:
Post-Production:
Adding Post-Processing
Effects and Music

In this part, you will delve into the final stages of perfecting your Unreal Engine cinematic masterpiece. *Chapter 13* unravels the intricacies of color management, fine-tuning additional camera settings, and executing the rendering process to bring your film to life. You'll then progress to *Chapter 14*, where you'll master the art of editing, seamlessly incorporating sound effects and music to elevate your project. Concluding with the essentials of exporting your film, this segment equips you with the skills needed to deliver a polished and professional cinematic production using Unreal Engine.

This part includes the following chapters:

- *Chapter 13, Exploring Color Management, Additional Camera Settings, and Rendering Your Shots*
- *Chapter 14, Adding Sound and Finalizing Your Virtual Film*

13

Exploring Color Management, Additional Camera Settings, and Rendering Your Shots

Color management is an integral part of any professional filmmaking production as its main role is to keep color consistent throughout the filmmaking process. This is achieved by setting it up using Unreal Engine's built-in rendering solution, Movie Render Queue, a powerful plugin that can produce high-quality multi-format cinematic renders. In this chapter, we will cover both of those topics, as well as exploring additional settings in Unreal Engine's virtual camera, providing you with enhanced control and creative options to refine your cinematography.

We will be covering the following topics:

- Understanding color management
- Exploring additional Unreal Engine camera properties
- Setting up Movie Render Queue
- Rendering your final shots

Technical requirements

To complete this chapter, you will need the technical requirements detailed in *Chapter 1* and the Unreal project we have been working on over the past few chapters.

You'll also need the following:

- A media player to view the rendered files. I recommend mrViewer: `https://alternativeto.net/software/mrviewer/about/`.

- The **Open Color IO** (**OCIO**) configuration files that are needed to set up color management when rendering the shots: `https://github.com/colour-science/OpenColorIO-Configs/releases/tag/v1.2`.

Understanding color management

In filmmaking, **color management** refers to the process of controlling and maintaining consistent colors throughout the various stages of production, from capturing the footage to the final display. It is crucial in filmmaking for several reasons:

- *Consistency*: Filmmakers aim for consistency in color across different shots, scenes, and even entire movies. This helps create a cohesive visual experience for the audience and avoids distracting shifts in color that can disrupt the narrative flow.

- *Creative control*: Color management allows filmmakers to have greater control over the look and feel of their film. By carefully manipulating color, directors and cinematographers can evoke specific emotions, enhance storytelling, and establish a unique visual identity for their project.

- *Accuracy*: Filmmakers want the colors in their films to accurately represent the intended artistic vision. This is particularly important when dealing with specific color palettes or when recreating real-world scenes. For example, a sunset should appear as it does unless a creative choice is made to alter it.

- *Compatibility*: Different devices, such as cameras, monitors, and projectors, may interpret and display colors differently. Color management ensures that the intended colors are faithfully reproduced across various devices, providing a consistent viewing experience for the audience.

- *Workflow efficiency*: Color management helps streamline the filmmaking workflow. It allows filmmakers to work with confidence, knowing that the colors they see during editing and post-production will translate accurately to the final output.

In practical terms, color management involves using standardized color spaces, calibration tools, and careful color grading techniques to achieve the desired results. This process typically includes steps such as setting up color profiles for cameras, monitors, and other equipment, as well as adjusting and fine-tuning colors during the post-production phase.

Overall, color management is an essential aspect of filmmaking that contributes to visual storytelling and ensures that the audience experiences the film as intended by the creators.

Color spaces

As mentioned in the previous section, color management involves using standardized color space. **Color spaces** refers to specific gamuts of color with a specific gamma curve. **Gamut** defines the total set of colors that can be represented within a given color space, while **gamma** defines the relationship between the numerical value of a color and its perceived light intensity.

Let's understand some of the color spaces:

- **Standard Red Green Blue** (**sRGB**), developed by Microsoft and HP in 1996, is a widely used color space standard that defines the range of colors displayed on digital screens, such as monitors, cameras, and printers. It is designed to ensure consistent and predictable color reproduction across different devices, making it a common standard for web graphics, digital photography, and general-purpose digital imaging.

- **Linear sRGB** is the color space that's used for the computer graphics rendering method commonly referred to as *linear workflow*.

- **Rec 709** (also known as ITU-R BT.709) is a standard color space for **high-definition television** (**HDTV**) that specifies the parameters for the production and broadcast of television content. Rec 709 defines the color space, gamma, and other characteristics to ensure consistent and accurate color representation in HDTV systems.

- **Academy Color Encoding System** (**ACES**, or **ACES2065**) is a standardized color management and image interchange system developed by the Academy of Motion Picture Arts and Sciences. It is designed to provide a consistent and reliable color framework for the entire filmmaking process, from image capture to post-production and final mastering.

- **Academy Color Encoding System – Computer Graphics** (**ACEScg**) is a color space within the broader ACES that was designed specifically for **computer-generated imagery** (**CGI**) and computer graphics workflows. ACEScg provides a linear color space, meaning the relationship between the numerical values and the actual intensity of light is linear.

Figure 13.1 shows a horse-shoe diagram (because of its shape) with all the colors representing all the colors the human eye can see. Inside the diagram, several different colored triangles represent the most common color spaces we've just discussed:

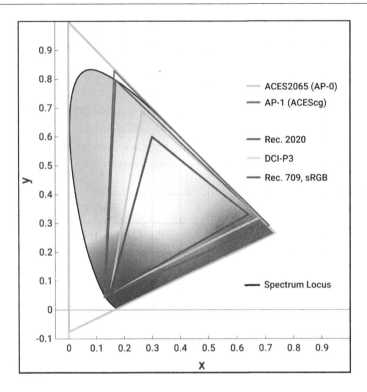

Figure 13.1: The color space diagram

The most important takeaway is that ACES2065 and ACEScg allow for an enormous amount of range and flexibility while remaining compatible with smaller color spaces. Since it's an industry standard and a good practice, we will be using the ACES/ACEScg color workflow in our final renders.

Color management workflow in Unreal Engine 5

Natively, Unreal Engine uses the sRGB/Rec 709 color space, but for it to comply with the ACES color space, it must be first converted from sRGB/Rec 709 into ACES/ACEScg using the **OCIO** color management system. OCIO is used in film and virtual production and guarantees that colors remain consistent throughout the entire pipeline. This encompasses camera capture, compositing applications, and the final render.

There are various ways of doing color conversion using OCIO in Unreal Engine. This includes doing the following:

- Applying color conversion to media sources such as captured clips or live feeds to match computer-generated elements in Unreal Engine

- Applying color conversion to the Viewport while working in the Editor to ensure consistency with the chosen color space

- Choosing to apply a color space transformation (sRGB/Rec 709 to ACES/ACEScg) to the render in Movie Render Queue when exporting

Movie Render Queue (**MRQ**) is Unreal Engine's image sequence and movie rendering solution. It is built for high-quality rendered images, simplified integration into production pipelines, and user extensibility. We will adopt this third option simply because it is the most convenient and straightforward process.

There are generally two workflows when exporting renders out of Unreal Engine:

- *The compositing-editing workflow*: This involves using Movie Render Queue to generate render passes that will be composited in applications such as Adobe After Effects or Nuke, before exporting them to a non-linear editing application such as DaVinci Resolve.

- *The editing workflow*: This is the same as the previous workflow, but it involves bypassing the compositing stage:

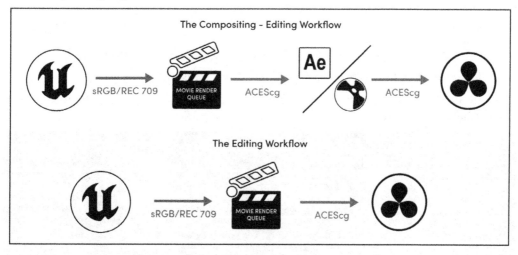

Figure 13.2: Two render workflows for Unreal Engine

In our workflow, we will be using the second option. We will accomplish this by setting up Movie Render Queue with the ACES/ACEScg color space while utilizing the OCIO color management system. We'll do this in the *Setting up Movie Render Queue* section.

In the next section, we will switch gears and delve into additional Unreal Engine 5 camera properties that I believe you will find useful in enhancing your shots. These properties are by no means necessary for you to use in the film, but they provide a deeper level of control and creativity for those seeking to fine-tune their cinematography. Understanding and experimenting with these features can open up new possibilities!

> **Note**
>
> Although the topic of color management and the science behind it can go to greater lengths, you now know enough to progress to the next stage. However, if you'd like to learn more, here's a good read: `https://www.linkedin.com/pulse/aces-color-management-pipeline-computer-graphics-visual-onni-li/`.

Exploring additional Unreal Engine camera properties

As discussed previously in this book, Unreal Engine's **Cine Camera Actor** mimics real-world cameras. Although we have already learned about some of its important properties, such as **Current Aperture**, **Current Focal Length**, and **Manual Focal Distance**, let's look at some additional properties.

Lookat Tracking Settings

Lookat Tracking Settings allows **Cine Camera Actor** to track a selected actor in the scene. When this feature is enabled, it will override the camera's rotation and aim/track the selected actor. Let's learn how to use it:

1. Open the A_New_Beginning project, and then open **Master_Sequence**.

2. Jump into **Shot_06**, where we have the shuttle flying across the landscape.

3. In the **CAM_06** properties, under **Lookat Tracking Settings**, click the **Enable Look at Tracking** checkbox:

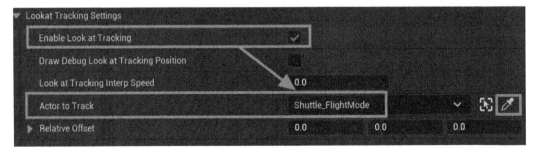

Figure 13.3: Enable Look at Tracking

4. Then, for **Actor to Track**, you can either use the drop-down list to choose the actor to track or use the eyedropper tool to click on an actor in the Viewport. Either way, choose the **Shuttle_FlightMode** actor.

5. Now, scrub the timeline and see how the camera tracks the shuttle!

6. You can also use *X*, *Y*, and *Z* **Relative Offset** values to reframe/offset the shot if needed.

Go ahead and use this feature for the other shots if you think it contributes to the storytelling process.

Filmback (Sensor Size)

Back in *Chapter 2*, I covered key camera properties. The first on the list was **Filmback/Sensor Size** – there, I mentioned what it was and how it is used to control the depth of field.

Additionally, the **Filmback** properties in **Cine Camera Actor**, such as zooming, aperture settings, and depth of field, can be changed just like real-world cameras. Let's find out how:

1. With the project still open, open **Shot_05** (the **EXT_Space** scene).

2. From the **Viewport** menu, click on **Perspective** and enable **Cinematic Viewport**:

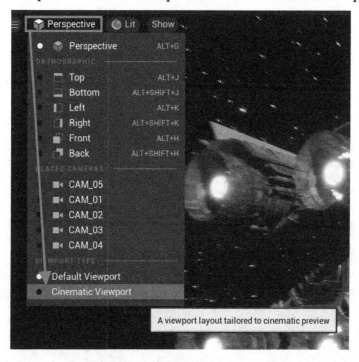

Figure 13.4: Changing to the Cinematic Viewport view

3. The Viewport will now go into the currently selected **Filmback** mode, which is **16:9 Digital Film**, and will show playback preview and controls, as shown in *Figure 13.5*:

Figure 13.5: Changing to the Cinematic Viewport view

Let's learn more about these controls:

- *1*: The name of the current sequence and current camera
- *2*: A draggable time bar that syncs with the sequencer playhead
- *3*: The current camera's **Filmback** properties, including the current preset in use, **Zoom Factor / Focal Length**, **Aperture**, and **Squeeze Factor** (the latter of which you can learn more about in the *Lens Settings* section)
- *4*: A mirror of the playback controls that are available in the Sequencer
- *5*: The current frame

Having the current **Filmback** properties in the Viewport can be useful when you're changing the camera properties on the fly. Now, let's start changing the **Filmback** presets.

4. Select **CAM_05**. Then, in the **Details** panel, select the **Filmback** category, and click the down arrow to reveal the default list of presets containing common real-world camera sensor sizes:

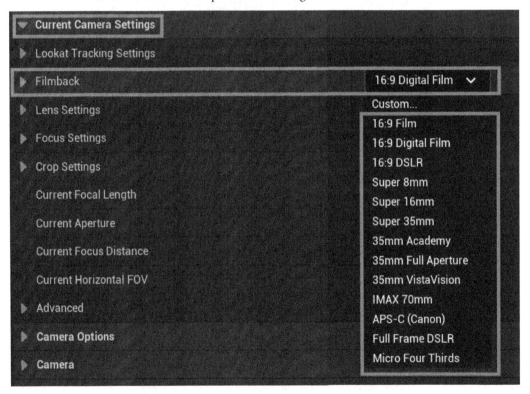

Figure 13.6: Cine Camera Actor – Filmback properties

5. Click on any of the presets to see the aspect ratio of the Viewport change. Also, notice how the sensor width and sensor height change as you select the presets.

For your reference, *Figure 13.7* shows all the Unreal Engine 5 Filmback presets, with their sensor width/height and aspect ratios:

Flimback Preset	Sensor Width/Height	Sensor Aspect Ratio
16:9 Film	24.0mm x 13.5mm	1.77778
16:9 Digital Film	23.76mm x 13.365mm	1.77778
16.9 DSLR	36.0mm x 20.25mm	1.77778
Super 8mm	5.79mm x 4.01mm	1.44389
Super 16mm	12.52mm x 7.58mm	1.651715
Super 35mm	24.88999mm x 18.66mm	1.333869
35mm Academy	21.945999mm x 16.002001mm	1.371453
35mm Full Aperture	24.892mm x 18.9121mm	1.316194
35mm Vista Vision	37.719002mm x 25.146mm	1.5
IMAX 70mm	70.410004mm x 56.630001mm	1.243334
APS-C(Canon)	22.200001mm x 14.8 mm	1.5
Full Frame DSLR	36.0mm x 24.0mm	1.5
Micro Four Thirds	17.299999mm x 13.0mm	1.330769

Figure 13.7: Cine Camera Actor Filmback presets and aspect ratios

> **Note**
>
> If you have a project that requires you to mimic a real-world camera, you can manually key it in the **Sensor Width** and **Sensor Height** slots. **Sensor Aspect Ratio** will be automatically calculated based on the width and height. Here's a good resource for such information for cinema and television cameras: `https://vfxcamdb.com/`.

Film Overlays

Another tool that I find useful is **Film Overlays**, which is available at the top right of the Viewport once you enable **Cinematic Viewport**:

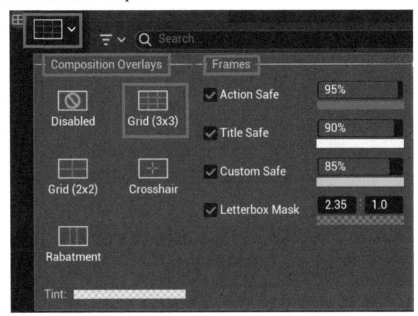

Figure 13.8: Film Overlays

The **Film Overlays** menu contains visual guides for composition and framing and composition:

- **Composition Overlays** refers to layout guides such as **Grid (3x3)**, which follows the rule of thirds, **Grid 2x2**, and others

- **Frames** refers to the square boxes near the edge of the frame, which you can use to place elements and titles so that they stay visible on all screens

Figure 13.9 shows the result of the **Action Safe**, **Title Safe**, **Custom Safe**, and **Letterbox Masking** overlays being enabled, plus the **Grid 3x3** (rule of thirds) frame:

Figure 13.9: Enabled overlays

These overlays are just visual guides and will not appear in the final render. To remove the overlays, just disable them by unticking the respective checkboxes.

Lens Settings

In *Chapter 2* of this book, we also discussed the various types of real-world camera lenses, their focal length, and their aperture (F-stop). The **Lens Settings** category is where we can set the lens parameters to mimic any real-world camera lenses:

Figure 13.10: Lens Settings

Let's go through the parameters:

- **Lens Settings**: A convenient drop-down list of real-world camera lenses. Using any of the presets shown will change the **Focal Length Range** and **Diaphragm Blade Count** properties of the lens:

Figure 13.11: The effects of using different lens presets

When using a shorter focal length (a smaller number), the wider (zoomed-out) the framing will be; on the other hand, the longer the focal length (a larger number), the narrower (zoomed-in) the framing will be.

- **Min Focal Length** and **Max Focal Length**: These options set the minimum and maximum values of the lens focal length, respectively. For example, to emulate a **Zoom** lens, set the **Min** value to **24** and the **Max** value to **70**. To emulate a prime lens, set both to the same value.

- **Min FStop** and **Max FStop**: This sets the minimum and maximum aperture range for this camera, respectively. It is best to set this to a low value to emulate a shallow depth of field.

- **Squeeze Factor**: This is used to emulate anamorphic lens effects. To do so, set **Squeeze Factor** to a higher number, such as **2.0**, and see the result, as shown in *Figure 13.12*:

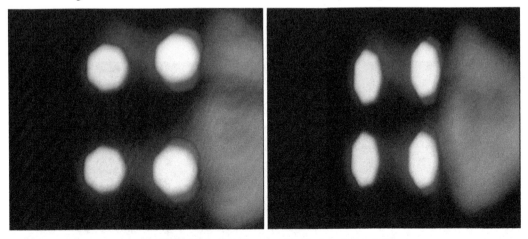

Figure 13.12: Setting Squeeze Factor from 1.0 to 2.0

- **Diaphragm Blade Count**: To control the light entering through the camera lens, a mechanism with overlapping metal blades (as shown in *Figure 13.13*), known as the iris, opens and closes within the lens. This action alters the size of the lens opening, influencing the shape of the Bokeh effect. The Bokeh effect is determined by the number of blades involved, shaping the overall appearance of the Bokeh:

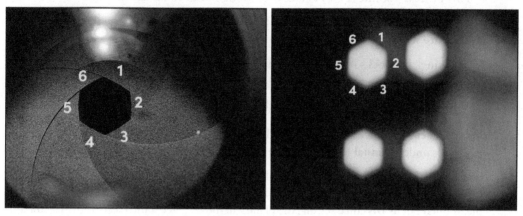

Figure 13.13: Diaphragm Blade Count

Focus Settings

In filmmaking, the **Focus Settings** properties of a camera refer to the adjustments that are made to bring a subject into sharp clarity. Achieving proper focus is crucial for capturing clear and sharp images. Different cameras may have varying focus settings. For **Cine Camera Actor** in Unreal Engine 5, these settings are available in the **Focus Settings** category:

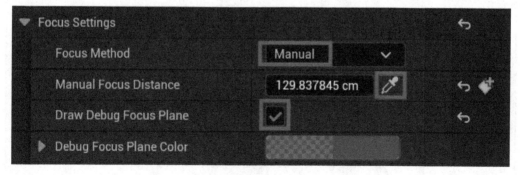

Figure 13.14: Focus Settings

Let's look at some of them:

- **Focus Method**: This controls the depth of field and contains the following options:

  - **Do not override**: This relieves the camera's ability to control the depth of field and allows **Post Process Volume (PPV)** to take over depth of field controls.

  - **Manual**: This allows the depth of field to be controlled manually using the **Manual Focus Distance** settings.

  - **Tracking**: This locks focus on a specific actor (an automated way of keeping focus on a moving object in your scene).

  - **Disabled**: This disables the depth of field entirely so that everything will be in focus.

- **Manual Focus Distance**: This allows the depth of field to be controlled manually by changing the values under **Manual Focus Distance** or by using the eyedropper tool.

- **Draw Debug Focus Plane**: This will enable a visual guide for setting the focus or depth of field. As you use it, you will notice a purple-colored rectangular plane. Then, when changing the **Manual Focus Distance** setting, the plane will move. Once it intersects with an actor, this is where the focus will be set:

Figure 13.15: Using Draw Debug Focus Plane on Adam and Eve

> **Note**
>
> I find **Draw Debug Focus Plane** to be the most effective method when setting the depth of field/focus, but be sure to uncheck **Draw Debug Focus Plane** to avoid it being visible in the final render.

In this section, we looked at additional camera properties to help enhance your shots with a deeper level of control so that you can fine-tune your creativity. In the next section, we will begin setting up Movie Render Queue so that we can start the rendering process.

Setting up Movie Render Queue

As we discussed previously, Movie Render Queue is the solution for rendering image sequences and movies. It is designed to produce high-quality rendered images that can be seamlessly integrated into production pipelines and allow for user customization.

In Unreal Engine 5, Movie Render Queue can produce the Apple QuickTime .mov video format using the **Apple ProRes [10-12bit]** plugin, but more importantly, it can also produce image sequences such as .bmp, .exr, .jpg, and .png. Let's look more closely at image sequences.

Why should we use image sequences?

Image sequences have an advantage over video file formats for the following reasons:

- Most editing and compositing applications, such as Adobe After Effects, Nuke, and DaVinci Resolve, work better and faster with individual frames as opposed to videos.

- There is no interlacing, images are less compressed, and it is easier to carry out the denoising process, compared to videos, which are often interlaced and compressed, which will make the denoising process slow.

- In the case of a system crash or power outage mid-render, it is faster and more convenient to start rendering the image from the last good frame instead of having to start from scratch. This is the render workflow we will be adopting in our rendering process.

With that, let's look at how we can enable Movie Render Queue via the plugin manager.

Enabling Movie Render Queue

Movie Render Queue is a plugin that must be enabled before use. Let's do that now:

1. Open the A_New_Beginning project, and then open **Master_Sequence**.

2. In the top-right corner of the interface, click **Settings** and choose **Plugins**:

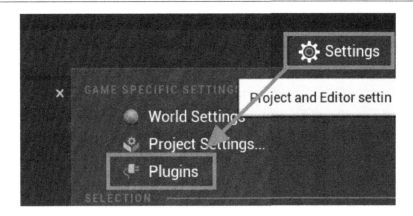

Figure 13.16: Accessing the plugins manager

3.　In the **Plugins** popup, type `movie`. Then, from the results, enable the **Movie Render Queue** and **Movie Render Queue Additional Render Passes** plugins:

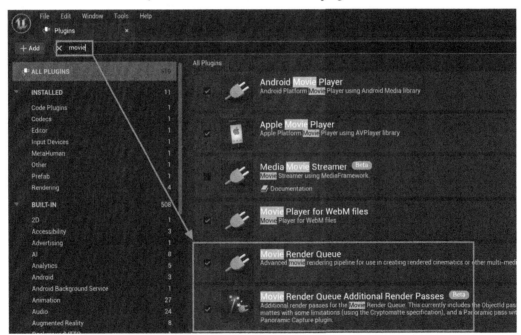

Figure 13.17: Enabling the Movie Render Queue and Movie
Render Queue Additional Render Passes plugins

> **Note**
>
> The **Movie Render Queue Additional Render Passes** plugin allows for separate render passes to be generated for use in a compositing application such as Nuke or Adobe After Effects. Though we are enabling the plugin now, we won't be using it. If you would like to learn more about it, here is a good resource: `https://docs.unrealengine.com/5.2/en-US/cinematic-render-passes-in-unreal-engine/`.

4. While we are here, there is another plugin that needs to be added. Search for `Apple` and enable the **Apple ProRes Media** plugin. When this plugin is enabled, it will appear in the configuration settings of Movie Render Queue:

Figure 13.18: Enabling the Apple ProRes Media plugin

5. You'll now need to restart the application, so click the **Restart** button at the bottom corner of the plugin manager.

With the plugins enabled, let's open Movie Render Queue and familiarize ourselves with the interface.

Opening Movie Render Queue

There are two ways to open Movie Render Queue:

*   The first option is from the main menu bar, by clicking **Window | Cinematics | Movie Render Queue**:

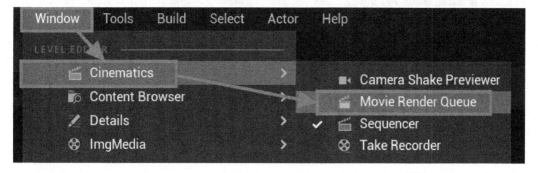

Figure 13.19: Opening Movie Render Queue using the main menu

*   Alternatively, in the Sequencer, click the three ellipses beside the clapperboard icon and choose **Movie Render Queue** to make it the default renderer. Then, click on the clapperboard icon again to open the Movie Render Queue interface:

Figure 13.20: Opening Movie Render Queue using the Sequencer

The **Movie Render Queue** pop-up panel will now be displayed in the center of the application:

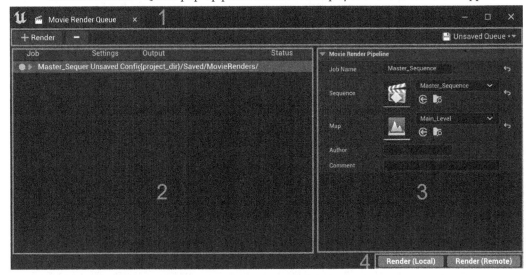

Figure 13.21: The Movie Render Queue interface

Let's break down the interface:

- **Menu toolbar** (**1**): This menu contains the functions for adding and removing render jobs, and saving the current job list.

- **Jobs** (**2**): This is the list of sequences to be rendered in the order in which they are queued. This list contains the configuration settings for each job (we will look at configuration in detail in the next section).

- **Job details** (**3**): Here, you can click on any of the items in the queue to reveal the job's details, such as **Job Name**, **Sequence**, **Map,** or the level it corresponds to, plus **Author** and any **Comment** details attached to the job.

- **The render options (4):** Here, you can either click **Render (Local)**, which will render the job locally on your machine, or **Render (Remote)**, which will render in a separate process (in the background) on your machine.

Now it's time to finally configure Movie Render Queue and do a quick render.

Configuring Movie Render Queue

Now that we are familiar with Movie Render Queue, let's start configuring it for our first rendering process for a Playblast. A **Playblast** will provide us with a low-resolution render but a realistic idea of our final render without requiring the time needed for a formal render. This is also a good way to check for timings such as camera animation, light illumination and position, particles, and more.

We are going to render the Playblast in a QuickTime (.mov) file format – hence why we installed the Apple ProRes plugin earlier.

Let's begin:

1. With the A_New_Begining project and **Master_Sequence** still open, click the clapperboard icon to open Movie Render Queue.

2. Upon opening **Master_Sequence**, it will be added to the **Jobs** listing automatically. Under **Settings**, click on **Unsaved Config**. This will open the **Render Settings** panel:

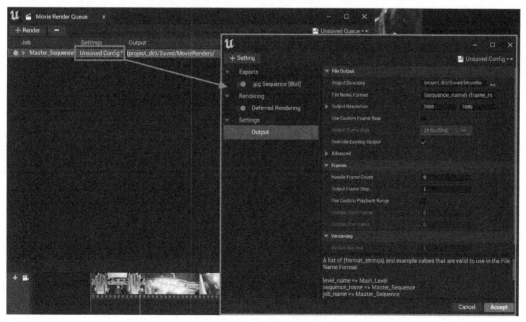

Figure 13.22: Opening the Render Settings panel

Here's a closer look at the **Render Settings** panel:

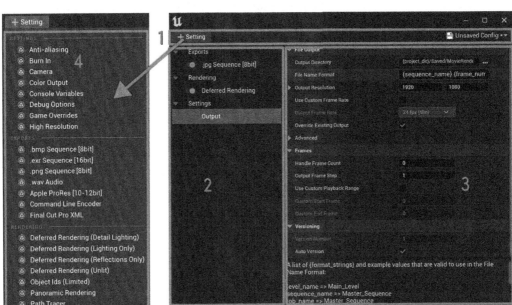

Figure 13.23: The Render Settings panel's interface

Let's run through the interface quickly:

- **Toolbar** (**1**): The toolbar contains the menu for additional settings and loading or saving the current settings as a preset.

- **Settings list** (**2**): This panel shows the current settings to be applied to the job, including the toggle switch to enable or disable them. The settings are divided into three categories – **Exports**, **Rendering**, and **Settings**.

- **Settings details** (**3**): This panel shows the properties of the selected item from the settings list.

- **Settings list details** (**4**): Clicking the green + button on the toolbar will reveal all the settings options.

3. Since we're rendering using the QuickTime `.mov` file format, in the **Exports** section, delete the **.jpg Sequence [8bit]** settings by pressing the *Delete* button on your keyboard.

4. Then, using the green + button, add the **Apple ProRes [10bit]** codec and change the **Codec** field to **Apple ProRes 422 HQ** – this codec will produce a lower - resolution, but quicker, render:

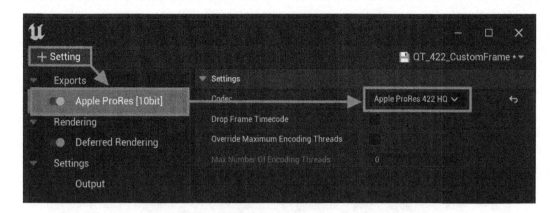

Figure 13.24: Adding the Apple ProRes 422 HQ codec

5. Next, click on **Output**. In **Output Directory**, click the three dots, navigate to your desktop, and create a new folder called `TestRenders`. Then, select the folder:

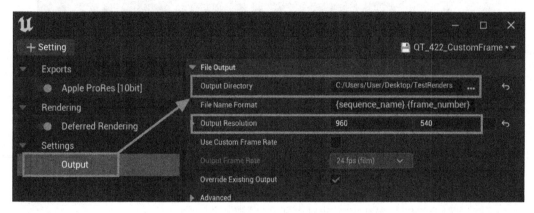

Figure 13.25: Configuring the output settings

Note

By default, Movie Render Queue will place the renders in a **Saved** folder in the Unreal project folder. From my experience, it's better to create a separate folder for all your renders; the desktop is a good temporary location.

6. In **Output Resolution**, change the values from **1920** and **1080** (full HD) to **960** and **540** (half HD). There is no point in rendering a full HD resolution for test renders; as you might be doing this several times, you will save time and disk space in the long run.

Since this project is a multi-shot project, I strongly suggest breaking up the test renders into different shots. This will allow us to preview the individual shots and make changes to only the necessary shots. I find it a time-saver as we do not need to re-render the entire film over and over again if there are mistakes.

7. Enable **Use Custom Playback Range**. Then, for **Shot_01**, set **Custom Start Frame** to **1** and **Custom End Frame** to **119** (making the shot a total of 119 frames):

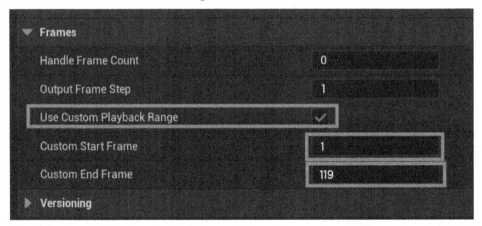

Figure 13.26: Setting the frame range

8. Before we close this panel, let's save these settings as a preset so that we can reuse it again without the need to re-enter the information. At the top-right corner of the settings panel, click on **Unsaved Config** and select **Save As Preset**.

9. Choose a folder of your choice and type `AppProRes_422_CustomFrame` (this is a good preset name as it references the settings we chose earlier). Then, click **Accept**:

Figure 13.27: Setting the render preset

10. Now, back in the **Movie Render Queue** panel, click **Render (Local)**. It will take several minutes for the render to complete:

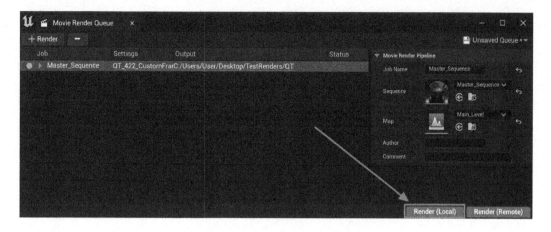

Figure 13.28: Test rendering the shots

11. Once completed, rename the rendered shots according to the respective shot's name – for example, **Shot_01**.

> **Note**
>
> mrViewer is a highly recommended media player as it also allows for image sequence playback, including the EXR format, just like you would a video. The download link is provided in the *Technical requirements* section.

12. To continue rendering the rest of the shots, back in Movie Render Queue, click on the preset we saved earlier. Then, in the **Output** tab, change the **Custom Start** and **Custom End** frames for each shot, as listed here:

Shot Name	Start Frame	End Frame	Total Frames
Shot_01	1	119	119
Shot_02	120	239	119
Shot_03	240	359	119
Shot_04	360	479	119
Shot_05	480	575	95
Shot_06	576	695	119
Shot_07	696	864	168
Shot_08	865	983	118
Shot_09	984	1223	239

Figure 13.29: List of frame ranges for the test renders

> **Note**
>
> These frame ranges are only applicable if you have followed the steps in this book. If you have created your own storyboard or have a different frame range, then you'll need to adjust the parameters accordingly so that they align with your customized storyboard or specified frame range.
>
> It's also worth noting that rendering **Shot_06** to **Shot_09** will take much longer due to it being an open world and the shots consist of MetaHumans.

Once the test renders are complete, carry out any necessary adjustments – such as camera animation, light position, material editing, and more – and render them again. Then, view them using the mrViewer media player. Once you're pleased with the results, it is time to carry out the final renders. We'll do just that in the next section.

Rendering your final shots

The time has finally arrived for us to carry out the final renders. Before doing so, here are some important points to consider:

- For the final renders, we will be using the industry-standard EXR file format. EXR files are significantly larger than a JPG or PNG image, with a single rendered image being approximately 7 MB. As such, the entire film will end up being around 8,400 MB (8.4 GB), so ensure that you have enough disk space.

- We'll be using OCIO to color manage with ACEScg color space for the final render; we will configure this in Movie Render Queue (note that this is optional).

- Employ the per-shot rendering method we covered in the previous section to safeguard yourself from wasting unnecessary time in re-rendering shots, just in case Unreal Engine decides to quit mid-render.

- Be patient; the final renders will take time.

Now, we will configure the OCIO manager, which we'll require when we set up Movie Render Queue for the final renders.

Setting up the OCIO configuration file

As mentioned earlier in this chapter, we will be using the ACEScg color management workflow in our project. However, before we can do that, we need to configure the OCIO color manager. Let's set that up now:

1. Download the OCIO configuration file (available at `https://github.com/colour-science/OpenColorIO-Configs/releases/tag/v1.2`):

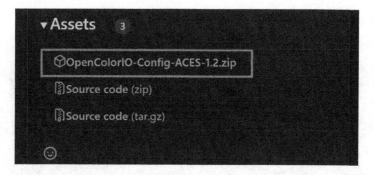

Figure 13.30: Downloading the OCIO 1.2 configuration file

2. Once downloaded, unarchive the file into a folder you can easily access.

3. Back in Unreal Engine, in the Content Browser, create a new folder and name it **OCIO_Config**.

4. Open the folder, right-click, and choose **Miscellaneous | OpenColorIO Configuration**:

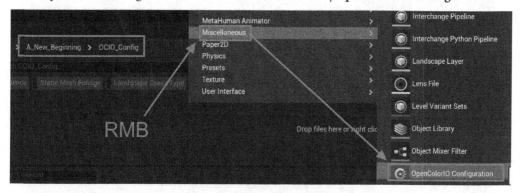

Figure 13.31: Creating the OCIO configuration file

5. Name the file `OCIO_Config`, then double-click to open it.

6. To load the config file, click the three dots marked in the following figure, browse to the OCIO config you downloaded earlier, and select **Open**:

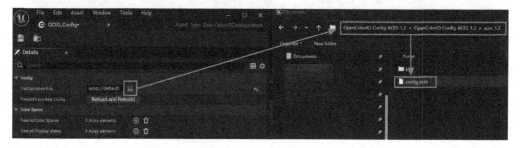

Figure 13.32: Loading the OCIO config file

7. Under the **Desired Color Spaces** section, click the + icon *twice*:

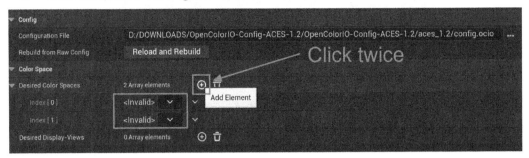

Figure 13.33: Setting the desired color space

8. Then, for **Index [0]**, click the down arrow, select **Utility**, and choose **Utility – Linear – sRGB** from the list:

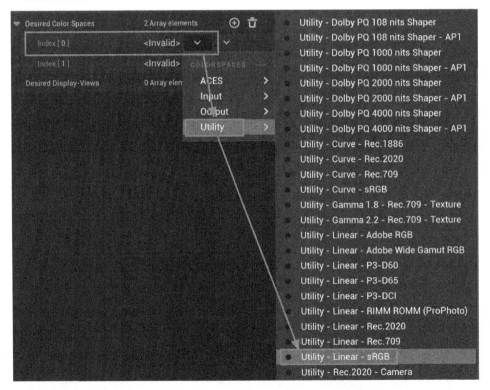

Figure 13.34: Choosing the Utility – Linear – sRGB color space

9. For **Index [1]**, click the down arrow and choose **ACES | ACES – ACEScg** from the list:

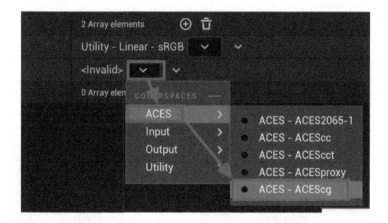

Figure 13.35: Choosing the ACES – ACEScg color space

10. Finally, click **Save** and close the panel.

With the OCIO color manager configured, we can start setting up Movie Render Queue.

Setting up Movie Render Queue

In the previous section, we configured Movie Render Queue for a test render using the Apple ProRes codec. For the final render, we are going to be using a similar technique, but we will add a few more settings to get the best images out of Unreal Engine. These include the following:

- **The EXR file format**: Otherwise known as **OpenEXR (EXtended Range)**, this is a **high-dynamic-range (HDR)** image file format developed by **Industrial Light & Magic (ILM)**. It is an open standard and is designed to store high-quality images containing a wide range of color and brightness values, as shown in *Figure 13.36*:

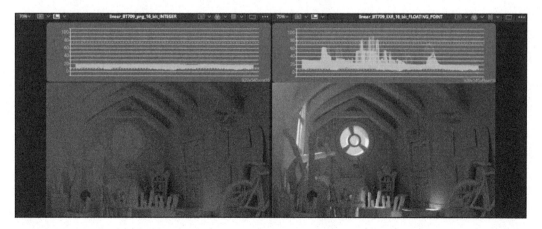

Figure 13.36: EXR file format (right) compared to a PNG (left)

The primary purpose of EXR is to accurately and efficiently represent the intense lighting conditions often found in CGI and visual effects in films.

- **Anti-aliasing methods**: This is a technique that's used in computer graphics to reduce visual artifacts such as jagged edges (or *jaggies*) that can occur when rendering images, especially at lower resolutions. These artifacts are a result of the limited resolution of the display or image, causing stair-step-like patterns along the edges of objects:

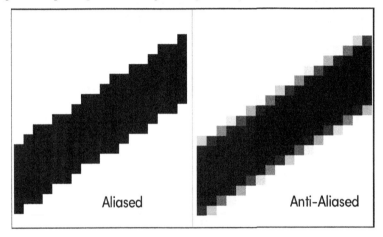

Figure 13.37: Aliased versus anti-aliased

The primary goal of anti-aliasing is to smooth out these jagged edges and create a more visually pleasing and realistic representation of the scene.

- **OCIO color management** (**OpenColorIO**): This is an open source color management system that's used in film and visual effects. It ensures consistent color across different software and workflows by managing color transforms between devices and spaces, which is crucial for accurate and uniform color representation in complex visual projects.

- **Command variables** (**CVARs**): This option enables console commands to be designated when the render begins. This is useful when you're trying to apply quality settings that are too computationally expensive for real-time preview in the Editor. Note that the variables will be reverted upon the render being completed.

There isn't a one-size-fits-all setting when it comes to final renders – the settings I'm about to show you are what I use regularly and have been successful in creating quality final renders. Depending on your computer specification, you may need to tweak the settings as you see fit for your projects. I also highly recommend that you read this article to get the best information on the settings: `https://dev.epicgames.com/community/learning/tutorials/GxdV/unreal-engine-demystifying-sampling-in-movie-render-queue`.

With that in mind, let's start configuring Movie Render Queue:

1.   Open the A_New_Beginning project, then **Master_Sequence**.

2.   In the Sequencer, click the clapperboard icon. Then, in **Movie Render Queue**, under **Settings**, click the preset we made earlier, **AppleProRes_422_CustomFrame**:

Figure 13.38: Creating a new render preset

3.   You will now be taken back to the **Settings** panel. In the **Export** section, delete the **Apple ProRes [10bit]** codec, then click the + **Settings** button and add **.exr Sequence [16bit]** codec.

4.   Now, click the + **Settings** button again, and in the **Setting** section, add the **Anti-aliasing**, **Console Variables**, and **Color Output** settings:

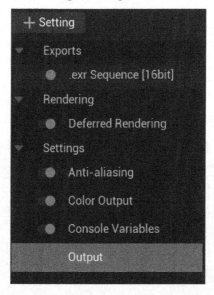

Figure 13.39: The EXR render workflow preset settings

5.   Select the **Anti-aliasing** option section and set the following properties:

- **Spatial Sample Count**: This works by rendering the same frames stacked on top, using the given number to increase the quality of the anti-aliasing. Set it to **1**.

- **Temporal Sample Count**: This works by rendering the given number of sub-frames between two rendered frames to increase motion blur quality; the more temporal samples, the smoother the motion blur, as shown in *Figure 13.40*. We will be setting this to **8**:

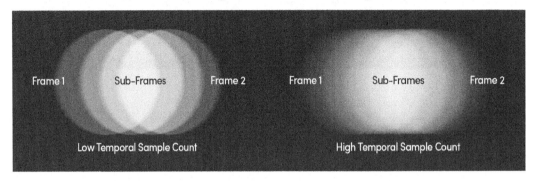

Figure 13.40: The effects of setting Temporal Sample Count

- **AntiAliasing Method**: Unreal Engine adopts several anti-aliasing methods (explained in detail through the link provided in the previous note box), but in our workflow, we will bypass these by enabling the **Override Anti-Aliasing** switch and setting it to **None**.

- **Engine Warm Up Count**: This indicates the number of frames to run before rendering begins. Typically, the warmup is useful when there are physics, particles, or other dynamic actors to settle into the right position before rendering begins. We will set this to **32**:

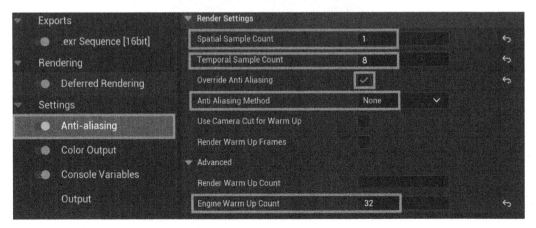

Figure 13.41: Anti-aliasing settings

6. Next, in the **Color Output** options section, beside **Configuration Source**, click the down arrow and select **OCIO_Config** (the file we created earlier):

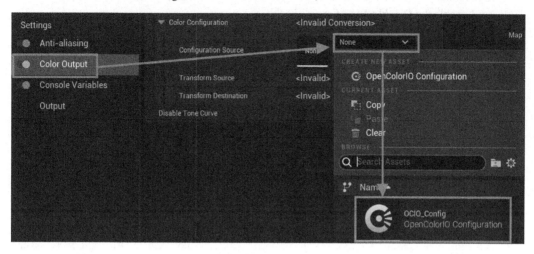

Figure 13.42: Selecting the OCIO_Config file

7. Then, in **Transform Source**, click the arrow and choose **Utility – Linear- sRGB**, and in **Transform Destination**, choose **ACES – ACEScg**:

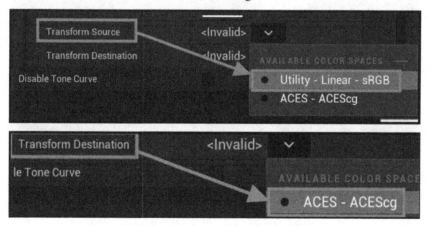

Figure 13.43: Selecting Transform Source and Transform Destination

8. As an alternative, if you do not wish to go down the ACES route – perhaps you are working on a personal project or color management is not a requirement – you can uncheck **Is Enabled** and enable the **Disable Tone Curve** checkbox:

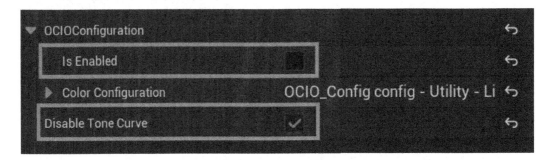

Figure 13.44: Disabling the ACES workflow

9. CVARs are not required to render your project, but by carefully choosing the right ones, you can improve the renders tremendously. There are hundreds of CVARs available for Unreal Engine, but you need to find the ones that suit your project. A list of CVARs and their descriptions can be found by clicking on the **Help** section and choosing **Console Variables**:

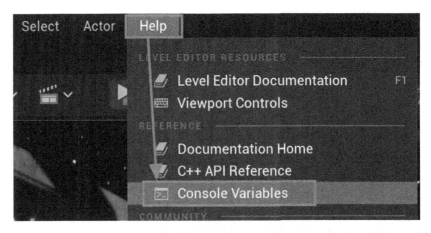

Figure 13.45: Accessing the list of CVARs

For this project, in the **Console Variables** section, add the suggested CVARs, as listed here:

- **r.MotionBlurQuality**: This defines the motion blur method, which allows you to adjust for quality or performance. Set it to **4.0**.

- **r.Tonemapper.Quality**: This defines the tonemapper quality (tonemapper was covered in *Chapter 12*). Set it to **5.0**.

- **r.DepthOfFieldQuality**: This allows you to adjust the depth of field quality. Set it to **4.0**:

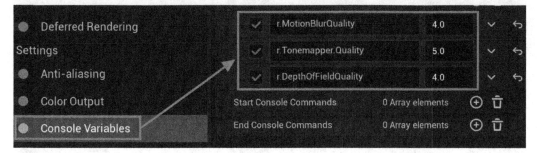

Figure 13.46: Adding CVARs

> **Note**
>
> A word of caution – CVARs can significantly add to the render time. I'd suggest rendering without the CVARS, then adding them one at a time to check whether the quality of renders improves. An extensive list of CVARs is available at the provided link under the SHOT ASSET and CVARS folders: https://packt.link/gbz/9781801813808.

10. Once you're done, in the **Output** section, select the folder you have designated to save the EXR image sequence – for example, **Desktop/FinalRenders/Exr/** – and set the output resolution to **1920 x 1080** (full HD).

11. Just like before, we will also enable **Use Custom Playback Range** and use the start and end frame ranges, as shown in *Figure 13.47*.

12. Before we click **Accept**, let's save this configuration as a preset – I used the name **EXR_Piz_AA1x8_Cvar_ACEScg_CustomFrames**:

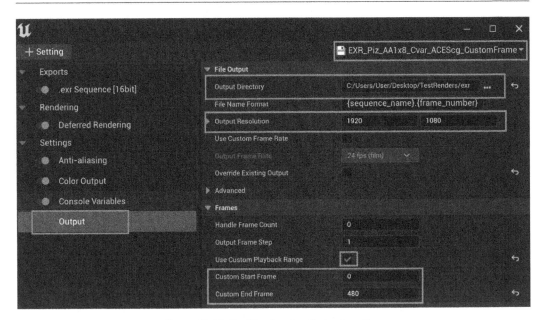

Figure 13.47: Configuring the Output section

The name refers to the fact that we're using the EXR file format with Piz compression, an anti-aliasing spatial sample count of 1 and a temporal sample count of 8, CVARs, the ACEScg color space, and custom frames enabled.

13. Finally, click **Render (Local)** to start rendering your first set of frames.

Phew – that was a lot to take in! Remember that if Unreal Engine decides to quit mid-render, check the last good frame number in the render folder, then continue from there by updating **Custom Start Frame** and **Custom End Frame**.

Summary

In this chapter, we explored the intricate domain of color management, gaining insights into various tools and techniques. We also uncovered additional features of Unreal Engine's virtual camera and delved into rendering pipeline techniques. The focus extended to utilizing Movie Render Queue to produce renders at a professional level.

In the next chapter, we will finally put the pieces together to complete our film with further color correction, music, and sound effects before sharing it with the world.

14

Adding Sound and Finalizing Your Virtual Film

Over the course of the past thirteen chapters, our focus has been deeply immersed in unraveling the intricacies of mastering Unreal Engine 5 and actively engaging in the creation of our virtual film. Now, the moment has arrived to reap the rewards of our dedicated efforts, as we stand prepared to unveil our production to the world.

In this section, our main goal is to incorporate Unreal Engine renders into our project using DaVinci Resolve, a comprehensive all-in-one suite for content creation. This professional application serves as an ideal option to finalize our film, offering industry-standard editing tools, a fully-fledged audio suite, and a solution for professional color correction and grading. Remarkably, all these features come at no cost.

So, in this final chapter, we will be covering the following topics:

- Setting up DaVinci Resolve for ACES Color Workflow
- Importing rendered image sequences
- Reviewing the DaVinci Resolve interface
- Exploring color correction and color grading
- Adding music and sound effects
- Exporting your film

Technical requirements

To complete this chapter, you will need the technical requirements detailed in *Chapter 1* and the Unreal Project we have worked on over the past few chapters. The link to the files for this chapter can be found here: `https://packt.link/gbz/9781801813808`.

You'll also need to download and install DaVinci Resolve 18, which you can access here: `https://www.blackmagicdesign.com/products/davinciresolve`.

Setting up DaVinci Resolve for ACES Color Workflow

As mentioned, we'll be using Blackmagic DaVinci Resolve 18 as the software to master our film. I've selected this for the following reasons:

- It is absolutely free! There is a paid Studio version with extra bells and whistles, but the free version will fit our requirements just the same.

- It is an all-in-one suite that allows audio and video editing, compositing, coloring, and exporting.

- It has a superior coloring suite and supports color management, which is exactly what we will need to complete the film.

- It supports multi-format media, including EXRs.

> **Note**
>
> This chapter is not about acquiring an in-depth knowledge of DaVinci Resolve but, instead, to teach you enough to complete the film. I suggest learning the basics of the application in the Blackmagic Design training portal at `https://www.blackmagicdesign.com/products/davinciresolve/training`.

With that, let's start setting up DaVinci Resolve for the ACEScg color workflow:

1. Open DaVinci Resolve (at the time of writing, I'm using version 18.6).

2. In the **Projects** panel, click the **New Project** button.

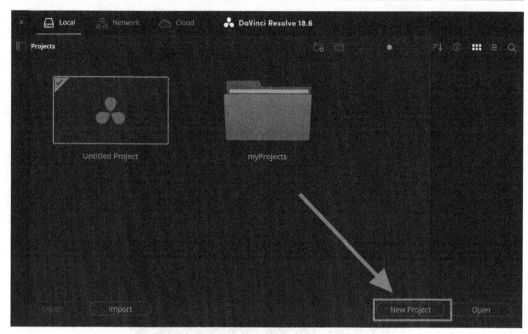

Figure 14.1: The DaVinci Resolve Projects screen

3.   When prompted for a project name, type A_New_Beginning_Edit_01.

4.   You'll now be presented with the main DaVinci Resolve interface. At the bottom of the screen, ensure that you're in the **Edit** workspace.

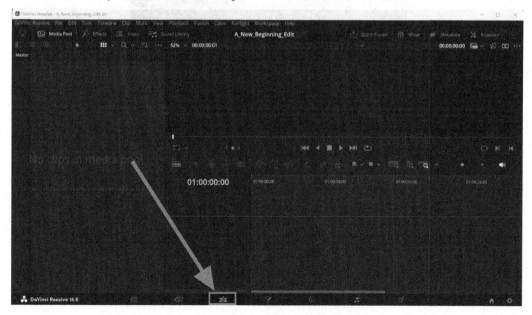

Figure 14.2: The DaVinci Resolve Edit interface

5.   From the main menu, select **File | Project Settings…**.

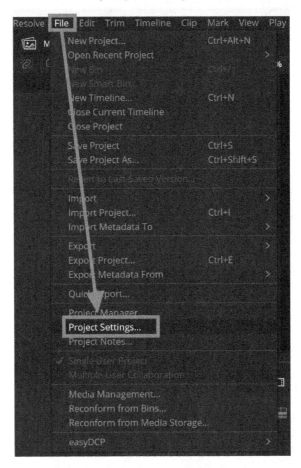

Figure 14.3: Accessing Project Settings…

6.   In the **Project Settings** panel, select the **Color Management** tab and apply the following settings:

- **Color science** to **ACEScct**
- **ACES version** to **ACES 1.2**
- **ACES Input Transform** to **ACEScg - CSC**
- **ACES Output Transform** to **Rec.709**

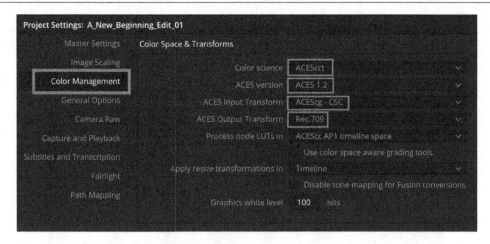

Figure 14.4: Setting the ACES Color space

7. Click the **Save** button at the bottom right of the panel.

That is how easy it is to set up the ACES color workflow in DaVinci Resolve. In the next section, we'll import all our rendered EXR sequences into the Editor.

Importing rendered image sequences

In this section, we will import all the rendered sequences into DaVinci Resolve to start assembling our final film. Let's get to it:

1. Ensure you're still in **Edit** mode. Then, in the **Master** panel on the left of the interface, right-click in the empty space and choose **Import Media…**:

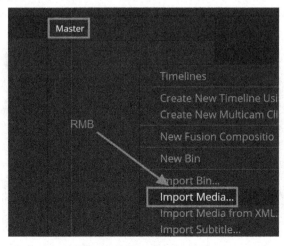

Figure 14.5: Importing media

The preferred method of importing will involve importing the film one shot at a time, simply because, in DaVinci Resolve, we intend to color-correct each shot individually for greater control.

2. Browse to the folder you created the renders in (e.g, `Final_Renders | Shot_01`). From there, manually select the first EXR image, press *Ctrl + A* to select the rest, and click **Open**.

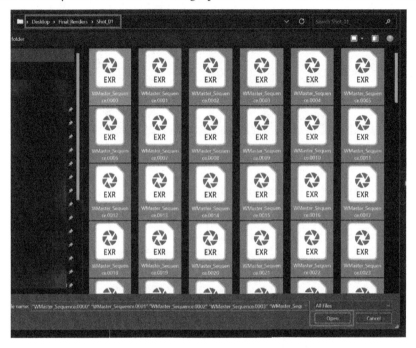

Figure 14.6: Selecting the image sequence

3. Once the shot is imported, it will be listed in the **Media Pool** panel. Using the *F2* key, rename the shot according to the renders from Unreal Engine.

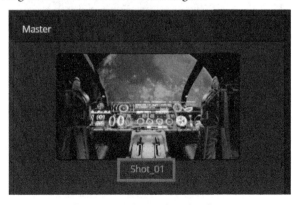

Figure 14.7: Renaming the shot

4. Continue doing so with the other eight shots, and then save your project (*Ctrl + S*).

5. Once all shots have been imported, select all of them, right-click on any one, and then select **Insert Selected Clips to Timeline**.

Figure 14.8: Inserting clips into the Timeline

6. In the **Create New Timeline** pop-up panel, keep every setting as default and click **Create**.

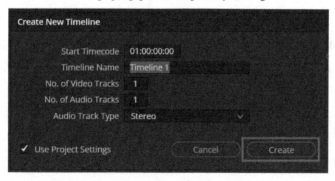

Figure 14.9: Creating the timeline

7. You'll now see the timeline, with all the shots lined-up in sequence. Save the project.

With all the shots now added to the timeline, let's get to know DaVinci's Resolve's interface.

Reviewing the DaVinci Resolve interface

DaVinci Resolve stands out as a highly robust editing suite equipped with numerous features. In this chapter though, you'll gain a concise overview of the suit, enabling you to efficiently utilize it to craft our final film. After that, you can dive in deeper by yourself.

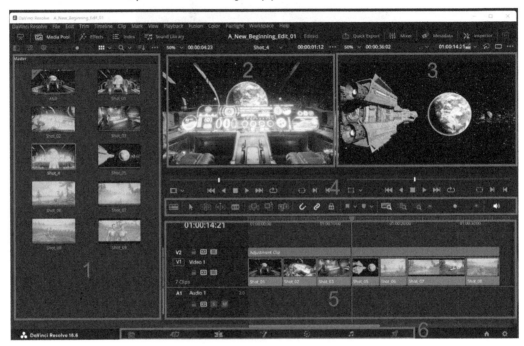

Figure 14.10: The DaVinci Resolve interface

However, before continuing here, let's familiarize ourselves with the interface layout:

1. **Media pool**: This panel displays and organizes all the imported footage.

2. **Source Viewer**: This displays the unedited footage before adding it to the timeline.

3. **Timeline Viewer**: This previews the clips already added to the timeline.

4. **Toolbar**: This features timeline editing modes, editing functions, and timeline zoom settings.

5. **Timeline**: This allows you to place and adjust clips used in the current edit.

6. **Workspace Switcher**: This has buttons to quickly switch from one workspace to another.

Now that you have a basic knowledge of the layout, let's start working on color-correcting the individual shots.

Exploring color correction and color grading

Color serves as a highly potent creative instrument, capable of shaping the style and expressing the mood of your film. With practice and learning, you can hone this skill and craft visually stunning images!

In *Chapter 12*, we employed various features of Unreal Engine's Post Process Volume to enhance shots, including effects such as Bloom, Chromatic Aberration, and Vignette. While we can perform a comprehensive post-process within Unreal Engine, we can also amplify the visual quality of each shot further by utilizing DaVinci Resolve. Our aim here is twofold:

- **Color correction**: This is a process that adjusts hue, saturation, brightness, contrast, and so on to bring consistency across all footage and correct color errors. We will accomplish this using DaVinci Resolve's color correction suite.

- **Color grading**: This is an artistic approach to adjusting color to create a stylized look and mood. This process can be achieved by using **lookup tables** (**LUTs**), a subject that was also explored in *Chapter 12*.

Figure 14.11: Color correction versus color grading

So, let's get started!

Reviewing the color page

To follow the instructions, you first need to be on the color page. So, at the bottom of the screen, in the Workspace Switcher, select **Color**. You'll now see the DaVinci Resolve color suite, as shown in *Figure 14.12*:

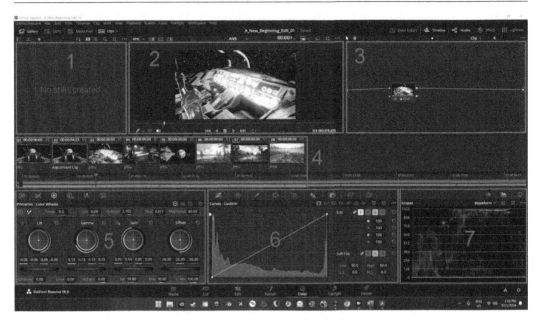

Figure 14.12: The DaVinci Resolve color page

Let's quickly understand the page layout:

1. **Gallery**: Color adjustments can be saved here, which can then be applied to other clips in the timeline
2. **Viewer**: Displays the frame at the current position of the playhead on the timeline
3. **Node Editor**: Links color corrections, image adjustments, and effects to produce distinctive visual styles
4. **Mini Timeline**: This area comprise clip thumbnails and a mini-timeline
5. **Primary adjustments**: This panel consists of standard color wheels and dials to adjust highlights, midtones, and shadows
6. Access to **Curves**: This panel provides access to the curves, which allows you to adjust tone, mapping the entire gamut or individual color channels
7. Access to **Scopes** and the **effect keyframes** (**7**): This panel provides access to various **color correction** scopes and the **Effect Keyframes** panel

Now, we are ready to carry out the color-correction process.

Color-correcting shots

Color correction is a vast subject that takes years to master, involving a deep understanding of color theory, software tools, and practical experience in achieving precise and visually appealing color grades. In this section, we will cover the basics of achieving the results we need to make our shots visually compelling and consistent across different scenes:

1. In the mini-timeline, ensure that we have the playhead on Shot_01.

2. In the Node Editor, right-click on the default color node and choose **Add Node | Add Serial**. This will add a second **Color** node to the **Node Editor** panel.

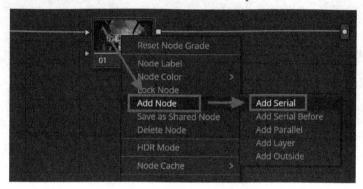

Figure 14.13: Adding a serial node

3. Click the second node, select **Node Label**, type Color Correction, and press *Enter*.

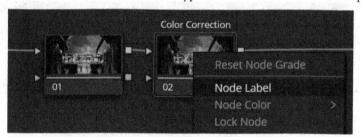

Figure 14.14: Adding a label

To explain what we're doing, in DaVinci Resolve, we create nodes that will keep all the color adjustments. We are going to adopt a non-destructive process by using this second node instead, keeping the default node untouched if we need to start over.

Since Shot_01 to Shot_05 are all located in the same vicinity, we will color-correct Shot_01, and then copy the adjustments and paste onto the other shots.

4. For Shot_01, drag the playhead to the four-second timeframe (when the HUD lights up). Then, in the **Primary** panel, using the dial, adjust **Gamma** to **0.01** on all four channels. This will brighten up the shot. If there is a need to start over, use the **Reset** button to reset all adjustments as default.

Figure 14.15: Adjusting Gamma

5. To save this adjustment and apply it to the rest of the shots, right-click in the **Viewer** panel and select **Grab Still**. This action will add the adjustment we made to the **Gallery** panel.

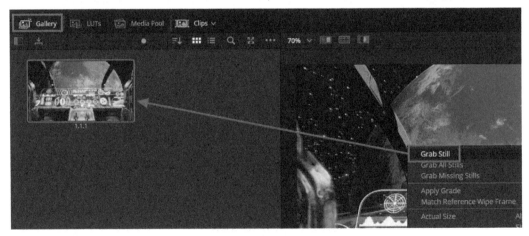

Figure 14.16: Grabbing a still

6. Next, in the mini-timeline, holding the *Ctrl* key, select Shot_02, Shot_03, Shot_04, and Shot_05. With all of them selected, right-click on the saved grabbed still and select **Apply Grade**.

Figure 14.17: Applying the adjustment

7. Scrub the mini-timeline to check the adjustment on all five shots. This is the quickest way to apply the same adjustment to multiple clips. When you are happy with the results, save the project.

Now that you have a basic idea of the workflow, you can go ahead and make further adjustments as you see fit. Color correction is an iterative process, so take your time and be creative. You can add as many nodes to the Node Editor as you want – experiment away. To delete a node, just tap *Delete* on your keyboard. When you are happy with the results, save the project.

Next, let's work on the EXT_Planet shots. I find them a tad warm (more red and yellow) and a little too dim for my taste, so let's change that:

8. Select Shot_06 (the one with the shuttle traversing the landscape) in the Node Editor, create a new node, and add a label – for example, Color Correction.

9. For this shot, increase the **Gamma** value to 0.04 on all four channels. This time, change the **Temp** value to -200.0 as well.

Figure 14.18: Adjusting Temp and Gamma

Changing the **Temp** value will *cool down* the shot by adding blue to the overall image, as shown in *Figure 14.19*:

Figure 14.19: Shot_07 before and after

10. Save this adjustment and add it to the other shots, as you did earlier. Continue to adjust the colors as necessary, and when you are happy with the results, save your project.

In the next section, we will start the color-grading process by first downloading some LUTs.

Downloading free LUTs

In filmmaking, color grading can play a significant role in conveying emotions, setting the tone, and enhancing storytelling. For example, a filmmaker might use warm tones to create a cozy and inviting atmosphere in a romantic scene, while cooler tones might be employed to evoke a sense of tension or suspense.

For this process, we are going to take a different approach. We'll be utilizing LUTs to achieve the results. After doing a bit of research online, I came across a website offering free LUTs – FreshLUTs (`https://freshluts.com/`). So, let me show you how to import LUTs into DaVinci Resolve:

1. Navigate to FreshLUTs and create an account (it's free).

2. Once you've registered, click on **Browse LUTs** and find a LUT you think suits the look you're going for. As an example, I chose **Fresh Look** (`https://freshluts.com/luts/1536`). Then, download it to a folder on your desktop.

3. Back in DaVinci Resolve, open the **Color** page and click the **LUTs** button (at the top-left) to open the **LUTs** panel.

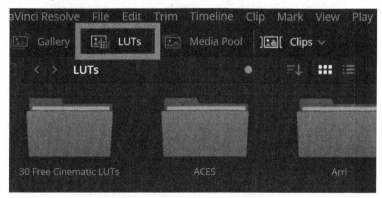

Figure 14.20: Accessing the LUTs panel

4. In the **LUTs** panel, right-click on any of the folders, and select **Open File Location**. This will take you to the folder where all the DaVinci Resolve default LUTs are located.

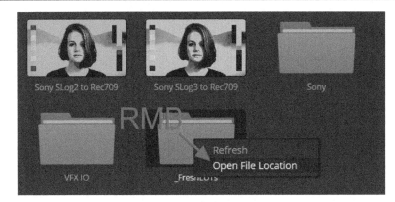

Figure 14.21: Accessing the LUT files' location

5. In the file directory structure, click the **LUT** directory, create a new folder there (e.g., _ FreshLUTs), and copy your downloaded LUT into it.

Figure 14.22: Adding downloaded LUTs

6. Returning to the **LUTs** panel, right-click in the panel and select **Refresh** – you'll now see the new folder you created with the downloaded LUT, available for you to use.

Figure 14.23: Refreshing the LUTs panel

Download as many LUTs as you need, as we will be experimenting with them in the next section.

Color grading with LUTs

Now that we have some LUTs available at our disposal, we can now apply them to our shots. Unlike color correction, where we apply color nodes to each of the shots, for grading, we will apply the color nodes using an adjustment layer. Let me show you what I mean:

1. In the Workspace Switcher, click the **Edit** page icon.

2. If the **Edit** page still looks like *Figure 14.10*, then click the **Effects** icon in the top-left corner of the interface:

Figure 14.24: Accessing the Effects panel

This will give you access to the **Effects** presets on the lower-left of the interface (although, do note that if you are using the free version of DaVinci Resolver, not all effects will be available to you).

3. Now, in the **Effects** preset, select the **Effects** tab. From there, select the **Adjustment Clip** effect, and drag it into the **Video 2** track in the timeline. This will add an **Adjustment** layer on top of the **Video 1** track, where we have all our shots.

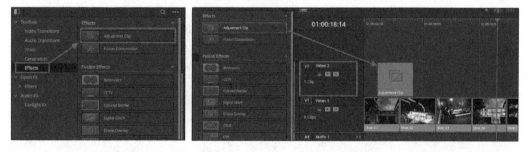

Figure 14.25: Adding an Adjustment layer to the Video 2 track

An **Adjustment** layer is a transparent layer that we lay on top of our shot(s). When there is an effect or any color correction applied to the **Adjustment** layer, it will affect all the underlaying layers. We will add the LUTs via a **Color** node to this **Adjustment** layer, and we will specify which shots will be affected by the LUT.

4. In the timeline, drag the **Adjustment** layer's left-edge to the beginning of the **Video 2** track, and then drag the right edge so that it aligns with the end of **Shot_5**, as shown in *Figure 14.26*.

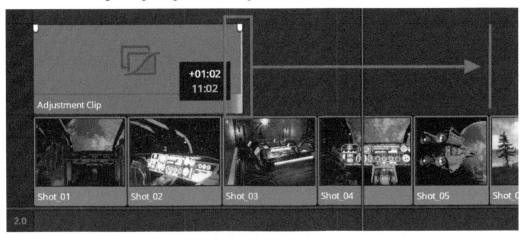

Figure 14.26: Configuring the Adjustment layer

By adjusting the **Adjustment** layer over the top of the shots, you can specify which shots are going to be affected by the LUT; let's work on the **Space** scenes first.

5. Ensure the **Adjustment** layer is selected, and then go back to the **Color** page. From there, in the **Nodes** panel, create a new **Color** node and label it as LUT.

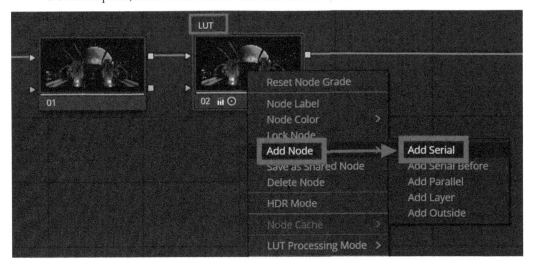

Figure 14.27: Adding a Color node for LUT

6. From the **LUTs** panel, drag and drop the LUT you chose onto the new **Color** node. Once done, you'll see a square icon beside the node number. That indicates that you've just applied an LUT to the **Color** node.

Figure 14.28: Adding the LUT to the Adjustment layer

7. Either scrub the mini-timeline or jump back to the **Edit** page to inspect the effect of the LUT you just applied.

8. Remember that you can change LUTs by just dragging and dropping on **Color** nodes. Also, here are some helpful keyboard shortcuts – use *Ctrl + D* to bypass (enable/disable) color corrections on a selected color node and *Shift + D* to bypass all color corrections.

9. Continue to add or remove LUTs to your shots using the **Adjustment** layer until you find the one that suits the look you're going for.

As you can see, LUTs are quick and easy to use, but what if you cannot find the perfect LUT? In the next section, I'd like to show how to create your own LUTs.

Generating your own LUTs

Generating your own LUTs is a fairly simple process. Let me show you how:

1. Back in the **Color** page, select any of the clips (above the mini-timeline) that you have added color nodes to and are happy with the results of. Then, right-click on the clip and select **Generate LUT**.

Figure 14.29: Creating an LUT

2. You can choose between **17 Point Cube**, **33 Point Cube**, and **65 Point Cube**. The bigger the number, the more accurate the results when applying the LUT. Think of them as good, better, and best, respectively.

Without getting too technical, I'd suggest choosing the highest possible preset. *Figure 14.30* shows the difference in size of the three aforementioned LUTs. It seems that **65 Point Cube** holds more data and so is probably more accurate, which is why we will choose that option here (but I urge you to experiment with your shots).

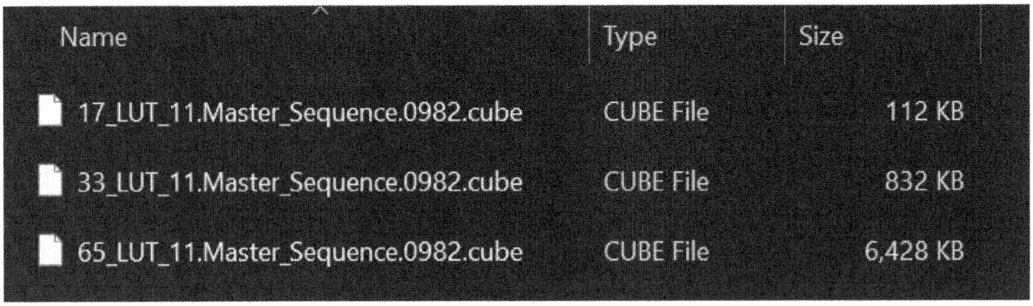

Name	Type	Size
17_LUT_11.Master_Sequence.0982.cube	CUBE File	112 KB
33_LUT_11.Master_Sequence.0982.cube	CUBE File	832 KB
65_LUT_11.Master_Sequence.0982.cube	CUBE File	6,428 KB

Figure 14.30: Comparing exported LUTs

3. You can now import the saved LUTs into the **LUTs** panel using the method described earlier, or you can upload them to `FreshLUTs.com` to share with the world!

At this point, you now have a basic understanding of the color grading workflow, including using and creating your own LUTs. Remember that this is just one way of doing it; there are many other ways, and I'm sure you'll find a way that suits your workflow. In the next section, we will finally start the process of adding music and sound effects to your film.

Adding music and sound effects

Music in film plays a vital role in creating a cohesive cinematic experience by intensifying moods, defining characters, and guiding emotional responses.

In this section, we're finally going to make our film come to life with music and sound effects. The genre of our film can be defined as science fiction, adventure, and mystery, but I'll admit it will be challenging for us to look for royalty-free music that is suitable for our film (unless, of course, we compose a piece, but that is beyond the scope of this book). There are strict copyright laws in place to protect an artist's original work, so you have to be careful when choosing your music.

To find royalty-free music, I usually use these websites:

*   Epidemic Sound (subscription-based): `https://www.epidemicsound.com/`
*   Free Music Archive: `https://freemusicarchive.org/`

- Incompetech: `https://incompetech.com/music/royalty-free/music.html`

- FreeSound: `https://freesound.org/`

You'll find all the music and sound effects I used in the project and the completed DaVinci Resolve project file if you downloaded the book's project files.

Importing music and sound effects

In this section, we will start adding the soundtrack and sound effects to our edit. But first, let's open the completed film in DaVinci Resolve:

1. From the downloaded project file, in the `DaVinci Resolve` folder, open the `A_New_Beginning_Final` project.

Figure 14.31: Opening the completed DaVinci Resolve project

2. Then, hit the **Play** button to view the entire edit.

    As you can see and hear, I have added the music and sound effects tracks that I downloaded from the sites mentioned earlier. I shortened the four-minute music track to fit the one-minute film by cutting it into smaller soundbites, and I chose the appropriate sound effects for each shot. I have also labeled each sound effect accordingly.

3. Now, let's open the last project you saved and continue with importing the audio files. In the main menu, click **File | Project Manager…**.

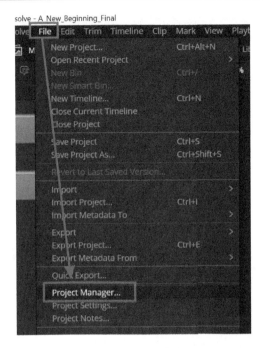

Figure 14.32: Accessing the Project Manager pop-up

4. In the **Project Manager** pop-up, double-click on the last project you saved – A_New_
    Beginning_Edit_01.

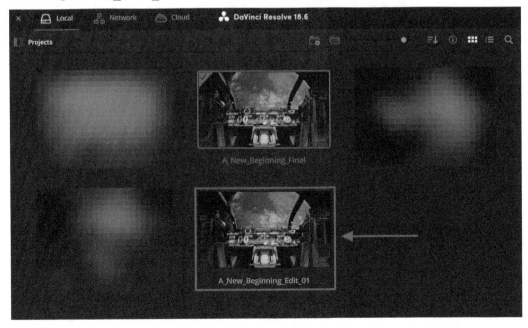

Figure 14.33: Opening the project via the Project Manager

5. Create three bins (essentially folders) by right-clicking in the **Media Pool** area and choosing **New Bin**. The bins will be called **SHOTS**, **MUSIC**, and **SFX**.

Figure 14.34: Creating a new bin/folder

6. Select all the **Shots** clips and drag them into the **SHOTS** bin (organization is key!)

7. Next, double-click the **MUSIC** bin, and in the panel, right-click and select **Import Media**. From the downloaded project files, select `Lost Frontier.mp3` and `Lost Frontier Edited.mp3`, and then click **Open**.

8. Now, continue with the sound effects from the downloaded project file, adding them all to the **SFX** folder.

Now that we have imported all the audio files, let's move on to adding them to the timeline.

Adding audio files to the timeline

The DaVinci Resolve timeline is divided into two sections – the **Video** tracks and the **Audio** tracks. We used the **Video** tracks earlier when we added all of our shots, and now, we will add the music and sound effects to the **Audio** tracks.

However, currently, there is only one track. Let's add some more:

1. In the **Audio 1** track, right-click in the empty area, and select **Add Track | Stereo**. The music we will use is a stereo audio file, hence the stereo audio track.

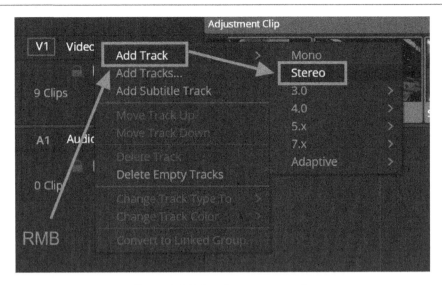

Figure 14.35: Creating a stereo track

2. Then, click once on the **Audio 1** text and rename it MUSIC.

3. Now, let's add five more tracks for the sound effects. Right-click in the empty area under the **MUSIC** track. Then, in the pop-up panel, for **Number of tracks**, type 5; for **Insert Position**, choose **Below MUSIC**; and for **Audio Track Type**, choose **Mono**. Finally, click **Add Tracks**.

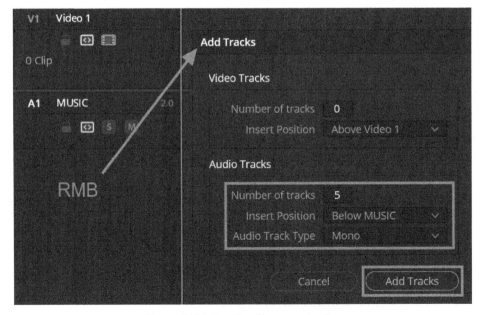

Figure 14.36: Creating five mono tracks

We are using **Mono** tracks for the sound effects, as the audio clips downloaded from FreeSound. org are mostly in mono (if you are unaware, this is music that is recorded and/or played back using one audio channel, as opposed to stereo, which uses two audio channels).

4. It is good practice to label tracks, so rename the new **Audio** tracks accordingly (e.g., SFX 1 to SFX 5).

5. From the **MUSIC** bin, drag the Lost Frontier Edited.mp3 soundtrack onto the **MUSIC** track in the timeline. You will see that it extends slightly beyond all our shots – this has been reserved for the end titles.

    This is the edited version of the original four-minute soundtrack. If you have experience in audio editing, you can use the provided original soundtrack and edit as you see fit, but remember to leave room for the end titles.

6. Start adding the sound effects according to the shots by dragging and dropping the sound effects files onto the SFX tracks – I've labeled the files sequentially so that you can add them accordingly. Refer to the completed edit if you are unsure, but there is no stopping you from downloading and adding your own sound effects.

    To help you do this, follow these tips:

    - Particularly on smaller screens, you may find yourself utilizing the zoom buttons:

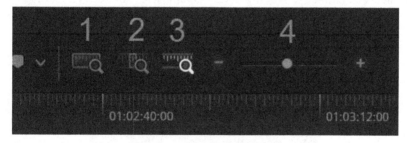

Figure 14.37: The zooming features

Let's break down the preceding screenshot from left to right:

- **(1) Zoom to full extent**: This will always display the whole duration of the timeline
- **(2) Detailed zoom**: This scales the timeline to a closer, zoomed view centered on the playhead
- **(3) Custom zoom**: This allows you to set your own zoom scale in the timeline
- **(4) Zoom slider**: Use this slider to zoom in and out on the playhead location

- Just like editing the video clips, you can trim the audio clips by dragging the ends of the clip with the mouse

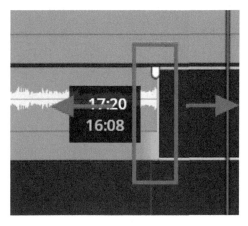

Figure 14.38: Trimming the clips

- To increase and reduce the volume of any audio clips, hover the mouse over the audio's volume level (white line) until you see a volume icon, and then either drag up to increase or down to reduce the volume

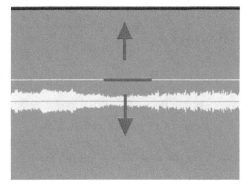

Figure 14.39: Adjusting the audio volume

- Optionally, you can color-code the tracks by right-clicking on any of the tracks and choosing the color of your choice – this gives more of a visual reference while editing

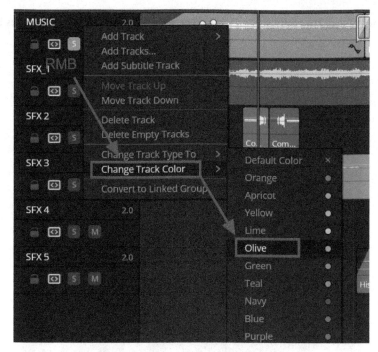

Figure 14.40: Changing the track color

You now have the basic skills of importing, adding, and editing audio files in your project. In the next section, you will learn how to add the end titles.

Adding end titles

Our film is almost ready to be exported, but it is missing one crucial ingredient – titles! We won't need any opening titles, as we want our viewers to keep guessing the story until the reveal at end.

Adding titles is just as easy as adding video clips. Let's start the process:

1. If you're using the Lost Frontier Edit.mp3 version of the soundtrack, drag the playhead to the **55:09** time mark, where there is a slight volume increase in the music; this is exactly where we will reveal the film title.

    You can jump to this exact time in the timeline by clicking the timecode window in the top-right corner of the viewer and typing in 5590.

Figure 14.41: The timecode window

2. With the playhead at **55:09** seconds, open the **Effects** panel and click the **Titles** tab.

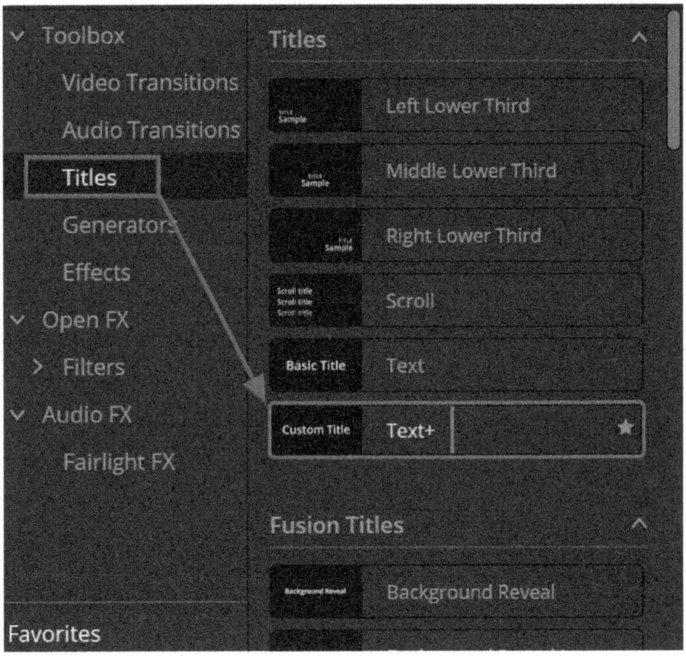

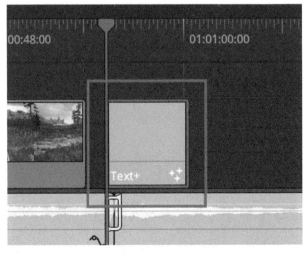

Figure 14.42: Adding a placeholder title

3. In the **Titles** section, drag the **Text+** placeholder title to the playhead on the **Video 1** track. You'll now have a five-second **Text+** placeholder title in the timeline.

Figure 14.43: The first custom title in the timeline

4. While the title clip is selected in the timeline, click the **Inspector** icon in the top-right corner of the interface, which will reveal the **Title Settings** panel. Here, you can add the film title, change the font and font size, and make any other necessary adjustments.

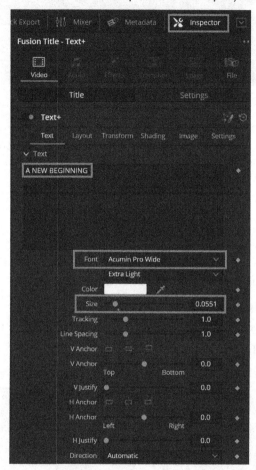

Figure 14.44: Customizing the title

5. Duplicate the title clip by using the *Alt* + left mouse button + drag shortcut to add as many credits as you need (don't forget to credit the music!).

6. To add a fade-in (cross-dissolve), from the **Effects** panel, access **Video Transitions** and drag the **Cross Dissolve** effect to the beginning and the end of the clip.

Figure 14.45: Adding the cross-dissolve

That is about all you need to know about adding titles. Spend as much time as you need to polish your edit. In the next session, our final session, we will export our film!

Exporting your film

The time has finally come for us to export our film! Luckily, in DaVinci Resolve, this process is as simple as it gets:

1. Using the Workspace Switcher, click in the **Deliver** page.

2. In the **Render Settings** panel, choose the **H.264** preset.

3. Add the export filename – I have chosen A_New_Beginning_Final.

4. Click **Add to Render Queue**.

5. Then, in the top-right corner of the **Deliver** page, in the **Render Queue** panel, click **Render All**.

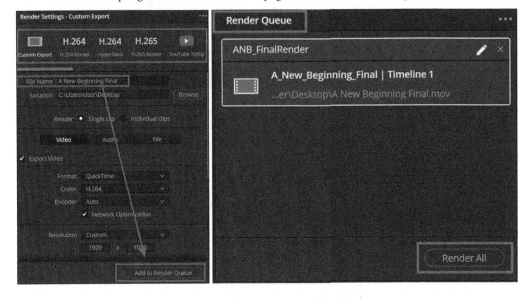

Figure 14.46: The Render Settings panel

> **Note**
>
> If you are interested in getting in-depth technical information about the render settings, I highly recommend you visit the DaVinci Resolve training page, which has a video dedicated to delivering content: `https://www.blackmagicdesign.com/products/davinciresolve/training`.

Since the film is a little over a minute long, it will only take a few seconds to export it. Once the render is completed, open the rendered movie using mrViewer to check the playback. If you feel it still needs tweaking (it usually does), feel free to jump back into DaVinci Resolve to refine it. If you are happy with the final render, congratulations! You've done a great job completing your virtual film!

Summary

Huge congratulations to you for reaching this point in your journey and finishing this book!

Armed with the skills acquired in this book, you're now equipped to craft your own 3D content and animations, bringing to life your very own virtual film within Unreal Engine 5. Unleash your creativity without bounds, with time and effort being your only limitations.

I'm deeply grateful that you chose to embark on this journey alongside me. Whether this marks the beginning of your filmmaking venture or not, I extend my best wishes. May the insights shared in this book provide a sturdy foundation for you to expand upon.

For those already entrenched in filmmaking, I trust that I've offered valuable alternatives by introducing the Unreal Engine 5 pipeline, particularly in areas such as enhancing visual effect capabilities and revolutionizing the way you approach real-time rendering for unparalleled cinematic experiences.

> **Note**
>
> For any help or support, you can join me on the book's Discord channel: `https://discord.com/invite/QbCS2ed2bs`.

Appendix
Creating Material IDs Using Blender

As an Unreal Engine artist, you also need to hone some 3D software skills, especially when augmenting 3D models downloaded from sites such as Sketchfab (`https://sketchfab.com/`) or CGTrader (`https://www.cgtrader.com/`) – my go-to sites for 3D models.

Often, you'll find that the downloaded 3D models either aren't compatible with Unreal Engine or are in a format that is not suitable to be imported straight into Unreal Engine. As such, you'll have to edit them in a **Digital Content Creator** (**DCC**) such as Maya, 3ds Max, or Blender. In our case, we will utilize the open source application Blender. Blender is free to download and use. Over the years, the software has found its place in the mainstream 3D industry and, in my opinion, is on a par with most industry-standard applications.

In this appendix, you will learn how to quickly create Material IDs in Blender.

We will cover the following topics:

- Understanding Material IDs
- Getting to know the Blender interface
- Importing the cryo-cryo-pod 3D object
- Defining surfaces for Material ID application
- Exporting to FBX

Technical requirements

To follow along with this appendix, you will need to have Blender downloaded and installed on your computer. You can find Blender using this link: `https://www.blender.org/download/`. I'm using Blender 3.5.1, but this workflow will work with any future versions of Blender.

> **Note**
>
> If you would like to understand more about Blender, there is a very well-written Blender 3.5 manual at `https://docs.blender.org/manual/en/latest/interface/index.html`.

Understanding Material IDs

In the context of 3D computer graphics, a material ID (also known as a material identifier or material index) is an attribute assigned to different parts or surfaces of a 3D model. It is used to define and differentiate between various materials or shaders applied to different portions of the model.

Let's say you have a 3D model of a car consisting of separate objects, such as the body, windows, wheels, and headlights. To apply different materials to each component, you would assign a unique material ID to each part, as follows:

- **Body**: Material ID 1 (assigned color: red)

- **Windows**: Material ID 2 (assigned color: transparent)

- **Wheels**: Material ID 3 (assigned color: black)

- **Headlights**: Material ID 4 (assigned color: yellow)

Material IDs are particularly useful when you want to apply complex materials or textures to specific regions of a 3D model, as they provide a convenient way to differentiate between different material assignments and achieve more realistic and visually appealing renders.

So, now that you understand the concept, let's dive into the creation of these Material ID maps.

Getting to know the Blender interface

When you open Blender, you will see this interface:

Appendix Figure 1: Blender 3.5.1 interface

Blender has some similarities to Unreal Engine in terms of the UI. Here is a breakdown of the areas we will be using in this section:

- **Menu**: Akin to any other software, this is where you access all the functionality of Blender.

- **Object/Edit Mode**: You will be using this function quite often as it toggles from **Object Mode** to **Edit Mode**. The keyboard shortcut is the *Tab* key. This is very useful to remember.

- **Toolbar**: The toolbar contains buttons for the various tools.

- **3D Viewport**: Like Unreal Engine, Blender has a 3D Viewport too.

- **Outliner**: The same as in Unreal Engine, all 3D objects that exist in the 3D Viewport will be listed here.

- **Properties**: This is similar to the **Details** panel in Unreal Engine.

The Blender UI is not that much different from Unreal Engine. You'll find it easy to navigate and follow the instructions for creating Material IDs, which we will attempt next.

Importing the cryo-pod 3D object

Before we begin, let's figure out what we're trying to achieve. In *Chapter 4*, we added a cryo-pod 3D object to the scene. When I downloaded the object, I felt that there were not enough surfaces we could assign materials to. As such, we will load the object into Blender and assign Material IDs to various surfaces to make it suit our scene better.

In this section, we will import the downloaded cryo-pod object and start assigning the surfaces with Material IDs.

To add a Material ID, do the following:

1. Open Blender 3.5.1. Once you see the splash screen, click once in the Viewport to make it go away.

2. In the Outliner, select the camera, cube, and light and press *Delete* (we won't be needing them).

3. Go to **File** | **Import** | **FBX (.fbx)**. Using the **Blender File View** window, browse to the downloaded project files, open the **scifi-cryogenic-sleep** folder, and choose `chamber.fbx`.

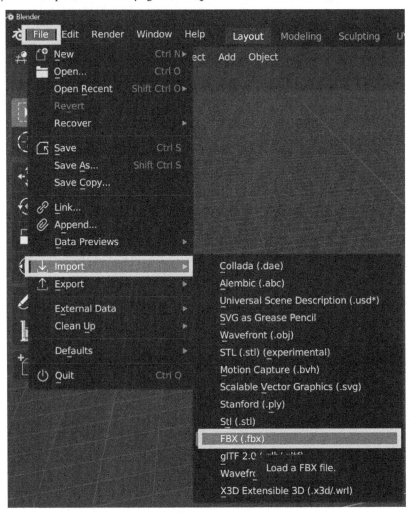

Appendix Figure 2: Importing the cryo-chamber FBX file

4. The 3D object will be added to the Viewport but it will be zoomed out. To zoom in, press the period key (.) on the numpad, or go to **View | Frame Selected** (note the object must be selected for this shortcut to work):

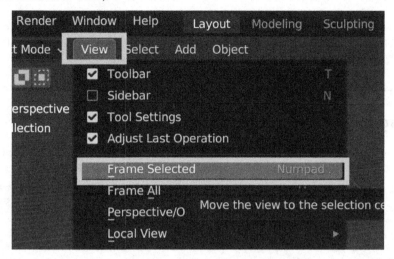

Appendix Figure 3: Zooming into the 3D object

> **Note**
>
> Navigation in Blender is slightly different compared to Unreal Engine. Here are some key combinations you must know:
>
> - To orbit in the Viewport, click and drag with the **Middle Mouse Button** (**MMB**)
> - To pan in the Viewport, press *Shift* and MMB
> - To zoom in and zoom out, use the mouse scroll wheel
> - To select an object, just click on it with the **Left Mouse Button** (**LMB**)
> - To deselect, just click away from the 3D object

5. In the Outliner (the top-right panel), there are a few objects listed. Let us edit them to make their use clear:

    - Select the **base_branca** object, press *F2*, and rename it Main_Body
    - Select **cama** and rename it Bed
    - Select **tampa** and rename it Glass
    - Select **human** and delete it (using the *Delete* key on the keyboard)

6. To save the 3D object, use the **File | Save As…** (or *Shift + Ctrl + S*) command and save the object in the same **scifi-cryogenic-sleep** folder as before. Name it `Cryo-Pod.blend` (note you are now saving it as a Blender 3D object, not an FBX just yet).

Notice that we could only rename the three main parts of this 3D object. If we were to import this object into Unreal Engine, we would be able to apply materials only to these three objects, which would not allow us to make the cryo-chamber look the way we want it.

Before we start creating the Material IDs, let's identify the surfaces we plan to add the Material IDs to.

Defining surfaces for Material ID application

In this section, we will identify surfaces we would like to assign the materials to. In Blender, this is a very straightforward task. I have identified a few, as shown in *Appendix Figure 4*:

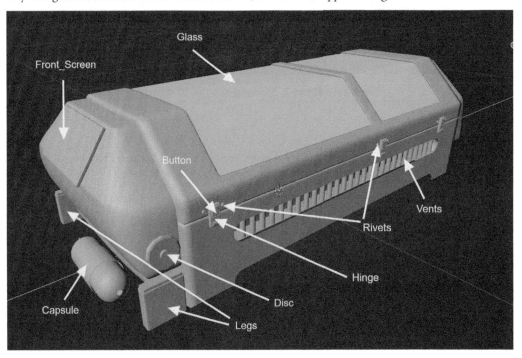

Appendix Figure 4: Material ID parts for the cryo-chamber

There are *nine* parts of the cryo-pod that you will need to create Material IDs for. Although I do not recommend applying this many materials to an object due to draw calls, we will use this as a *practice-makes-perfect* scenario. The more practice you get, the better you will remember how to do it.

Let's continue with the process:

1. With the 3D object still open and selected in Blender (it should have an orange outline), in the Outliner, select the **Bed** object. In the **Properties** panel, click the **Material Properties** icon (beach ball icon), then rename **lambert1** to Bed:

Appendix Figure 5: Renaming materials for all objects

2.   We will do the same for the **Glass** and **Main_Body** objects. Select the **Glass** object, then, in the **Material** properties, rename **m_acrilico** to Glass. Select the **Main_Body** object and rename **m_brancos** to Main-Body.

3.   Press the *Tab* key on the keyboard to go into **Edit Mode** – the mode where we will be able to select individual vertices, edges, or faces.

Use the *1*, *2*, and *3* keys across the keyboard to switch to these modes. Try it a few times. Press *3* to go into **Face Mode** (we will only be using **Face Mode** for now).

4.   Let's work on the disc first. With the cursor in the + mode, draw a rectangle across the disc area, as seen in the following screenshot (you may zoom in using the scroll wheel to help):

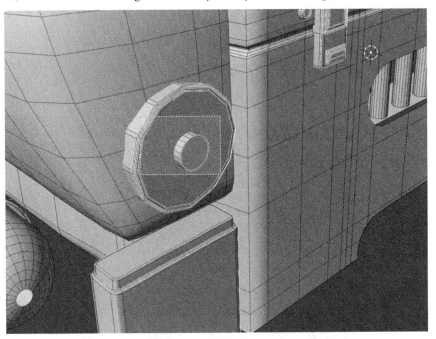

Appendix Figure 6: Selecting the disc in Edit Mode

5.   Once the mouse is released, parts of the disc (polygons) will be selected, but we need to select the rest of the disc. So, press *Ctrl* + *L* to select the rest of the disc area.

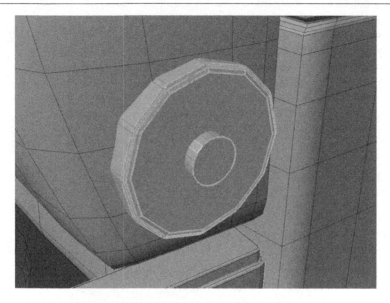

Appendix Figure 7: The selected disc polygons

Ctrl + L is a key combination you must remember for the rest of the parts. You can also use **Select | Selected Linked | Linked**.

6. With the rest of the disc selected, in the **Properties** panel (bottom right), click on the **Material Properties** icon (if the panel is not active).

7. Click on the + (**1**) sign and click **New** (**2**) to make a new material. Blender will assign **Material.001** as the default but we will rename it Disc.

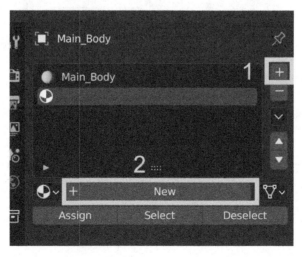

Appendix Figure 8: Creating a new material slot

8. Once renamed, you can assign a color to the material using the **Base Color** slot. I assigned a bright yellow. Then click on the **Assign** button to assign the material.

Appendix Figure 9: Assigning a color to the newly created material

> **Note**
>
> The color you assign to the various parts is just to identify them visually. Later, in Unreal Engine, we will apply materials to them. So, use as many different colors as you like.

So, we have selected and named all the surfaces of the area, but the assigned areas aren't viewable in accordance with the color we applied to them. Let's remedy that.

9. Change the Viewport shading mode to **Material Preview Mode** by pressing the *Z* key and choosing **Material Preview Mode**. You can also achieve this by clicking on the **Viewport Shading** sphere icon at the top right of the interface, as shown here:

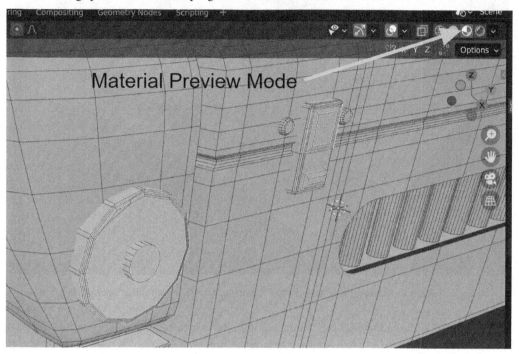

Appendix Figure 10: Switching to Material Preview Mode

10. Save the project with *Ctrl + S*.

Congratulations! You've just created your first Material ID in Blender. You are not done yet; you have eight more to go! Using the same technique, assign the rest of the materials on your own. I have prepared a completed version of the `Cryo-Pod-Final.blend` file, which you'll find in the same folder, in case you want to open it in Blender and have a look at it.

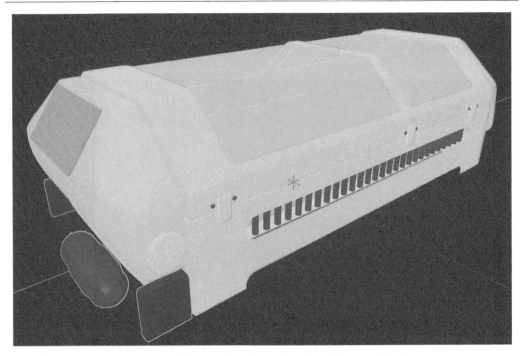

Appendix Figure 11: The completed cryo-chamber with material assignment

As I mentioned, creating Material IDs is not a complicated process. Once you've finished assigning the Material IDs, next, to be able to import them into Unreal Engine, we will need to export the 3D object as an FBX file format.

Exporting to FBX

To import the cryo-chamber into Unreal Engine, it needs to be saved as a `.fbx` file. Let's do that now:

1. Once you've completely assigned all the materials, press the *Tab* key to go back to **Object Mode**. Then select **File | Export | FBX**.

2. In the **Blender File View** panel, name the file `Cryo-Pod_UE.fbx` and save it in the same folder as before.

3. You can now close Blender and enter Unreal Engine!

Following these exercises allows you to effortlessly allocate Material IDs to 3D objects obtained from external sources that may lack sufficient surfaces for material assignment.

Index

Other Books You May Enjoy

If you enjoyed this book, you may be interested in these other books by Packt:

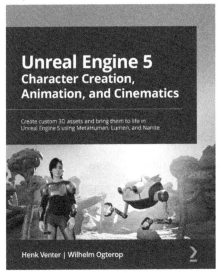

Unreal Engine 5 Character Creation, Animation, and Cinematics

Henk Venter | Wilhelm Ogterop

ISBN: 978-1-80181-244-3

- Create, customize, and use MetaHuman in a cinematic scene in UE5.

- Model and texture custom 3D assets for your movie using Blender and Quixel Mixer

- Use Nanite with Quixel Megascans assets to build 3D movie sets.

- Rig and animate characters and 3D assets inside UE5 using Control Rig tools.

- Combine your 3D assets in Sequencer, include the final effects, and render out a high-quality movie scene.

- Light your 3D movie set using Lumen lighting in UE5.

Blueprints Visual Scripting for Unreal Engine 5

Marcos Romero | Brenden Sewell

ISBN: 978-1-80181-158-3

- Understand programming concepts in Blueprints.

- Create prototypes and iterate new game mechanics rapidly.

- Build user interface elements and interactive menus.

- Use advanced Blueprint nodes to manage the complexity of a game.

- Explore all the features of the Blueprint editor, such as the Components tab, Viewport, and Event Graph

- Get to grips with OOP concepts and explore the Gameplay Framework

- Work with virtual reality development in UE Blueprint

- Implement procedural generation and create a product configurator.

Packt is searching for authors like you.

If you're interested in becoming an author for Packt, please visit `authors.packtpub.com` and apply today. We have worked with thousands of developers and tech professionals, just like you, to help them share their insight with the global tech community. You can make a general application, apply for a specific hot topic that we are recruiting an author for, or submit your own idea.

Share Your Thoughts

Now you've finished *Virtual Filmmaking with Unreal Engine 5*, we'd love to hear your thoughts! Scan the QR code below to go straight to the Amazon review page for this book and share your feedback or leave a review on the site that you purchased it from.

`https://packt.link/r/1-801-81380-9`

Your review is important to us and the tech community and will help us make sure we're delivering excellent quality content.

Download a free PDF copy of this book

Thanks for purchasing this book!

Do you like to read on the go but are unable to carry your print books everywhere?

Is your eBook purchase not compatible with the device of your choice?

Don't worry, now with every Packt book you get a DRM-free PDF version of that book at no cost.

Read anywhere, any place, on any device. Search, copy, and paste code from your favorite technical books directly into your application.

The perks don't stop there, you can get exclusive access to discounts, newsletters, and great free content in your inbox daily

Follow these simple steps to get the benefits:

1. Scan the QR code or visit the link below

https://packt.link/free-ebook/9781801813808

2. Submit your proof of purchase

3. That's it! We'll send your free PDF and other benefits to your email directly

Made in the USA
Coppell, TX
09 June 2024

33313748R00267